The Prayers of Peter Marshall

Edited and with Prefaces by
CATHERINE MARSHALL

John Doe, Disciple

PETER MARSHALL

Edited and with Introductions by
CATHERINE MARSHALL

Preface by PETER JOHN MARSHALL

GUIDEPOSTS ASSOCIATES, INC.
Carmel, New York

THE PRAYERS OF
PETER MARSHALL

Edited and with Prefaces by
Catherine Marshall

GUIDEPOSTS ASSOCIATES, INC.
Carmel, New York

THE PRAYERS OF PETER MARSHALL

The quotations in the prayers on pages 99 and 113 are condensed and reprinted from *A Diary of Private Prayer* by John Baillie; used by permission of the publishers, Charles Scribner's Sons.

Guideposts edition published by arrangement with McGraw-Hill Book Co., Inc.

ACKNOWLEDGMENTS

Grateful acknowledgment is hereby made to the Fleming H. Revell Company for their kind permission to reprint the following prayers originally used in *Mr. Jones, Meet the Master, Sermons and Prayers of Peter Marshall:* "For Those Who Serve," "Newness of Life," "For a Renaissance of Faith," "The Humanity of Jesus"; to the McGraw-Hill Book Company for the following prayers, which first appeared in *A Man Called Peter:* "We Confess Before Thee," "The Cry of the Human Heart," "For More Faith"; to the *Washington Evening Star* for permission to quote three paragraphs from an article by Harold B. Rogers dated January 5, 1947; and to Mrs. Daniel A. Poling and the National Council of Churches of Christ in America for permission to quote the prayer for the World Day of Prayer Service for 1948, used in the Senate prayer for February 13, 1948.

I wish to express my deep appreciation to Miss Margaret Bradley, my most efficient secretary, who typed the manuscript; to Miss Kathryn Campbell and Mr. Edward MacConomy (the latter of the Legislative Reference Division of the Library of Congress) who helped with the background research work in connection with the Senate prayers; to Mrs. Alma Deane MacConomy, Mrs. George Markley, and Mrs. Eugene Campagna who gave me many valuable suggestions in the final selection of the pastoral prayers; to Miss Sara Leslie who helped with the format of the book.

In public prayer one's mind instinctively recalls many passages from Scripture, hymns, and well-loved authors. I have tried to find all such quotations in the prayers and to give proper credit. If any such quotations still remain unacknowledged, the publisher or I will appreciate information to that effect and will be happy to give the usual credit in all future editions of the book.

C. M.

CONTENTS

Prayers for Special Days

Prayers for the Nation and the World

Part Two. The Senate Prayers

PART ONE

The Pastoral Prayers

ON THE THRESHOLD OF TIME

Early in the year 1947 many Americans began to realize that a man with an extraordinary talent for prayer had been made Chaplain of the United States Senate. Immediately, Peter Marshall's Senate prayers began to receive a great deal of national publicity.

Thus the nation at large suddenly "discovered" and grew enthusiastic about what Dr. Marshall's congregations had long known. For these congregations in Covington and Atlanta, Georgia, and in the Nation's Capital, their minister's pastoral prayers had always been a unique experience in worship.

In the process of editing the prayers for this book, it has been easy to recapture my first fresh impressions of the prayers as I, then a college student, originally heard them in Atlanta's Westminster Presbyterian Church in the winter of 1932.

It was immediately apparent to me that the morning prayer was for this young minister not just another customary, trite part of his order of service. The prayer period was approached in a leisurely fashion with an unmistakable sincerity and an undercurrent of anticipation approximating excitement.

"The most precious moments of our morning worship are the moments we spend with the Risen Lord," Peter would say before he began to pray. "We cannot see His form, but we can feel His presence. He knows all about you—your hidden perplexity, your secret shame. He waits by appointment, anxious to speak to you reassuringly, comfortingly, forgivingly. You may tell Him your needs now in your own way." Then a period of silence would follow.

Peter *knew* Christ was there, and he was somehow able to

3

transmit that knowledge to the waiting congregation bowed before him. That was why hungry-hearted people would make almost any sacrifice to get to Westminster Church.

It was also obvious that Peter Marshall confidently expected things to happen as he prayed. Burdened consciences were going to be forgiven; burdened minds were going to be unloaded of worry and tension. The sick were going to be healed. The lonely were going to find a Friend. The aged were going to receive the benediction of a strange, new peace.

It was this expectation of answered prayer that accounted for the undercurrent of excitement. And it worked! It was because many individuals in those congregations actually did have experiences of specific needs met that people came to regard these prayers as rare spiritual treasure.

There were other initial impressions—the young minister always clasped his big laboring-man's hands around the pulpit microphone in a characteristic gesture; his eyes were closed; he used no written prayer or even notes. The prayers flowed from the depths of his soul clothed in a rare beauty of language; yet there was the paradox of a simple dignity combined with a homey, down-to-earthness. . . . "Our heads swell so much easier than our hearts," he might say. Humor often crept in. . . . "We thank Thee, Lord, that there is no weather in heaven."

Those were my first impressions. At the end of Peter's ministry as at the beginning, all of this was still characteristic of him. Yet as the years went on, his prayers revealed a deepening of the channel of Peter's own Christian experience.

In Atlanta his prayers had been largely directed to the individual's needs. He spent little more time than does the average minister on petitions concerning the Nation or its leaders.

In Washington this changed. It was as if Peter saw all of life as from the perspective of a mountaintop. Three tributaries of interest, easily traceable in his later prayers, were the result.

First, he came to have a profound concern for his adopted

country—more than a concern, a passion reminiscent of that of the seers and the prophets of ancient Israel. There was born in Peter's heart an ineffable yearning over America. He longed to see us "cast off all Pharisaical garments, lay down the overcoats of our smug complacence"; put aside self-interest and false pride, and become truly righteous, so that the United States of America might rise to her God-appointed destiny of world leadership.

There is little wonder that Dr. Marshall was called to serve on Capitol Hill. Without realizing it, he had been preparing for that task for years. The proof is that well over half of the total wordage of his pastoral prayers left to us are the outpouring of his heart on this patriotic note.

Peter's second great concern was for plain homespun virtues of honesty, integrity, and goodness of the individual. This was a natural corollary of his eagerness for righteousness on a national scale. He saw clearly that we can never achieve nationally what we are unwilling to accede to individually. Over and over he kept calling us back to these basic realities because he well knew that God is more impressed by an honest income-tax return than by any amount of too-stereotyped churchgoing.

The third strand of Peter's concern was that we be "more kindly affectioned, one to another, more patient, more understanding, forgiving one another even as God for Christ's sake has forgiven us." As searing tongues of misunderstanding and hatred leaped out to engulf the earth in World War II, this emphasis became an ever-recurring note in Peter's praying.

Because Peter did not write his prayers out, most of them are now lost to us. Were it not for the interest and ingenuity of three individuals, this collection of his pastoral prayers would not have been possible. In Atlanta, Peter Marshall's secretary, Ruby Coleman Daughtry, once took down a few of his prayers in shorthand. In Washington there was a girl in the State Department to whom Dr. Marshall's prayers were soul sustenance. She conceived the idea of taking them down in shorthand during the church service. It proved to be hard dictation to get. A few words were irretrievably lost here and there. Nevertheless, the result was a group of prayers from which most of those included here are taken.

Of Miss Elizabeth McNaull's notes on these prayers, eighteen of them Dr. Marshall subsequently corrected and edited himself, and included with his sermons which were then being printed locally in pamphlet form.

The only other pastoral prayers left to us are a residue of thirteen prayers recorded on tape along with the Sunday morning sermons. This was a labor of love undertaken by Mr. Jack Ingram of Dallas, Texas, during the winter of 1947–1948, while he was stationed in Washington. Otherwise, I have only fragments of prayers jotted down by unidentified individuals.

The pastoral prayers were, of course, quite long. In order to make them more readily usable by families and for individual devotions, I have taken the liberty of dividing them topically into prayers for various needs and occasions.

Dr. Marshall had a way of speaking to the deepest needs of our hearts, because he actually was pouring out before the Throne of Grace the deepest needs of his own heart. In these particularly personal portions of the prayers, I have changed the "we" of the public prayer to the even more personal "I." Otherwise the language is entirely Peter Marshall's.

In the prayer of Sunday morning, December 26, 1948, there are these words: "We all need Thee so much. Grant that in the new year, if we shall live through it. . . ."

Did Peter Marshall have some intimation that the adventure men call dying was for him only thirty days away? I cannot be sure.

Perhaps it was just that he had so often seen death rudely interrupt men and women in the thick of life. Perhaps it was that he himself had long since quietly accepted the idea (since his first heart attack) that death stood always just at his elbow.

Whatever the reason, toward the end of the prayer there

crept in an almost incredible sentence . . . "We are standing," Peter prayed, "on the threshold of time."

We are indeed—every one of us. That is why these prayers, breathed from the depths of a man's soul, speak with surety to your heart and mine.

Catherine Marshall

Washington, May 20, 1954

Prayers for Personal Needs

When We Feel Forsaken

Our Father, sometimes Thou dost seem so far away, as if Thou art a God in hiding, as if Thou art determined to elude all who seek Thee.

Yet we know that Thou art far more willing to be found than we are to seek. Thou hast promised "If with all Thy heart ye truly seek me, ye shall ever surely find me." And hast Thou not assured us that Thou art with us always?

Help us now to be as aware of Thy nearness as we are of the material things of every day. Help us to recognize Thy voice with as much assurance as we recognize the sounds of the world around us.

We would find Thee now in the privacy of our hearts, in the quiet of this moment. We would know, our Father, that Thou art near us and beside us; that Thou dost love us and art interested in all that we do, art concerned about all our affairs.

May we become aware of Thy companionship, of Him who walks beside us.

At times when we feel forsaken, may we know the presence of the Holy Spirit who brings comfort to all human hearts when we are willing to surrender ourselves.

May we be convinced that even before we reach up to Thee, Thou art reaching down to us. These blessings, together with the unexpressed longing in our hearts, we ask in the strong name of Jesus Christ, Our Lord. Amen.

The Humanity of Jesus

May our prayer, O Christ, awaken all Thy human reminiscences, that we may feel in our hearts the sympathizing Jesus.
> Thou hast walked this earthly vale and hast not forgotten what it is to be tired, what it is to know aching muscles, as Thou didst work long hours at the carpenter's bench.
> Thou hast not forgotten what it is to feel the sharp stabs of pain, or hunger, or thirst.
> Thou knowest what it is to be forgotten, to be lonely.
> Thou dost remember the feel of hot and scalding tears running down Thy cheeks.

O we thank Thee that Thou wert willing to come to earth and share with us the weaknesses of the flesh, for now we know that Thou dost understand all that we are ever called upon to bear.

We know that Thou, our God, art still able to do more than we ask or expect. So bless us, each one, not according to our deserving, but according to the riches in glory of Christ Jesus, our Lord. Amen.

I Need Thee, Lord

I do need Thee, Lord. I need Thee now. I know that I can do without many of the things that once I thought were necessities, but without Thee I cannot live, and I dare not die.

I needed Thee when sorrow came, when shadows were thrown across the threshold of my life, and Thou didst not fail me then. I needed Thee when sickness laid a clammy hand upon my family, and I cried to Thee, and Thou didst hear. I needed Thee when perplexity brought me to a parting of the ways, and I knew not how to turn. Thou didst not fail me then, but in many ways, big and little, didst indicate the better way. And though the sun is shining around me today, I know that I need Thee even in the sunshine, and shall still need Thee tomorrow.

I give Thee my gratitude for that constant sense of need that keeps me close to Thy side. Help me to keep my hand in Thine and my ears open to the wisdom of Thy voice.

Speak to me, that I may hear Thee giving me courage for hard times and strength for difficult places; giving me determination for challenging tasks. I ask of Thee no easy way, but just Thy grace that is sufficient for every need, so that no matter how hard the way, how challenging the hour, how dark the sky, I may be enabled to overcome.

In Thy strength, who hast overcome the world, I make this prayer. Amen.

Teach Us How to Pray

LORD, teach us to pray. Some of us are not skilled in the art of prayer. As we draw near to Thee in thought, Our spirits long for Thy Spirit, and reach out for Thee, longing to feel Thee near. We know not how to express the deepest emotions that lie hidden in our hearts.

In these moments, we have no polished phrases with which to impress one another, no finely molded, delicately turned clauses to present to Thee. Nor would we be confined to conventional petitions and repeat our prayers like the unwinding of a much-exposed film. We know, our Father, that we are praying most when we are saying least. We know that we are closest to Thee when we have left behind the things that have held us captive so long.

We would not be ignorant in prayer and, like children, make want lists for Thee. Rather, we pray that Thou wilt give unto us only what we really need. We would not make our prayers the importuning of Thee, an omnipotent God, to do what we want Thee to do. Rather, give us the vision, the courage, that shall enlarge our horizons and stretch our faith to the adventure of seeking Thy loving will for our lives.

We thank Thee that Thou art hearing us even now. We thank Thee for the grace of prayer. We thank Thee for Thyself. Amen.

The Soul Tonic of Prayer

FATHER, I am beginning to know how much I miss when I fail to talk to Thee in prayer, and through prayer to receive into my life the strength and the guidance which only Thou canst give. Forgive me for the pride and the presumption that make me continue to struggle to manage my own affairs to the exhaustion of my body, the weariness of my mind, the trial of my faith.

In a moment like this I know that Thou couldst have worked Thy good in me with so little strain, with so little effort. And then to Thee would have been given the praise and the glory. When I neglect to pray, mine is the loss. Forgive me, Lord.

Let not, I pray, any future forgetfulness of mine, or a false sense of self-sufficiency, any spiritual laziness, or doubt of Thy faithfulness keep me from taking everything to Thee in prayer.

And now, I thank Thee that the fresh breath of heaven is even now blowing away the close, damp air of all my failure, of every doubt and fear. I ask Thee for that soul tonic of prayer that shall reburnish my faith, brighten my hope, revive and rekindle my love. In Thy name, I pray. Amen.

To Make Life an Adventure

O LORD Jesus, I remember that Thou hast said, "Lay not up for yourselves treasures upon earth, where moth and rust doth corrupt. . . ." O God, deliver me from falling in love with things. Help me rather to love people, to love principles, to love righteousness, to love Thee.

Thou hast commanded me "to seek first the Kingdom of God and His righteousness," and then hast made me a promise that if my heart and mind and soul and will were thus dedicated, I should receive as dividends the very things I seek—an abundant ministry unto all my needs.

O God, help me to believe this. Help me to practice it, that I may find for myself that the promise is true, that all my needs shall be met.

Thou hast invited me "to ask, to seek, to knock"—assuring me that if I ask, it shall be given unto me; if I seek, I shall find; if I knock, it shall be opened unto me.

Help me to believe that, O God. Give me the faith to ask, knowing that I shall receive. Give me the faith to seek, believing that I shall surely find. Give me the faith and the persistence to knock, knowing that it shall be opened unto me.

Help me to live the Christian life in daring faith and humble trust, that there may be worked out in me, even in me, Thy righteousness and goodness. With a sense of adventure, I make this prayer. Amen.

For More Faith

FORGIVE us, O God, for our small concept of the heart of the Eternal, for the doubting suspicion with which we regard the heart of God.

Give to us more faith. We have so little . . . we say. Yet we have faith in each other—in checks and banks, in trains and airplanes, in cooks, and in strangers who drive us in cabs. Forgive us for our stupidity, that we have faith in people whom we do not know, and are so reluctant to have faith in Thee who knowest us altogether.

We are always striving to find a complicated way through life when Thou hast a plan, and we refuse to walk in it. So many of our troubles we bring on ourselves. How silly we are . . .

Wilt Thou give to us that faith that we can deposit in the bank of Thy love, so that we may receive the dividends and interest that Thou art so willing to give us. We ask it all in the lovely name of Jesus Christ our Saviour. Amen.

Confession

O LORD, I come to Thee out of my great need. Thou hast pledged Thy word that whosoever cometh to Thee shall in no wise be cast out.

I dare to pray that something will happen to me in Thy presence. Lord, I know I need to be changed! For the visions that once swept across the leaden skies of monotony, like white-winged gulls, have dimmed and faded, and I would see them again. Open Thou my eyes!

Shame fills my heart as I remember the aspirations that I have breathed before Thee, the vows I made, the resolves that were born, the seedlings of consecration that were planted in my heart. I blush to remember the withering blight that touched them all—my failures, my shortcomings.

Lord, I confess before Thee that:

I have had longings and nudgings from Thee which I did not translate into action;

I have made decisions without consulting Thee, then have blamed Thee when things went wrong.

I have said that I trusted Thee, yet have not turned my affairs over to Thee.

I have been greedy for present delights and pleasures, unwilling to wait for those joys which time and discipline alone can give.

I have often sought the easy way, have consistently drawn back from the road that is hard.

I have been fond of giving myself to dreams of what I am going to do sometime, yet have been so slow in getting started to do them.

Forgive me for all the intentions that were born and somehow never lived. These, Lord Jesus, are sins, grievous in Thy sight, grievous even in mine.

And now I claim Thy promise to change me. Do Thou for me what I cannot do for myself. Lead me into a new tomorrow with a new spirit. Cleanse my heart, create within me new attitudes and new ideas, as only Thou canst create them.

For these good gifts, I thank Thee, Lord. Amen.

For True Repentance

FORGIVE me, Lord Jesus, for the things I have done that make me feel uncomfortable in Thy presence. All the front that I polish so carefully for men to see, does not deceive Thee.

For Thou knowest every thought that has left its shadow on my memory. Thou hast marked every motive that curdled something sweet within me.

I acknowledge, with sorrow and true repentance, that
I have desired that which I should not have;
I have toyed with what I knew was not for me;
I have been preoccupied with self-interest;

I have invited unclean thoughts into my mind and
   entertained them as honored guests;
My ears have often been deaf to Thy whisper;
My eyes have been often blind to the signs of Thy
   guidance.
Make me willing to be changed, even though it requires surgery of the soul, and the therapy of discipline.

Make my heart warm and soft, that I may receive and ac-
cept now the blessings of Thy forgiveness, the benediction of
Thy "Depart in peace . . . and sin no more." In Jesus' name.
Amen.

Cleanse Me, O God

"If we confess our sins, he is faithful and just to forgive
us our sins, and to cleanse us from all unrighteousness."
I JOHN 1:9

FATHER, over and over again I have fallen into the same
temptations. It does seem as if I am slow to learn Thy ways
and Thy laws.

I blush to recall my vows to Thee: never again to do what I
have just come from doing, not again to stain myself in the
same mudholes.

Yet, O Lord, stained as I am, and conscious of my own
weakness, I have no choice but to pick myself up again, to
ask Thee to forgive me once more and make me clean again.

I thank Thee, O Lord Jesus, for the glory of the Gospel of
the Second Chance. I would claim from Thee that chance to
begin all over again.

Thou hast heard my prayer of confession. Now I claim Thy
promise to forgive me and to cleanse me. From this moment
I accept that forgiveness and that cleansing by faith, because

I believe that Thy promise is the "word of a Gentleman of the most strict and sacred honor."

And now I ask for Thy spirit to come into me like cool fresh air to revitalize me, to shock me into a new discipleship, to invigorate me for a new life in Christ Jesus, my Lord. Amen.

For Restoration

FATHER, I have lost the feeling of Thy presence. Yet deep in my heart I know that it is not because Thou didst leave me, but because I have wandered from Thee.

"All we like sheep have gone astray. We have turned every one to his own way." I confess that I have found that way hard and wearisome. My feet are tired of wandering. My heart is sick of being lost. I would return to Thee now and be led of Thee in Thy way, that I may walk once more with a sense of direction and a clear light upon my path.

O my Father, receive me—Thy prodigal child; prodigal because I have wandered in a far country, prodigal in my forgetfulness of Thee, prodigal in all the blessings I have taken for granted. Now, bowing before Thee, I acknowledge them all.

And now I arise and come back to Thee, my Father, knowing that Thou art even now running to meet me, placing over my shoulders the robe of Thy love, placing upon my hand the ring of Thy forgiveness, pressing upon me the kiss of a divine love that knows no limit—a love which loved me while I was yet a sinner—a love that brought Jesus to Calvary.

I thank Thee for that love; I thank Thee for this restoration. I thank Thee that Thou art still my Father, that I am still Thy child. Amen.

For the Death of the Old Self

O ur Father, we believe that Thou wilt hear our prayers, that Thou wilt be sympathetic without coddling; Thou wilt have mercy without condoning; Thou wilt forgive, but not without a price.

Thou Thyself hast paid that price on Calvary's hill, and we, too, must pay a price if we would know Thy peace—the price of full confession, the price of real repentance, and the price of the crucifixion of the things within us that destroy our peace of mind.

Make us willing, Lord Jesus, to pay that price, remembering that without the shedding of blood there is no remission of sin, that without hard work there is no accomplishment, that without real effort there can be no achievement, and without the crucifixion of our old selves there can be no victory. Amen.

To Be a New Person

> "Therefore if any man be in Christ, he is a new creature: old things are passed away; behold, all things are become new." II CORINTHIANS 5:17

I know, Father, that I must come to Thee just as I am. But I also know that I dare not go away just as I came.

Often I have known failure—failure in the moral realm, failure in ethics, failure in my attitudes, failure in my disposition.

I have confessed all these defeats to Thee, and Thou hast graciously forgiven me. Yet I know, Lord, that merely to forgive me will not suffice. For unless I am changed, I shall do these same things again. At last I know, Lord, that only Thou canst correct that within me which makes me do wrong.

Where I am blind, Thou must give me sight.

Where I fail to heed Thy voice, Thou wilt have to do something about my deafness.

Even where I deliberately choose to do what I know is wrong, Thou wilt have to do something about my will.

So, Lord, I acknowledge my total dependence upon Thee. Make me over into the person Thou dost want me to be, that I may yet find that destiny for which Thou didst give me birth. For His help, who is plenteous in mercy, I give Thee my gratitude. Amen.

For a Grateful Heart

LORD, I pause to look back on the long way Thou hast brought me, on the long days in which I have been served, not according to my deserts but according to my desires and Thy loving mercies. Let me meditate upon the dark nights through which I have come, the sinister things from which I have been delivered—and have a grateful heart. Let me meditate upon my sins forgiven, for my shame unpublished—and have a grateful heart.

I thank Thee, O Lord, that, in Thy mercy, so many things I feared never came to pass. Fill my heart with thankful praise. Help me to repay in service to others the debt of Thy unmerited benefits and mercies. May the memories of sorrows that disciplined my spirit keep me humble and make me grateful that my God is no celestial Santa Claus but a divine Saviour. In His name I offer this sacrifice of praise. Amen.

Lord, in my Success I Need Thee

LORD, forgive me that when life's circumstances lift me to the crest of the wave, I tend to forget Thee. Yet, like an errant child, I have blamed Thee with my every failure, even as I credit myself with every success.

When my fears evaporate like the morning mist, then vainly I imagine that I am sufficient unto myself, that material resources and human resources are enough.

I need Thee when the sun shines, lest I forget the storm and the dark. I need Thee when I am popular, when my friends and those who work beside me approve and compliment me. I need Thee more then, lest my head begin to swell.

O God, forgive me for my stupidity, my blindness in success, my lack of trust in Thee. Be Thou now my Saviour in success. Save me from conceit. Save me from pettiness. Save me from myself! And take this success, I pray, and use it for Thy glory. In Thy strength, I pray. Amen.

To Be Consistent

LORD, what is the matter with us that we are so fitful and moody, so changeful—one moment professing our love for Thee, and the next moment yielding to temptations that lure us away from Thee? One moment, cheerful, smiling, and kind, and the next, glum and surly. Lord, we do not understand ourselves! What strange creatures we are!

Yet we do not pray, our Father, that always everything should be the same, for we would get tired of unending sunshine, and long for a shower of rain.

We do not pray that our way may always lie on level places, for then we would long to see a mountain.

We do not pray that always our lot might be favored with pleasant strains of music, for then we would long for the ministry of silence.

But we do pray, O Lord, that there might be some pattern of consistency in our relations with Thee. Teach us how to maintain life on an even keel, that with a balanced life of faith and trust in Thee, and kindness and love toward each other, we shall not be at one moment up in the sky and at the next at the bottom of a well.

Help us to walk with our hand in Thy hand, knowing that Thou Thyself didst come down from mountaintops to walk in the valleys. So may we not give way to despair when we too must return to the valley, but know that the trail will wind up again.

But whether on the mountaintop or in the valley, may we ever be aware that Thou art walking beside us. And if Thou art with us, what difference does it make where we are? In Thy name, we pray. Amen.

For Childlikeness

FORGIVE us, Lord, that as we grow to maturity, our faith is blighted with doubts, withered with worry, tainted with sophistication. We pray that Thou wilt make us like children again in faith—not childish, but childlike in the simplicity of a faith that is willing to trust Thee even though we cannot see what tomorrow will bring.

We ask Thee to give to each of us that childlike faith, that simplicity of mind which is willing to lay aside all egotism and conceit, which recognizes vanity for what it is—an empty show, which knows that we are incapable of thinking the thought of God, which is willing to be humble again.

Then may we feel once more as do our children who whisper their love to Thee, who trace with chubby little fingers the pictures of Jesus in a picture book—those pictures that portray Thee, Lord Jesus, with a hurt lamb in Thy arms or a child on Thy knee. Help us, even now, to feel again like that, that we may be as loving, as trusting, as innocent, as grateful, as affectionate.

And as we are willing to kneel again as children, then shall we discover for ourselves the glory Thou hast revealed, and find the wonder of it gripping our hearts and preparing them for Thy peace. So shall we, along with our children, enter into the Kingdom of God, and know it, and feel it, and rejoice in it. In Thy name, who didst dare to come to earth as a little child, we pray. Amen.

For One Burdened with Worry

"Rest in the Lord, and wait patiently for him;
And He shall give thee thy heart's desires. . . ." *

FATHER, teach me that, as Thy child, worry has no place in my life. I know that it helps nothing. I know that by worrying I cannot add a single cubit to my stature. I know that fretting overcomes no difficulty.

Often in the past, Lord, I have come to Thee with heavy heart and burdened life. And Thou hast answered my prayers and graciously lifted the burden from me. Yet with a strange perversion, I still refuse to leave my burdens with Thee. Always I gather them up—those heavy bundles of fears and anxieties—and shoulder them again.

Do now for what I cannot do for myself. With Thou break these habit patterns, reverse the direction of my negative thoughts, lift from me once again all anxieties and apprehensions.

Give me in their stead a calm and confident trust in Thee. Make me willing to live just one day at a time. May my heart re-echo to Thy promise that only as I rest in Thee can the desires of my heart be given me.

And now help me to do my part by placing a guard around my thoughts, by resolutely refusing to return to my old haunts of distrust. I thank Thee for Thy love for me and for Thy help. Amen.

* From the oratorio *Elijah,* by Mendelssohn.

To Live One Day at a Time

FATHER, some of Thy children find life hard. It is for them we would ask Thy help now. Many of them are burdened with loads that they need not carry. Many of them clutch black burdens of anxiety and worry, when no child of Thine need be anxious. There are many who carry loads of fear when there is nothing to fear; many who make themselves miserable when they might be filled with Thy peace.

We ask Thee, O Lord, to teach us all how to live without strain. We have to confess to Thee that most of the things we have worried about have never happened.

Teach us the secret of living just one day at a time, knowing that each day brings with it so much joy that we cannot fully explore it, so many blessings that we cannot even count them —much less enter into them all.

So help us to be like children, content to live fully each hour as it comes. Then shall we escape the corroding care, the agonizing worry that destroys our peace of mind, renders us unfit for happiness, and dishonors Thee. Then shall we be filled with joy and that peace which no circumstance can take from us. We thank Thee for Thy ceaseless bounty, for that joy and that peace. Amen.

For Quietness

". . . in quietness and in confidence shall be your strength. . . ." ISAIAH 30:15

FATHER, I ask Thee to take from me now all that does harass and annoy, all that has laid upon my heart burdens of anxiety and care. I thank Thee for the stillness of this time of prayer —this oasis in my busy day when I can relax before Thee, lay my burdens down, and hand over to Thee all my anxieties.

At this moment, I open my heart to receive Thy blessing, knowing that in Thy presence

the furrows are being smoothed from by brow,
the lines from my face,
the load from my heart,
the doubts from my mind,
the fears from my soul,

that I am at peace.

And now, I thank Thee, not only for quietness without, but for Thy quietness at the heart of the universe and for quietness within. In Thy peace, I pray. Amen.

When Perplexed

LORD, Thou hast said that our Father in heaven notes even the fall of a sparrow to the ground. Help us to believe, O God, that Thou are concerned not only with the rolling of the spheres in their orbits, but even with each of us, our doubts, and perplexities.

We remember all too well the bitter discoveries we have made when we have tried to run our lives our own way, when we try to steer our own craft. Wilt Thou come aboard, Lord

Jesus, and set us a true course, for we grow weary of life's demands, tired of our own blundering ways.

We seek a clear light to shine upon our troubled way. We ask Thee to give us clearer directions.

Where we have missed the way and wandered far, bring us back at whatever cost to our pride.

Take away our stubborn self-will, for we know that in Thy will alone is our peace. We seek that peace.

We pray in that name which is above every name, even Jesus Christ our Lord. Amen.

For Peace of Mind

FATHER, I know now, if I never knew it before, that only in Thee can my restless human heart find any peace.

For I began life without knowledge, but full of needs. And the turmoil of my mind, the dissatisfaction of my life all stem from trying to meet those needs with the wrong things and in the wrong places.

Help me so to live that my conscience shall not have to accuse, so that I may be saved the necessity of trying to mend that which need never be broken. I know that only then will the civil war within me cease.

May I be willing to have Thee with me in play as well as in work, knowing that with Thee I shall have peace and joy and no regrets. Through Jesus Christ, my Lord. Amen.

To Face the Future Without Fear

THOU knowest, Father, the things of which we are afraid—the terror by night, the arrow by day that takes us unawares and often finds us without a vital, ready faith.

We know that Thou hast not promised to surround us with immunity from all the ills to which flesh is heir. We only pray that when they come, if come they must, they shall find us unafraid and with adequate resources to meet them.

Give us a constant faith and a steady courage, that we may neither whimper nor in peevish petulance complain before Thee.

We thank Thee that Thou dost still rule over the world that Thou hast made. Kings and emperors come and depart. All the shouting and the tumult, the screaming hurricanes of time have not deviated Thee from Thy path.

Help us to remember, O Christ, that Thou art victorious—Christus Victor—reigning over all; that in due time, in Thine own good time, Thou wilt work all things together for good to them that love Thee, who are called according to Thy purpose.

May we find our refuge in that regnant faith, and so face the future without fear. Give to us Thy peace, through Jesus Christ, our Lord. Amen.

For Reconciliation with a Friend

> "So if you are offering your gift at the altar, and there remember that your brother has something against you, leave your gift there before the altar and go; first be reconciled to your brother, and then come and offer your gift." MATTHEW 5:23–24

FATHER, Thou knowest the misunderstanding that has risen between me and my friend. Harsh and thoughtless words have been spoken. I know that this rift grieves Thee, that Thou wouldst be far more impressed with a sacrifice of reconciliation on my part than with any vows of loyalty or material gift I could make Thee.

I dare not make this a prayer for Thee to change ———; my friend is Thy responsibility. I know that always I must begin with *my* responsibility—myself and my own shortcomings.

In subtle ways I confess to Thee that I have used friendship to cushion and make comfortable my own ego. All too often I have sought my friend for my own pleasure and convenience; all too seldom have I thought of what pleasure I could give.

Thou hast asked me to love my neighbors and friends to the extent that I love myself. That, Lord, would be a lot of loving!

Enable me now to let all false pride go. Give me the grace of the oustretched hand and the open heart. Give me the courage that will enable me to go to ——— and be the first to say, "I have been wrong here and here. I am sorry. Forgive me."

Help me not to take myself too seriously. Grant to me objectivity and a quiet mind and a sense of humor.

Go Thou ahead of me to fling out a bridge of good will, to cast down all roadblocks of misunderstanding. And bless to Thy glory and the happiness of all concerned this gesture of good will undertaken in Thy name. Amen.

For Release from Resentment

LORD Jesus, Thou knowest me altogether. Thou knowest that I have steadily refused to forgive this one who has wronged me, yet have had the audacity often to seek Thy forgiveness for my own wrongdoing.

The acids of bitterness and a vengeful spirit have threatened to eat away my peace. Yet I have stubbornly rationalized every unlovely motive. I have said, "I am clearly in the right. It is only human to dislike a few people. This one deserves no forgiveness." How well I know that neither have I ever deserved the forgiveness which Thou hast always freely granted me.

So, Lord Jesus, I ask Thee now for the grace to forgive this hurt. Even now, I am divided about it, only partially willing to release it.

But Thou canst manage even my reluctance, my loitering feet. Take now my divided will and make it of one piece, wholly Thy will.

And Lord, I give Thee this emotion of resentment which clings as if glued to my heart. Wrest if from me. Cleanse every petty thought. Make me sweet again.

I dare to ask that Thou wilt not only forgive me to the extent that I have forgiven _____, but that Thou wilt bless _____ to the degree that Thou hast blessed me. For these great mercies I thank Thee, in Thy name, who gave me the supreme example in forgiving even those who slew Thee. Amen.

For More Love

Father, as I draw near to Thee in prayer, I am aware of the poverty of my love for Thee.

I have often given my heart to unworthy causes.

I have loved money and sought my security in it.

I have loved comfort and ease.

I have loved power and influence over others.

How strange it is that of all the things we humans love, our Lord, who is love and goodness and grace, should Himself receive so little love.

Yet I cannot manufacture the love I should bear Thee, even as I have not manufactured the love I feel for others. Thou art the giver of love. Except Thou bestow it, I cannot have it.

And so, my Father, wilt Thou give me the gift of love? Then I shall love Thee, and loving Thee, shall love other men—and compassion shall rise within me, warm and sweet.

But I ask not merely to love those easy to love. Help me to love those who are hard to live with. Give me a concern for the needs of others, not on the basis of barter or exchange—not love given for love received—but love given to the unlovely for Christ's sake.

Then shall my love partake of Thine, who dares to own me still. In the name of Him who is the King of Love. Amen.

For Our Family

Lord Jesus, we would thank Thee that Thou hast blessed our home with the gift of young life, for we know that through our children Thou wouldst remind us of God.

We do resolve, by Thy help, to honor Thee in all our relationships—in our home, so that it may be Thy temple; in our

hearts, where Thou dost love to dwell; in our place of business, that it may become an adventure in living our faith.

And now, Lord, we place every member of our family in Thy
care and keeping. We think of ⸺ and ⸺ and ⸺.
Bless them every one. Be with us all throughout this day—in
our work and in our play. In Jesus' name. Amen.

For the Young

Lord Jesus, we pray for youth in careless abandon, in love
of liberty, and in joy of life, especially those particular young
people whom we name now before Thee. . . . Help them to
find that discipline by which life can alone be successfully
lived, and character achieved. May they learn that just as
steam is effective when contained in the walls of a cylinder,
so will youthful energies be effective when controlled.

We ask Thee to
> protect them physically; throw around them the golden
>   aura of Thy protecting presence;
> be Thou their Teacher; be Thou their Guide;
> send into their lives the specially chosen companions and
>   friends Thou dost want them to have;
> save them from any costly blunders that would haunt
>   them down the years.

Give to them that joy and happiness that shall enable them
to go out to meet life, bearing with them those lasting satisfactions which only Thou canst bestow.

We thank Thee, Lord. Amen.

For Our World in Need

Our Father, I think of all the pain and heartache, the tears and sorrow, the greed and cruelty unloosed around the world. Help me to be an instrument of Thine to alleviate the pain, by this day:

> returning good for evil,
> returning soft answers for sharp criticisms,
> being polite when I receive rudeness,
> being understanding when I am confronted by ignorance and stupidity.

So may I, in gentleness and love, check the hasty answer, choke back the unkind retort, and thus short-circuit some of the bitterness and unkindness that has overflowed Thy world. I ask this in the name of Jesus, who alone can give me the grace so to act. Amen.

For My Tongue

> "Whoever considers he is religious, and does not bridle his tongue, but deceives his own heart, his religion is futile." JAMES 1:26—Moffatt

I NEED Thee, O Lord, for a curb on my tongue; when I am tempted to make carping criticisms and cruel judgments, keep me from speaking barbed words that hurt, and in which I find a perverted satisfaction.

> Keep me from unkind words and from unkind silences.
> Restrain my judgments.
> Make my criticisms kind, generous, and constructive.
> Make me sweet inside, that I may be gentle with other people, gentle in the things I say, kind in what I do.

Create in me that warmth of mercy that shall enable others to find Thy strength for their weakness, Thy peace for their strife, Thy joy for their sorrow, Thy love for their hatred, Thy compassion for their weakness. In Thine own strong Name, I pray. Amen.

Free Me, Lord, from Materialism

FORBID it, Lord, that our roots become too firmly attached to this earth, that we should fall in love with things.

Help us to understand that the pilgrimage of this life is but an introduction, a preface, a training school for what is to come.

Then shall we see all of life in its true perspective. Then shall we not fall in love with the things of time, but come to love the things that endure. Then shall we be saved from the tyranny of possessions which we have no leisure to enjoy, of property whose care becomes a burden. Give us, we pray, the courage to simplify our lives.

So may we be mature in our faith, childlike but never childish, humble but never cringing, understanding but never conceited.

So help us, O God, to live and not merely to exist, that we may have joy in our work. In Thy name, who alone can give us moderation and balance and zest for living, we pray. Amen.

In Sickness

"Hitherto have ye asked nothing in my name: ask, and ye shall receive, that your joy may be full."   JOHN 16:24

LORD Jesus, Thou art the Lord of Lords, the King of Kings. Thou art still the ruler of this universe. Thou art its Great Architect.

In the beginning, Thou didst design every part of it—from the twinkling of the great stars to the molding of the petals of the wayside flowers; from the coloring of the heavens to the tint of the butterflies' wings, even to this body of mine which is the Temple of Thy Spirit. Hear me now as I pray for Thy healing touch.

I confess that in my desperation and my need, I have wondered about the Providence of God. Forgive, I pray, this lack of trust in His power and in His love.

I acknowledge my unworthiness to ask Thee for any good gift. Yet I ask not on any merit of mine, but because of the claim purchased for me on the Cross.

Thou who didst Thyself explore all the vast treasures of pain on that Cross, bestow upon me Thy grace.

I have known Thee as the Saviour of my soul; now I would know Thee as the Saviour of my body. I would find in Thee this day the Great Physician.

I pray simply and humbly, with a deep conviction that Thou canst still heal and that Thou dost want to heal me. As I discover Thy strength in this time of weakness, may I never forget Thy mercy nor cease to give Thee thanks as health returns. In Thy lovely name, I pray. Amen.

For Those in Pain

THIS morning, O Christ, bird songs pour in through the open windows of hospitals. There are pain-glazed eyes looking out to where trees—dressed in the green lace of spring—are eloquent of recurring life.

Thou, O Christ, art the author of this new life. Wilt Thou even now visit the sick as Thou were even wont to do? Lay upon fevered brows the cool fingers of Thy love. May those who suffer, whom we name now before Thee, feel Thy presence at their bedsides, and have the realization at this moment of Thy touch, bringing to them new life and strength and health.

We thank Thee for the healings that have come, for the restorations that have been received, for many prayers answered. We thank Thee that Thou dost still heal today. We thank Thee that Thou dost still heal today. We thank Thee for this, the sweetest word of the gospel message, that Thou dost come with healing in Thy wings.

We thank Thee that Thou has heard and answered this prayer, born of our faith in Thee as the Great Physician. In Thy name, we pray. Amen.

For All Prisoners

LORD Jesus, who didst come to liberate the captives, remember the prisoners, we pray, those locked up in jails, those confined to the huts of the chain gangs.

Release from the prisons of their own making all those who struggle with habits that bind them. If Thou wilt make them free, they shall be free indeed. Release them, we pray.

And Lord, remember the captives of illness, weakness, and

pain. Loose them from that bondage into the heritage of health which is Thy perfect will for them.

Remember in Thy mercy the prisoners of sorrow who know not comfort, the prisoners of loneliness who know no solace of friendship. Thou who wast a friend to the friendless, Thou who wert a man of sorrows and acquainted with grief, remember them all most graciously.

Together we pray too for the peoples of other nations whose freedom has been stolen, whose liberties have been restricted or taken away, whose lives have known deep and dark shadows; for they too are prisoners; prisoners of human tyranny.

O God, let not the flares of freedom die out on the altars of their hearts that, having glimpsed that good life, they may not be disobedient to the vision nor forget the luster of the freedom yet to be.

For these great gifts we ask confidently, knowing that Thou didst come to earth to free us from "the bondage of corruption into the glorious liberty of the children of God." Amen.

For the Lonely

Lord Jesus, Thou hast walked earth's trails; Thou knowest the nostalgia of human life. Thou who hast been alone in the wilderness, bless now the members of the fraternity of loneliness.

To all who are bewildered, homesick, or ready to desert their post, give new courage. May they hear in the portals of their own souls the bugle call announcing the arrival of reinforcements.

May the friendship of Jesus of Nazareth be made known to them. May they find a welcome in this company of God's people. Wilt Thou guide and inspire them. Keep them from the mean and the low. Point them ever to the uplands of fellowship with Thee.

Transform for them their homesickness into new endeavors. Enable them to translate the affection of the heart into a new zest for living.

Direct our hearts that we may all be kindly affectioned one to another, abounding in love and sympathy, keeping back the unkind word, checking the hasty judgment, in all things being gentle and full of compassion in a world of hate. So may we walk softly before Thee and deal gently with one another, through Jesus Christ, our Lord. Amen.

In Time of Grief

FATHER, eyes blinded by the symbols of sorrow cannot see the stars. Even so, I, at this moment, can see nothing beyond my own grief.

I have been face to face with misery and loneliness in these days; with the strangeness of life and death that takes away a loved one and gives no explanation; with the mystery of a Providence I have tried to understand and cannot understand.

Thou, O Holy Spirit, Thou visitor in sorrow, Thou who art acquainted with human tears and broken hearts, sorely I need Thy help now.

Because my heart is sore, I have shut the door of my heart to my fellows, even to Thee. But I sense that withdrawal and the effort to dull my feelings is not the way toward healing. Help me now to dare to open my being wide to the balm of Thy loving Spirit, unafraid of any depth or height or intensity of overflowing emotion.

Thou hast promised to wipe away all tears from our eyes.

I ask Thee to fulfill that promise now.

Thou hast promised to bind up our wounded spirits.

I ask Thee to fulfill that promise now.

Thou hast promised to give us peace, not as the world gives but in the midst of our trouble.

I ask Thee to fulfill that promise now.

Thou hast promised to be with us alway.

I therefore thank Thee that Thou art walking beside me every step of the way.

I put my hand in Thine, and walk on into the future, knowing that it will be a good future because Thou art in it. Amen.

For Loneliness in Bereavement

FATHER, I am only human. I need the touch of human companionship. Sorely I miss those I love who are with Thee.

I pray, O Jesus, that Thou wilt reveal to me unseen presences. Help me to know how close my loved ones are. For if they are with Thee, and Thou art with me, I know that they cannot be far away.

Make real for me that contact of spirit with spirit that will re-establish the lost fellowship for which my heart yearns.

Give to me faith shining through my tears.

Plant peace and hope within my heart.

Point me with joy to the great reunion.

But until then, enable me to live happily and worthily of those who are with Thee. In the Name of Him who is the Lord of Life, I pray, Amen.

For Those Whose Hearts Are Broken

LORD Jesus, Thou hast been despised and rejected of men; be merciful to the disillusioned, to all those whose hearts have been wounded.

There are some for whom skies are dark, whose future is uncertain. These are Thy children with nameless griefs, weighed down in the bitterness of sorrow, living sorrows that have no graves and cannot be buried. There are hearts heavy with suspense, who wait in the twilight of an excruciating uncertainty.

Thou art a God who knowest every sin and shame of our lives and who loves us still. Be gracious now unto all these. Make them to feel the strength and the power of Thy grace that grants the ability to endure.

But, Lord, we pray not just that they will endure. We ask that even as a grain of sand in the oyster shell becomes—by patience and the grace of God—a pearl, so may the troubles of these, Thy children, yet become tokens of loveliness to glorify Thee. May they learn through these troubles what a wonderful God Thou art! Then shall we lift up our hearts, for Thou shalt cause a new light to shine in their eyes and a lilting song to return to their jaded hearts.

We know, Lord, that at the last all the lost chords of earth will be found in Heaven; all the broken melodies of our lives will be blended in the harmony and beauty of Thy glory. By this hope are we upheld and sustained; in this hope we live. In the strong name of Jesus Christ, our Lord. Amen.

For Those in the Evening of Life

Bless, O Lord, those who, nearing the end of their earthly pilgrimage, are sometimes tempted to wonder if they are forgotten; those who sorely need Thy companionship.

Sustain and gently lead them as they find the outward man declining and the strength of the body growing weak. May they—each step of the way—come to know and to love the Everlasting Arms, come to know that the Lord is indeed their Shepherd and will not forsake His sheep.

May they discover the uplift of the Everlasting Arms and the grace of God to sustain them, that they may be renewed in spirit and mount up with wings as eagles, that they may run and not be weary, that they may walk and not faint.

Help them to see by faith the twinkling lights of that celestial harbor in which their moorings shall be cast forever. Strengthen their faith and joy as they look forward to that haven where loved ones wait. How Thou must love them! Be gracious, our Father, be gracious unto them all, we ask in the name of Jesus, our Lord. Amen.

As We Look to the Future

> ". . . I will fear no evil: for Thou art with me; . . ."
> PSALMS 23:4

Lord Jesus, as we look into the future, let no fears assail us. Help us to be as confident that Thou wilt be with us in the future as we know Thou hast been in the past.

We know that our Christianity is no insurance policy against trouble, but rather the guarantee that Thou wilt be with us in the trouble. That should give us strong hearts and confident faith. For so long as Thou art beside us, loving us, helping us, what have we to fear?

Bless each one of us every day as we try to live like Christian men and women. Where we are inclined to be satisfied with ourselves as we are, make us willing to be changed.

Give us a more sincere kind of faith, a more virile, a more liveable faith, not alone a religion that smacks of Sunday, but the kind of faith that can be used on Monday and will not have evaporated by Saturday.

Hear us as we pray, standing on the threshold of time. Thou alone canst equip us for the tasks and the duties that are ours, that we may do our very best and quit us like men. In Thy strong name we pray. Amen.

Prayers for Special Days

On the Threshold of a New Year

OUR Father, grant that in the days of this new year we may feel Thy love, the love that surrounds us, the love that will not let us go but will ever bring us back—back to Thy side, back to Thy will, back to Thy way.

In that way we would walk, O Lord. For though all we like sheep have gone astray, like sheep, we are tired—tired of missing Thy path and stumbling along paths of our own choosing. Like sheep, we would return to the fold.

We would come back to Thee, confessing that we are not proud of the mistakes we have made, not too proud of our record as we look back over the last year. We are conscious not of our triumphs and successes but of our failures. We are in no boastful mood, O Lord, as we look into a new year. We seek now Thy forgiveness for our stupidity and our obstinacy, for the blindness of our hearts, for the wrong choices that grieved Thee and subtracted from our own happiness.

Wilt Thou forgive us, Father?

Humbly and gratefully we open our hearts to receive that great miracle of grace. We thank Thee for the fresh, strong wind of Thy Spirit which comes to bring us refreshment, cleansing, and perfect peace. Amen.

Lincoln's Birthday

OUR Father, we think this day of one upon whose shoulders in troubled times fell the mantle of great responsibility: a child of the South who became a leader of the North, in whose heart there lived that passion for union, that sense of brotherhood and unity that neither war's alarms nor the tides of politics nor the hatred of his foes could change or diminish.

And we thank Thee that now our whole nation unites in paying tribute to him who was humble before Thee. We thank Thee for his understanding heart and whimsical humor, and high resolve in all things to be on the side of God. We thank Thee that the memory of such a man is honored among us.

And we do pray that something of the spirit that was in Lincoln may indwell our leaders now, that they may see as clearly as he saw that only right makes right, that only as we are on the side of God can we hope that our affairs will prosper.

We pray that Thou wilt raise up among us now other men to walk as he walked, to talk as he talked, to rise above the undercurrents of politics, so that they may see the country as a whole and not be governed by pressure from this group or that, but may seek the common good and the will of God. In Thy name we pray. Amen.

For the Coming of Spring

WE GIVE Thee thanks for the loveliness of spring with its promise of summer.

Bird and blossom seem to tell us of the possibility of new life for our own souls. This spring day speaks to us of beginning again, of new beauty that can come to reburnish our own barren lives.

O Lord Jesus, may that transformation begin in us now as we sit before Thee—penitent and expectant. Amen.

Good Friday

As we look upon Thy Cross, O Christ, filled with wonder and with awe at the love that brought Thee to it, humbly we confess that we have no offering meet for such a love, no gift fit for such a sacrifice.

Thou wert willing to go to the Cross so that men might forever be haunted by its sign, might return to the foot of that Cross to be melted and broken down in the knowledge of Thy love for us and all men everywhere.

When we see a love like that—the love of God yearning for the hearts of His children, we know that only love can respond.

We acknowledge, O Lord, that there is so little in us that is lovable. So often we are not lovely in our thoughts, in our words, or in our deeds. And yet Thou dost love us still, with a love that neither ebbs nor flows, a love that does not grow weary, but is constant—year after year, age after age.

O God, may our hearts be opened to that love today. With bright skies above us, the fields and woods and gardens bursting with new life and beauty, how can we fail to respond? With the clear notes of bird songs challenging us to praise, with every lowly shrub and blooming tree catching new life and beauty, our hearts indeed would proclaim Thee Lord, and we would invite Thee to reign over us and make us truly Thine own. May Thy healing love invade our inmost hearts, healing sorrow, pain, frustration, defeat, and despair.

May this day create within us a love for Thee of stronger stuff than vague sentimentality—a love which seeks to know Thy will and do it. So grant that this day of hallowed remembrance may be the beginning of a new way of life for each of us, a new kind of living that shall be the best answer to the confusion and to the challenge of evil in our day. This we ask in Jesus' name. Amen.

Easter

"He is not here: for he is risen, as he said." MATTHEW
28:6

We THANK Thee for the beauty of this day, for the glorious
message that all nature proclaims: the Easter lilies with their
waxen throats eloquently singing the good news; the birds,
so early this morning, impatient to begin their song; every
flowering tree, shrub, and flaming bush, a living proclamation
from Thee. O open our hearts that we may hear it too!

Lead us, we pray Thee, to the grave that is empty, into the
garden of the Resurrection where we may meet our risen
Lord. May we never again live as if Thou were dead!

In Thy presence restore our faith, our hope, our joy.

Grant to our spirits refreshment, rest, and peace.

Maintain within our hearts an unruffled calm, an un-
broken serenity that no storms of life shall ever be
able to take from us.

From this moment, O living Christ, we ask Thee to go with
us wherever we go; be our Companion in all that we do. And
for this greatest of all gifts, we offer Thee our sacrifices of
thanksgiving. Amen.

Mother's Day

On THIS day of sacred memories, our Father, we would
thank Thee for our mothers who gave us life, who surrounded
us early and late with love and care, whose prayers on our
behalf still cling around the Throne of Grace, a haunting per-
fume of love's petitions.

Help us, their children, to be more worthy of their love. We

know that no sentimentality on this one day, no material gifts
—no flowers or boxes of candy—can atone for our neglect during the rest of the year.

So in the days ahead, may our love speak to the hearts who
know love best—by kindness, by compassion, by simple courtesy and daily thoughtfulness.

Bless her whose name we whisper before Thee, and keep
her in Thy perfect peace, through Jesus Christ, our Lord.
Amen.

Memorial Day

SAVE us, our Father, from either indifference or unseemly
revelry in this solemn hour, lest we mock those who lie in the
quiet places they liberated from the scourge, and their com-
rades in whose eyes are the shadowed memories of the horrors
they saw. Let us rather gird ourselves to finish the work they
began, that God's peace may yet come to all our troubled
world.

For the liberation of so many from the cruel hand of the op-
pressor, we give Thee thanks. As we were willing to make
sacrifices in war, so may we be willing to make sacrifices to
ensure a just and lasting peace. For those who are still in
bondage, we ask a speedy liberation.

Make us aware of the responsibility that rests upon us to
create peace in our own hearts, in our homes, in every as-
sociation with our fellows. Teach us that righteousness alone
exalteth a nation. Lead us; inspire us. Make us Thy people
to walk in Thy way, that this land may become in a new and
deeper way, God's own country. In the name of the God of
our Fathers, who is still our God, we pray. Amen.

For God's Blessing on a Marriage

Father, we know that Thou art the Author of Love; that the love which we bear each other is Thy gift to us, precious in Thy sight, precious in ours. Help us in the years ahead never lightly to regard that gift.

We know that the relationship into which we are about to enter is more than moonlight and roses, much more than the singing of love songs and the whispering of our vows of undying affection. We know that in Thy sight our marriage will be an eternal union. It is the clasping of our hands, the blending of our lives, the union of our hearts, that we may walk together up the hill of life to meet the dawn, together to bear life's burdens, to discharge its duties, to share its joys and sorrows.

We know that our marriage will stand and endure—not by the wedding ceremony or by any marriage license, but rather by the strength of the love which Thou hast given us and by the endurance of our faith in each other and in Thee, our Lord, the Master of our lives.

And now, as alone with Thee, we plight this troth: we do promise Thee, by Thy help, to be faithful and true to each other and to Thee who, having given us love and faith in Thee, hast given us all things.

We thank Thee that Thy blessing will go down the years with us as a light on our way, as a benediction to the home we are about to establish. May that home always be a haven of strength and love to all who enter it—our neighbors and our friends. We thank Thee. Amen.

Thanksgiving Day

Father, we around this table thank Thee:
> for Thy great gift of life,
> that Thy love for us is not dependent upon any unworthiness of ours,
> for good health,
> that we know neither hunger nor want,
> for warm clothes to wear,
> for those who love us best,
> for friends whose words of encouragement have often chased away dark clouds,
> for the zest of living,
> for many an answered prayer,
> for kindly providences that have preserved us from danger and harm.

We thank Thee that still we live in a land bountifully able to supply all our needs, a land which still by Thy Providence knows peace, whose skies are not darkened by the machines of the enemy, whose fields and woodlands are still unblasted by the flames of war, a land with peaceful valleys and smiling meadows still serene.

O help us to appreciate all that we have, to be content with it, to be grateful for it, to be proud of it—not in an arrogant pride that boasts, but in a grateful pride that strives to be more worthy.

In Thy name, to whose bounty we owe these blessings spread before us, to Thee we give our gratitude. Amen.

On a Winter's Day

W<small>E THANK</small> Thee, Lord, that there is no weather in heaven. Let not the dullness of this day get into our hearts or minds. May we be warm and cheerful, secure in the knowledge that Thou art still here, that no clouds can blot Thee out, no rain drive Thee away.

As winter blows her icy breath along the city's streets, our love goes out
> to all who need encouragement,
> to all who lack food and clothing,
> to all who are cold and cheerless,
> to all who long for home and friendship.

Help us, in our blessedness, to be more willing to share the good things of life. Give us generosity and that concern for others that shall mark us as disciples of Thine. Amen.

Christmas

W<small>E YEARN</small>, our Father, for the simple beauty of Christmas —for all the old familiar melodies and words that remind us of that great miracle when He who had made all things was one night to come as a babe, to lie in the crook of a woman's arm.

Before such mystery we kneel, as we follow the shepherds and Wise Men to bring Thee the gift of our love—a love we confess has not always been as warm or sincere or real as it should have been. But now, on this Christmas Day, that love would find its Beloved, and from Thee receive the grace to make it pure again, warm and real.

We bring Thee our gratitude for every token of Thy love,

for all the ways Thou hast heaped blessings upon us during the years that have gone.

And we do pray, Lord Jesus, that as we celebrate Thy birthday, we may do it in a manner well pleasing to Thee. May all we do and say, every tribute of our hearts, bring honor to Thy name, that we, Thy people, may remember Thy birth and feel Thy presence among us even yet.

May the loving kindness of Christmas not only creep into our hearts, but there abide, so that not even the return to earthly cares and responsibilities, not all the festivities of our own devising may cause it to creep away weeping. May the joy and spirit of Christmas stay with us now and forever.

In the name of Jesus, who came to save His people from their sins, even in that lovely name we pray. Amen.

For Our Children at Christmas

LORD Jesus, who didst take little children into Thine arms and laugh and play with them, bless, we pray Thee, all children at this Christmastide.

As with shining eyes and glad hearts they nod their heads so wisely at the stories of the angels, and a baby cradled in the hay at the end of the way of a wandering star, may their faith and expectation be a rebuke to our own faithlessness. Help us to make this season all joy for them, a time that shall make Thee, Lord Jesus, even more real to them.

Watch tenderly over them and keep them safe. Grant that they may grow in health and strength into Christian maturity. May they turn early to Thee, the Friend of children, the Friend of all. We ask in the lovely name of Him who was once a little child. Amen.

Prayers for the Nation and the World

Lord, We Confess as a Nation

O UR Father, bring to the remembrance of Thy people Thine ancient and time-honored promise: "If my people, which are called by my name, shall humble themselves, and pray, and seek my face, and turn from their wicked ways; then will I hear from heaven, and will forgive their sin, and will heal their land."

We—this company of Thy people assembled—would begin now to meet the conditions that will enable Thee to fulfill Thy promise.

May all of America come to understand that right-living alone exalteth a nation, that only in Thy will can peace and joy be found. But, Lord, this land cannot be righteous unless her people are righteous, and we, here gathered, are part of America. We know that the world cannot be changed until the hearts of men are changed. Our hearts need to be changed.

We therefore confess to Thee that:

Wrong ideas and sinful living have cut us off from Thee.
We have been greedy.
We have sought to hide behind barricades of selfishness; shackles have imprisoned the great heart of America.
We have tried to isolate ourselves from the bleeding wounds of a blundering world.
In our self-sufficiency we have sought not Thy help.
We have held conferences and ignored Thee completely.
We have disguised selfishness as patriotism; our arrogance has masqueraded as pride.
We have frittered away time and opportunities while the world bled.
Our ambitions have blinded us to opportunities.
We have bickered in factory and business, and sought to solve our differences only through self-interest.

Lord God of Hosts, forgive us! O God, by Thy guidance and Thy power may our beloved land once again become

54

God's own country, a nation contrite in heart, confessing her sins; a nation keenly sensitive to all the unresolved injustice and wrong still in our midst.

Hear this our prayer and grant that we may confidently expect to see it answered in our time, through Jesus Christ, our Lord. Amen.

For the President of the United States

We PRAY, Lord Jesus, for our President. We are deeply concerned that he may know the will of God, and that he may have the spiritual courage and grace to follow it.

Deliver him, we pray, from all selfish considerations.

Lift him above the claims of politics.

Fill him with the Spirit of God that shall make him fearless to seek, to know, to do the right.

Save him from the friends who, in the name of politics or even friendship, would persuade him from that holy path.

Strengthen and empower his advisers. Bring them, too, to their knees in prayer. May their example and their influence spread, that we, in these United States, may yet have a government of men who know Thee, the Almighty God, as their Friend, and who place Thy will first in their lives as well as in their prayers.

Hear and answer, we pray Thee, forgiving us all our unworthiness; cleansing us from every ignoble thought and unworthy ambition that we may be renewed in spirit and mind and heart, through Jesus Christ, our Lord. Amen.

For the Leaders of the Nation

Our Father, bless, we pray Thee, the leaders of this nation. Strengthen the courage of the representatives in Congress assembled—sincere men who want to do the right, if only they can be sure what is right. Make it plain to them, O Lord. And then wilt Thou start them out on the right way, for Thou knowest that we are hard to turn.

Forgive them for the blunders they have committed, the compromises they have made. Give to them the courage to admit mistakes. Take away from us as a nation and as individuals that stubborn pride which, followed by conceit, imagines itself to be above and beyond criticism.

Save our leaders, O God, from themselves and from their friends—even as Thou hast saved them from their enemies.

> Let no personal ambition blind them to their opportunities.
>
> Help them to give battle to hypocrisy wherever they find it.
>
> Give them divine common sense and a selflessness that shall make them think of service and not of gain.

May they have the courage to lead the people of this Republic, considering unworthy the expediency of following the people.

Save them from the folly of man-made schemes and plans. Give to them the faith and the courage together to seek God's inspired plan and, finding it, to propose it, knowing that when it is God-inspired, Thou wilt open the way for it through all obstacles.

As Thou hast made and preserved us a nation, so now mold us into a people more worthy of a great heritage. In Thy strong name we make these prayers. Amen.

For Our Land

Our Father, we pray for this land. We need Thy help in this time of testing and uncertainty, when men who could fight together on the field of battle seem strangely unable to work together around conference tables for peace.

May we begin to see that all true Americanism begins in being Christian; that it can have no other foundation, as it has no other roots.

To Thy glory was this Republic established. For the advancement of the Christian faith did the Founding Fathers give their life's heritage, passed down to us.

We would pray that all over this land there may be a return to the faith of those men and women who trusted in God as they faced the perils and dangers of the frontier, not alone in crossing the continent, in building their cabins, in rearing their families, in eking out a livelihood, but in raising a standard of faith to which men have been willing to repair down through the years.

Thou didst bless their efforts. Thou didst bless America. Thou hast made her rich. Wilt Thou also make her good?

Make us, the citizens of this land, want to do the right things. Make us long to have right attitudes. Help us to be Christian in our attitudes. Let all that we do and say spring out of understanding hearts.

Make us willing to seek moral objectives together, that in united action this nation may be as resolute for righteousness and peace as she has been for war.

Bless those who bear responsibility. May they be led by Thee to do that which is right rather than that which is expedient or politically wise. Save us from politicians who seek only their own selfish interests. Illumine the minds of management as well as labor, that there may be an end to selfishness and greed, to the stupidity of men who are unable to find in reasonable agreement solutions to the problems that plague us.

Bless this land that we love so much, our Father, and help her to deposit her trust, not in armies and navies, in wealth and material resources, or in achievements of the human mind, but in that righteousness which alone exalteth any nation, and by which alone peace can finally come to us. This we ask in that name that is above every name, Thy Son, Jesus Christ, our Redeemer. Amen.

For True Brotherhood

WE PRAY that Thou wilt teach us all how to live, that we may provide an example to all the world. Yet we confess before Thee the bigotry and the intolerance that plague us. We confess to Thee our disinclination to enjoy brotherhood, for we have withheld the spirit of it from many around us. O God, forgive us.

We remember that Thou didst bid us "to do good, to love mercy, to walk humbly with our God."

Give us such a vision of ministry that we can select for our philanthropy, for the expression of our love, these who cannot possibly recompense us at all.

Then only shall we discover what love really is, what brotherhood really means. Show us what Thou wouldst have us do today to make that discovery, we ask in the name of the Author of Love, even Christ Jesus, our Lord. Amen.

For Those in the Service of Our Country

WE, LORD Jesus, are children of God. Yet we would not be the sons and daughters of men were we not sometimes fearful, did not our hearts often ache and harbor anxiety for those we love who wear our country's uniform, who serve her in distant places.

Yet we know, our Father, that the Everlasting Arms reach out across the world. We know that the shadow of Thy wing covers all Thy children.

We are persuaded that in that world of the Spirit in which we really live neither persecution nor peril nor sword shall be able to separate us from Thy love.

We know that the bonds of the fellowship of prayer are real. We know that at the throne of grace we are all united, that our souls can mingle with those we love on earth even though separated by tumbling sea and dreary miles.

So now our minds and hearts reach out to be in spirit with those whom we name now before Thee; to surround them with our love and prayers and hopes. For them we ask:

support in time of need . . .

strength beyond their own . . .

confidence that Thou art their Shepherd, that Thou wilt never for a moment forsake them . . .

Thy strength in temptation, that they may be kept clean . . .

the gift of inner peace, a serenity that no tragedy can destroy . . .

that knowledge of God that shall assure them of eternal life, of peace and joy forevermore . . .

Thy gift of resoluteness in duty; gird them with courage; enable them to quit themselves like men who have deposited all their trust in their God . . .

a determination toward love, not hatred, that the fruits

of victory shall not wither . . .

salvation of body and soul, and if it be possible, bring them safely home.

We thank Thee that this ministry of intercessory prayer has linked our hearts and bound us even closer to those we love —closer to Thee and to them. May we feel Thy presence, and see by faith that day when the love of Christ shall live in the hearts of all men everywhere.

Hear, O God, not alone these prayers, but the unspoken inarticulate yearning of every seeking heart bowed before Thee. In the name of Jesus Christ, our Lord. Amen.

In a Time of National Danger

O LORD, when we, Thy children, are apprehensive about the affairs of our world, remind us that Thou art in Thy world as well as above and beyond it. Remind us that Thou art not indifferent. For Thou art not a spectator God, high and lifted up, serene and unperturbed. The feet that were wounded are still walking the trails of earth. The heart that was broken on the tree still feels every human woe.

Thus shall we not feel forsaken, nor give way to hopelessness. Thus we shall know that Thou hast a plan, and that Thy will shall one day be done on earth, not alone by those who love Thee and know Thee to be God, but by all, not in one nation or two, but in all the nations of the earth. Then shall every tongue confess that Christ is Lord, and every knee shall bow before Thee.

Sustain us with that hope and encouragement, that our prayer be not in vain when we pray "Thy Kingdom come." Come it will, however dark may be the present prospects for peace on earth—in the darkness of men's minds and the hardness of men's hearts.

We do pray that Thou, O Holy Spirit, where Thou dost find the doors of human hearts still closed before Thee, wilt knock the louder and wilt, in Thy own secret way, prevail upon the wills of men that they may do the will of God—ere it be too late.

All these things we ask in that name above every name, that name before whom all nations of the earth shall bow, Thy Son, Jesus Christ, our Redeemer. Amen.

Before a National Election

Lord Jesus, we ask Thee to guide the people of this nation as they exercise their dearly bought privilege of franchise. May it neither be ignored unthinkingly nor undertaken lightly. As citizens all over this land go to the ballot boxes, give to them a sense of high privilege and joyous responsibility.

Help those who are about to be elected to public office to come to understand the real source of their mandate—a mandate given by no party machine, received at no polling booth, but given by God; a mandate to govern wisely and well; a mandate to represent God and truth at the heart of the nation; a mandate to do good in the name of Him under whom this Republic was established.

We ask Thee to lead America in the paths where Thou wouldst have her walk, to do the tasks which Thou hast laid before her. So may we together seek happiness for all our citizens in the name of Him who created us all equal in His sight, and therefore brothers. Amen.

Gratitude for Our Heritage

WE GIVE Thee thanks, our Father, that Thou hast guided us safely over land and ocean, that in Thy kindly Providence Thou hast permitted our lot to be cast in this pleasant place, that we are privileged to live in a land founded under God.

We give Thee thanks that this land was settled by men and women who came here, as we did, in order that they might live in the light of freedom, in order that they might worship Thee according to the dictates of their consciences.

Help us never to forget, our Father, that all the rights and privileges we enjoy here have blood on them, that every good gift was bought and paid for in human sacrifice. This goodly heritage is ours by choice and by adoption. May we never lightly regard it! May we ever be grateful to those who in years past have labored and loved in order that we might have something to inherit. This we pray in humbleness and thanksgiving. Amen.

For World Peace

WE PRAY for our troubled world, wandering in the excruciating twilight of an uncertain peace. In our hearts we know that this is no true peace—rather suspicion and fear, animosity and greed.

We ask that Thy Spirit will strive mightily with the leaders of the nations as they seek a formula by which the peoples of the earth can live at peace with one another.

Impress upon their minds and hearts
    that until we are at peace with Thee, we can be at peace
      with no one else;

that freedom can exist nowhere unless it exists everywhere;

that the strength of this nation does not lie in armies or
navies, but in the integrity of her people;

that peace is born out of righteousness—and nothing else;

that the trouble with our world is still—people; that peace
is not possible until men's hearts—our hearts—and the
direction of our wills are changed.

Make us willing to be changed, whatever the cost to our
self-sufficiency, whatever the price to our insistence on having
our own way.

Wilt Thou reveal Thy will for America, that she may now
realize her destiny and place in Thy plan for the world?

O our Father, grant that the promised day may soon come
when culture and learning, education and pity, shall again
light all lamps that wars have extinguished; when all wander-
ers can return to their homes and their little gardens; when
"men to men the world o'er shall brothers be for a' that"; when
all of us may be united in the high adventure of building a
better world. In Thy name, who art the Father of us all, we
make this prayer. Amen.

For a Renaissance of Faith

Our Father, remove from us the sophistication of our age
and the skepticism that has come, like frost, to blight our
faith and to make it weak. Bring us back to a faith that makes
men great and strong, a faith that enables us to love and to
live, the faith by which we are triumphant, the faith by which
alone we can walk with Thee.

We pray for a return of that simple faith, that old-fashioned
trust in God, that made strong and great the homes of our

ancestors who built this good land and who in building left us our heritage. In the strong name of Jesus, our Lord, we make this prayer. Amen.

PART TWO

The Senate Prayers

SHEPHERD OF THE SENATE

On January 5, 1947, a telegram addressed to Dr. Peter Marshall was delivered to the door of the Presbyterian Manse on Cathedral Avenue in Washington. It read:

YOU WERE OFFICIALLY ELECTED CHAPLAIN OF THE U.S. SENATE JAN 4 STOP YOU SHOULD APPEAR AT THE OFFICE OF MR OCO THOMPSON FINANCIAL CLERK OF THE SENATE TOMORROW FORE-NOON AND HAVE THE OATH OF OFFICE ADMINISTERED TO YOU AND THEREAFTER OPEN THE SESSION OF THE SENATE WITH PRAYER AT 12:30 PM JAN 6 STOP

CARL A LOEFFLER SEC. OF SENATE

Thus—quite unpretentiously—Peter Marshall embarked on his duties as Senate chaplain. He felt strange, shy, and out of place that first morning as he hunted along the wide marble corridors of the Senate wing of the Capitol for Mr. Oco Thompson's office.

If someone had told Peter nineteen years before, as he was landing at Ellis Island as a quota immigrant, that he would someday be hunting for *anyone's* office in the Capitol on official business, it would have seemed fantastic indeed. In fact, the suggestion of such a thing did seem fantastic to him on the morning when Senator Kenneth Wherry first suggested it.

In this month of January, 1947, there was a Republican majority in Congress for the first time in fifteen years. Two of the men spearheading the Republican conference were Senator Styles Bridges of New Hampshire and the Majority Whip, Senator Kenneth Wherry of Nebraska. Senator Wherry came regularly to hear Dr. Marshall preach in the old red-brick church at H and New York Avenue, standing sentinel on its island in traffic. The New York Avenue Presbyterian Church was, moreover, Abraham Lincoln's old church. What

67

could be more appropriate, these men thought, than to have its minister as Senate chaplain for the new Republican Senate? It was Senator Wherry who posed the question to Dr. Marshall.

Peter insisted that he could not even consider such a post unless he had a most definite green light on it from the Chief. Several days of soul-searching on his part followed. Finally, he came to feel that God's hand was on this most unexpected invitation, and he agreed to let his name be proposed.

The quite unforeseen result was the first partisan fight on the floor of the Eightieth Congress—a matter of acute embarrassment to Peter.

An article by Harold B. Rogers in the *Washington Evening Star* of January 5, 1947, carried headlines: "DR. PETER MARSHALL ELECTED CHAPLAIN AFTER PARTY FIGHT; Senate Democrats Lose Move to Keep Dr. Harris in Post. The Senate late yesterday elected the Rev. Dr. Peter Marshall of the New York Avenue Presbyterian Church, as Chaplain of the Senate. . . ."

"During an extended debate over the subject shortly before adjournment, Democratic leaders contended that the chaplaincy should not be . . . subject to change with shift of party control.

"Republicans insisted there was no reflection whatever on Dr. Harris, and said Dr. Marshall had not been a candidate for the post. . . ."

When a reporter asked Dr. Marshall if he was a Republican or a Democrat, he replied, "Neither. I'm a native of Scotland, and as I was naturalized after I became a resident of the District in 1937, I've always been denied the right to vote."

Peter never felt quite right about this brush with party politics, until that day came two years later when he was re-elected by the Democratic majority. In the beginning, because of these political machinations, his attitude was a little rueful about the whole business of being chaplain.

He became even more rueful when, within a few days, he had sized up the job for himself. It seemed to him that the

Senators regarded the opening prayer as rather boring routine business. Ordinarily only a handful were on hand for the prayer; the rest were still in their offices or in committee meetings. Moreover, Peter missed the worshipful atmosphere created in his church service for the prayer by the reading of Scripture and the prayer-hymn. The atmosphere was scarcely made more worshipful by shuffling papers, shuffling feet, coughing, doors opening and closing.

All this made Peter wonder at first whether he had been mistaken about his green light and was simply wasting his time. On most days he had to be up on the Hill at noon. Though the prayer itself was brief, the time it took to get there and to return to his office at the church ate into his working day. The Chaplain, he found, was also expected to act in the capacity of a pastor to his Senatorial flock—to marry and conduct funeral services for members of Congress and their families, to baptize their children, to visit them when ill, to counsel with them if they wished it. The Senate has always had a chaplain for these duties. The first one took office on April 25, 1789. Dr. Marshall was the fifty-fourth chaplain—the first Presbyterian since 1879.

At the beginning, another difficulty troubled Peter. The Official Reporters of Senate Debate (the men responsible for getting all Senatorial discussion down on paper) requested of the new chaplain an advance copy of his prayer. This posed quite a problem, since Peter had never written out his public prayers. To do so seemed to him almost a denial of the reality of prayer, certainly of any heartfelt spontaneity. On the other hand, he did not wish to increase work for the overburdened reporters by forcing them to have to take his prayers down in shorthand and then transcribe them.

It was our friend Starr Daily who helped Peter solve this dilemma.* Mr. Daily's suggestion that God could best specifically guide Peter's prayers for the Senate in the quietness of his study, enabled him to make the adjustment involved in giving up his usual extemporaneous technique.

* See *A Man Called Peter*, pages 225 to 226.

Actually having to prepare the prayers in advance proved to be a fortunate discipline. It brought to full flower what *The New York Times* called "Dr. Marshall's pungent phrasing . . . and tart morsels of thought." (January 11, 1948)

Then there was the matter of the length of the prayers. "It's quite obvious," Peter smilingly commented at home to me, "that the Senators appreciate my prayers in inverse ratio to their length."

Dr. Marshall understood this and bowed to it. The result was that the longest prayer Peter ever prayed in the Senate—that of March 10, 1947, at the time of Mrs. Alben Barkley's death—took two minutes; the shortest, that which opened the Second Session of the Eightieth Congress—was exactly 36 words long and took a matter of seconds.

Peter's analysis concerning the inverse ratio of length to appreciation appeared to be correct. At any rate, it soon became apparent that the Senators were appreciative of his prayers. Soon after Dr. Marshall took office there came to be a noticeable difference in the number of Senators present in the Senate Chamber in time for the opening prayer.

The fresh, spontaneous quality of the prayers seemed to give the Senators a lift. Never before had most of these men heard any minister speak in public prayer about their "sulking as children will" (January 17, 1947); about their being "confused . . . and at cross-purposes with each other" (April 3, 1947). They had never heard the matter of obeying God spoken of as "a forced option—like eating—" (April 23, 1947). They were a bit rueful and yet amused when their chaplain suggested that they "quit waiting for the other fellow to change his attitude and his ways . . ." and get on with changing their own (April 24, 1947). And when he spoke of "the stubborn pride that keeps us from apology and confessing fault . . . to one another" (May 1, 1947), and "of the balloon tires of our conceit" (June 19, 1947), they marveled at his realistic analysis of human nature.

The Senators liked the complete absence of sanctimoniousness in Dr. Marshall. In his easy homespun colloquialisms they felt no effort to impress them with racy verbiage, but rather a man on intimate terms with his God, speaking to Him in a language that breathed an air of reality.

Many people (so they have told me since) whose daily routine included looking over *The Congressional Record,* acquired the habit of turning to the prayer first of all. Wire services like the Associated Press, periodicals such as *The Reader's Digest, The New Yorker,* and *This Week,* could not resist printing prayers like that of January 6, 1948, or that of May 14, 1947.

But there were far more significant results of these prayers than mere publicity. In his prayers, Dr. Marshall emphasized one point above all. This was that the Senators could secure God's specific guidance, wisdom, and help. Increasingly, individual men began coming to their chaplain to talk about how this principle could be applied to various legislative problems.

One of the most appreciative members of Dr. Marshall's Senatorial flock was Senator Arthur Vandenberg. Peter's usual daily routine was to leave his hat and coat in the Reporter's Office, chat for a few minutes with his friends there—Mr. John D. Rhodes, "Scottie" MacPherson, and others—and then go on to the Vice President's office to greet Senator Vandenberg. The two men usually spent about ten minutes talking, then walked together into the Senate Chamber.

Perhaps the relationship of the two men is best told in Senator Vandenberg's own words:

". . . he [Peter Marshall] was a very precious friend whom I came to know intimately during the past two years when I was serving as President of the Senate and he as Chaplain. We had a very beautiful relationship, a most intimate one, in which I am sure he gave his heart to me as I gave mine to him. I never knew a more rugged character. I never had a more delightful companion. . . ."

The Senator from Michigan was at that time in need of the quality of friendship which Peter gave him. Some of his colleagues in the Senate considered Vandenberg somewhat withdrawn and unapproachable. Perhaps it was because he had so much on his heart and mind that he sometimes gave this impression. In his private life there was the problem of Mrs. Vandenberg's poor health. As the months went on, it became clear that her illness was very serious.

In Vandenberg's public life he carried a great load. In January, 1945, there had been his dramatic conversion from isolationism. In a courageous public statement he had said in effect, "I've been wrong. I now publicly renounce isolationism." It was a permanent conversion; from then on he never wavered in his bipartisan leadership toward world responsibility.

In foreign policy, therefore, the record of the Eightieth Congress was an imposing one. It ended a hundred and fifty-two years of United States peacetime isolationism. It approved aid to Greece and Turkey; authorized ECA. It took the major inconsistencies out of the Truman Doctrine and placed it in the framework of UN. Both Senate and House members took their responsibilities seriously; over two hundred of them abandoned vacations to trudge over Europe on their own investigations. These events and other more everyday occurrences were the soil out of which grew Peter Marshall's Senate prayers. In order to re-create the setting I have interpolated between some of the prayers a few explanatory notes.

Peter had deep and honest admiration for Senator Vandenberg. Vandenberg, on his part, one day confided to Peter, using the Dutch nickname he had adopted, "Dominie, I've been a little disillusioned with preachers. You have restored my faith."

It would be presumptuous to try to measure or even to analyze the effect of Dr. Marshall's prayers. The results are God's results; He alone can measure them. Only He knows how many of Peter's prayers in the Senate were specifically answered. Only He knows the truth about how much difference prayer makes in the affairs of men and nations. Only He knows to what extent Vandenberg drew inner strength and inspiration from his friendship with Dr. Marshall during those crucial years.

God still works in mysterious ways. He uses a variety of instruments to make all things work together for good. At the very least then, the Senate prayers were one of God's instruments, one of many appointed factors all weaving a pattern toward the good which God willed for those early postwar days.

The government copy of the Senate *Prayers* bore the following Foreword by the Hon. Arthur H. Vandenberg:

"Rev. Peter Marshall was Chaplain of the Senate for two years while I presided as President *pro tempore* in the absence of a Vice President. Thus it was my daily privilege to greet him each noon when the Senate convened and to present him to my colleagues for his daily prayer. This duty swiftly became a precious privilege for me and this routine quickly became an inspiration. My Chaplain became my intimate and priceless friend.

"Dr. Marshall was a rugged Christian with dynamic faith. He was an eloquent and relentless crusader for righteousness in the lives of men and nations. He always spoke with courage, with deepest human understanding, and with stimulating hope. To know him was to love him. His sudden and untimely death was a loss of major magnitude to countless friends in whose hearts his memory will long and vividly survive.

"I count it a rare privilege to be permitted this foreword to his Senate prayers."

           ✻   ✻   ✻

Quite apart from the inherent value of the prayers which follow, Dr. Marshall's Senate chaplaincy was a significant milestone in his own life and ministry.

When, as a college student, I had first heard him preach, I had been haunted by a sense of destiny for him. The call to go to Washington had only served to heighten that feeling.

Then, when Peter received the invitation to become Chaplain of the Senate, I found myself in the grip of an inner conflict. Nineteen months before, my husband had suffered a severe heart attack. Though he had made a fine recovery, too heavy a work schedule was as a Damoclean sword hanging over his head. I knew that the Senate chaplaincy on top of the duties of his regular pastorate, would greatly add to his burdens.

Even then, however, there was the deep intuitive knowledge that this new ministry was meant to be. It was part of Peter's God-appointed destiny. I knew that fear, even for those we love, is always petty, while a sense of destiny is a personal testament of faith. There could be little question of the decision; faith must always triumph over fear.

Now in retrospect, I know how surely God led us. For January 6, 1947, when Dr. Marshall first stood on the floor of the Senate to pray, marked the beginning of what was to become an ever-widening ministry.

It was at that time that the nation at large began to hear about Peter Marshall. Then on that dismal winter's day in January, 1949, when he left us so suddenly, it looked as if his ministry was forever cut off.

But God's ways are never our ways, and God had quite a different plan. Someday the whole story can be told—a fairy-tale sort of story, so incredible that no other explanation for it seems possible apart from the golden alchemy of a loving God. Suffice it to say here that through the printed word Peter Marshall is preaching to more people today than he could ever have reached in a lifetime from the pulpit of any church.

No longer can any one church or denomination or nation claim Peter Marshall. For in the six years since his death, his ministry has leaped over all boundaries to become a cherished part of the heritage of Christendom around the world. I'm quite sure Peter knows about all this, has marveled at it, and rejoiced in it. In fact, it's exactly as he would have it.

Catherine Marshall

Washington, June 8, 1954

Eighthieth Congress

MONDAY, JANUARY 6, 1947

The Republican majority in Congress was in an oppose-Truman mood. Peter Marshall was not an astute follower of politics. "My interest, if any, is in public issues, not party politics," he said in an interview. Nevertheless he caught the atmosphere and its spiritual causes immediately.

He knew that the spirit of both Republicans and Democrats would have to be changed if we were to secure the best legislation for the country.

He also knew that facing this Eightieth Congress were tangles far too difficult of solution for any human wisdom. Therefore Peter's great desire was to bring to these men an awareness of and receptivity to God and His will for the specific issues before them.

O LORD our God, if ever we needed Thy wisdom and Thy guidance, it is now—as the Congress begins a new session, standing upon the threshold of a new year, fraught with so many dangerous opportunities.

We pray that Thou wilt bless these men chosen by the people of this Nation, for Thou knowest them, their needs, their motives, their hopes, and their fears. Lord Jesus, put Thine arm around them to give them strength, and speak to them to give them wisdom greater than their own. May they hear Thy voice and seek Thy guidance.

May they remember that Thou art concerned about what is said and done here, and may they have clear conscience before Thee, that they need fear no man. Bless each of us according to our deepest need, and use us for Thy glory, we humbly ask in Jesus' name. Amen.

WEDNESDAY, JANUARY 8, 1947

ETERNAL Father of our souls, grant to the Members and the officers of this body a sacred moment of quiet ere they take up the duties of the day. Turn their thoughts to Thee and open their hearts to Thy Spirit that they may have wisdom in their decisions, understanding in their thinking, love in their attitudes, and mercy in their judgments.

Let them not think, when this prayer is said, that their dependence upon Thee is over, and forget Thy counsels for the rest of the day.

Rather from these moments of heart-searching may there come such a sweetness of disposition that all may know that Thou art in this place. From this holy interlude may there flow light and joy and power that will remain with them until night shall bring Thy whispered benediction, "Well done, good and faithful servant."

So help us all this day, through Jesus Christ our Lord. Amen.

FRIDAY, JANUARY 10, 1947

LORD Jesus, Thou hast promised to give us the Holy Spirit if we are willing to open our hearts and let Him in. Make us willing now that things of eternal significance may begin to happen here.

We know deep down in our hearts that without Thy guidance we can do nothing, but with Thee we can do all things. Let us not be frightened by the problems that confront us, but rather give Thee thanks that Thou hast matched us with this hour. May we resolve, God helping us, to be part of the answer, and not part of the problem. For Jesus' sake. Amen.

MONDAY, JANUARY 13, 1947

SAVE this moment, O Lord, from being merely a gesture to custom or convention, and make it a real experience for each one of us in this place, as we call upon Thee for guidance and for help.

We have felt Thee near and beside us in the exalted experience of worship in church; make us now to feel Thy nearness in the business of the day—the Unseen Delegate, present and voting. Vote through these men, we pray Thee, O Jesus, that what they say and what they do may be in accordance with Thy will for this land that we love so much.

Thou hast said: "When ye stand praying, forgive, if ye have aught against any." Give us the grace to lay aside all bitterness or resentment we may be nursing in our hearts, lest their acid eat into our peace and corrode our spirits.

Thou hast said: "It is more blessed to give than to receive." Give us the grace today to think not of what we can get but of what we can give, that a new spirit may come into our work here, with a new vision and a new purpose, that Thou wilt delight to bless.

We ask these things in Thine own name and for Thy sake. Amen.

WEDNESDAY, JANUARY 15, 1947

OUR Father who art in heaven, we acknowledge that Thou dost govern in the affairs of men. And if a sparrow cannot fall to the ground without Thy notice, how can we think Thou art indifferent to what we say and do here?

If this day Thou dost want us to do, or not to do, any particular thing, we pray that Thou wilt make it plain to us, for Thou knowest how blind we can be, and how stubborn, in our own intentions. We pray for Thy help in our thinking and Thy love in our hearts. Through Jesus Christ our Lord. Amen.

FRIDAY, JANUARY 17, 1947

O LORD our God, before whom one day we shall all have to give account, lend us Thine aid, that this day's work may be well pleasing unto Thee.

If there be any here sulking as children will, deal with and enlighten him. Make it day about that person, so that he shall see himself and be ashamed. Make it heaven about him, Lord, by the only way to heaven—forgetfulness of self—and make it day about his neighbors, so that they shall help and not hinder him.

Forgetful ourselves, help us to bear cheerfully the forgetfulness of others. Give us courage, and faith, and the quiet mind. Give life to our good intentions, lest they be stillborn. Bless us in all that is right, and correct us in all that is wrong. We ask of Thee this help and mercy for Christ's sake. Amen.

MONDAY, JANUARY 20, 1947

O LORD our God, we remember Thy promise that wheresoever two or three are gathered together in Thy name, there Thou art in the midst of them. We claim that promise this morning, and pray that each one of us may be aware of Thy presence, for Thou knowest our needs and how inadequate we feel ourselves to be in the presence of world problems and the challenges of this hour. If Thou wilt help us, O Lord, then shall we be better than we are, wiser than we know, and stronger than we dream.

In this prayer, we bring unto Thee the Members of this body, its officers and its servants, for Thy blessing; men who feel the weight of responsibility and the need of divine guidance; men who often are sorely tempted and who need the support of Thy grace. Bestow upon them the courage to do the right as Thou hast given them to see the right, and make it clear unto us all, for Jesus' sake. Amen.

WEDNESDAY, JANUARY 22, 1947

> "Dear Lord and Father of mankind,
>   Forgive our feverish ways;
> Reclothe us in our rightful mind,
> In purer lives Thy service find,
>   In deeper reverence, praise.
>
> Take from our souls the strain and stress,
> And let our ordered lives confess
> The beauty of Thy peace."

DELIVER us, O Lord, from the foolishness of impatience. Let us not be in such a hurry as to run on without Thee. We know that its takes a lifetime to make a tree; we know that fruit does not ripen in an afternoon, and Thou Thyself didst take a week to make the universe.

May we remember that it takes time to build the nation that can truly be called God's own country. It takes time to work out the kind of peace that will endure. It takes time to find out what we should do, what is right and what is best.

Slow us down, O Lord, that we may take time to think, time to pray, and time to find out Thy will. Then give us the sense and the courage to do it, for the good of our country and the glory of Thy name. Amen.

FRIDAY, JANUARY 24, 1947

O FATHER in heaven, ere we become involved in the routine of the day, we pause to seek Thy help. Experienced in the ways of men, we know all too little of the ways of God.

But Thou knowest us, each one of us, by name and by our needs. Turn our wayward minds and hearts to Thee. Forgive the faults and failures of the past and set us free from them. Forgive, O Lord, our failure to apply to ourselves the standards of conduct we demand of others. Forgive our slowness to see the good in our fellows and to see the evil in ourselves.

In our differences may we be kind; in our agreements may we be humble, that Thy will may be done in us, and through us in our beloved land. For Jesus' sake. Amen.

MONDAY, JANUARY 27, 1947

> "... when we give ourselves to lesser loyalties and spend our time and our energies in that which is less than ... the best. ..."

The Congress was faced with decisions that would affect world peace for generations to come—what to do about China after our effort to back Chiang Kai-shek appeared to be failing; what to do about atomic control, the Marshall Plan for aid to Europe, grave labor trouble, etc.

Yet, at such a time, much discussion and effort were expended on issuing 3-cent airmail postcards on "good, stiff paper"; a bill to recondition the vessel Prowler *and return it to the Pomperang Council of the Boy Scouts of Bridgeport, Connecticut; a bill to authorize Federal funds for fighting cattle grubs, etc., etc.*

O LORD our God, before whom all our pretenses fall away, who knowest our secret thoughts and our hidden fears, bless us this day with Thy Spirit and help us to discharge our duties faithfully and well. Ever sensitive to the hurting of our own feelings, may we be sensitive also to our grieving of Thy Holy Spirit when we give ourselves to the lesser loyalties and spend our time and our energies in that which is less than the highest and the best.

We pray for the President of the United States, the members of the Cabinet, the representatives of the people, the judges of the land, and all those in authority, that it may please Thee so to rule their hearts that they may rightly use the trust committed to them for the good of all people.

Raise up among us, we pray Thee, fearless men who know that only in the doing of Thy will can we find our peace. So make it plain to us this day, and give us the courage to do it. All this we beg for Jesus Christ's sake. Amen.

WEDNESDAY, JANUARY 29, 1947

O GOD of Truth, who alone canst lead men into the truth that is freedom and joy, be Thou our teacher as we seek to find the way of life in times that bewilder and challenge.

Teach us better to know ourselves, that, knowing our weaknesses, we may be on guard. Teach us better to understand other people, that we may view their shortcomings with charity, their virtues with appreciation, and their kindness to us with gratitude.

Be with Thy servants in this place, in all things great and small, so that small things become great and great things become possible. Father of mercies, bless their loved ones and their families, and make their homes sanctuaries of love and peace where they may find spiritual resources for the strain and pressure of their duties here.

Give us now Thy spirit to guide and direct our thinking, that when the day's work is over we may merit Thy "Well done." Through Jesus Christ our Lord. Amen.

FRIDAY, JANUARY 31, 1947

ALMIGHTY God, creator of all things, giver of every good and perfect gift, hear us this day as we seek Thy blessing upon our deliberations.

We acknowledge before Thee our shortcomings, our selfishness, our smugness, and our pride. Forgive us wherein we have come short of Thy will for us and for our Nation. Create within us clean hearts, and renew right spirits, that we may do better and be better. Forgive us our forgetfulness of the world's sore need and our contentment with things as they are.

Hear us when we pray for all those in places of influence and authority, that they may do right. Guide those who lead us; and touch Thy servants with Thy Holy Spirit, that their faith may be revived, their hope renewed, and their vision made clear and challenging. Give to them the conviction that with Thy help all things are possible—even the most difficult things that baffle us now. God forbid that any of us here should add to the problems of the hour, but rather resolve, by Thy help, to become part of the answer. So help us, God, for Jesus' sake. Amen.

MONDAY, FEBRUARY 3, 1947

"Amid all the pressures brought upon them. . . ."

Much of the pressure during this month of February was brought by powerful industrialists who had descended on Washington to demand high tariffs. Production capacity of the Nation had been increased by World War II, and the United States was in a position to supply the rest of the world with many commodities, and thus lead the way to recovery. But if economic nationalism were allowed to continue, other countries would have no chance at all to get back on their feet.

Our Father, as we come before the Throne of Grace this day, we would not weary Thee with our constant begging. We would not be like petulant children seeking diplomas without study, or wages without work.

We thank Thee for lessons to learn and for work to do. May we apply ourselves to both.

As Thy servants here sincerely seek to do right, make it plain to them. Knowing that criticism will come, help them to take from it what is helpful and to forgive what is unjust and unkind. Amid all the pressures brought upon them, may they ever hear Thy still small voice and follow Thy guidance for the good of all the people, that Thy will may be done in this Nation, through these Thy servants. For Jesus' sake. Amen.

WEDNESDAY, FEBRUARY 5, 1947

Our Father, in the midst of the complicated situations of life and the unsolved problems of the world, deliver Thy servants from any sense of futility. Let them feel the support of the prayers of hosts of true patriots throughout this land and, above all, the uplift of the Everlasting Arms.

Cause them to understand that God's power has never been obstructed by difficulties, nor His love limited by the confusion of human plans. May the very failure of man's best resources impel us toward the resources of God.

Cleanse our hearts of selfishness. Grant that all questions immediately before us may be made so plain that we shall have no forebodings as we make our decision, nor vain regrets after it is made. For Jesus' sake. Amen.

FRIDAY, FEBRUARY 7, 1947

Forgive us, O God, for all our boasting and our presumptuous sins of pride and arrogance, for these are days that humble us.

By Thy grace we become more and more aware of our limitations and our weaknesses.

Let us not mistake humility for an inferiority complex, but help us to understand that with the proud and the self-sufficient Thou canst do nothing until Thou hast brought them to their knees.

We need Thy help, our Father, and we seek it humbly. We want to do right, and to be right; so start us in the right way, for Thou knowest that we are very hard to turn. Shed forth Thy grace upon us, O Lord, that each man here may say, "I can do all things through Christ which strengtheneth me." We ask it in His name. Amen.

MONDAY, FEBRUARY 10, 1947

O LORD, teach us to number our days that we may apply our hearts unto wisdom. Time is short, and no one of us knows how little time he has left. May we be found using wisely our time, our talents, and our strength.

Break to us this day the "bread of life." Our hearts are hungry, as are the hearts of people everywhere. Save us from thinking, even for a moment, that we can feed our souls on things. Save us from the vain delusion that the piling up of wealth or comforts can satisfy.

Save these, Thy servants, the chosen of the people, from the tyranny of the nonessential, from the weary round of that which saps strength, frays nerves, shortens life, and adds nothing to their usefulness to Thee and to this Nation. Help them to give themselves to the important and to recognize the trivial when they see it. Give them the courage to say "No" to everything that makes it more difficult to say "Yes" to Thee. For Jesus' sake. Amen.

TUESDAY, FEBRUARY 11, 1947

WE THANK Thee, Almighty God, for the rich heritage of this good land, for the evidences of Thy favor in the past, and for the Hand that hath made and preserved us a nation.

We thank Thee for the men and women who, by blood and sweat, by toil and tears, forged on the anvil of their own sacrifice all that we hold dear. May we never lightly esteem what they obtained at a great price. Grateful for rights and privileges, may we be conscious of duties and obligations.

On this day we thank Thee for the inspiration that breathes in the memory of Abraham Lincoln, and we pray that something of the spirit that was his may be ours today. Like him, may we be more concerned that we are on Thy side, than that Thou art on ours. In our hearts may there be, as there was in his, "malice toward none and charity for all"; that we may, together, with Thy blessing and help, "bind up the nation's wounds, and do all which may achieve and cherish a just and lasting peace among ourselves and with all nations." Through Jesus Christ our Lord. Amen.

FRIDAY, FEBRUARY 14, 1947

O THOU Great Architect of the Universe, whom, by the revelation of Thy Son our Lord, we may address as our Father, help us to understand what that means. As we are now united in our praying, so may we be united in our working, that, as a team, we may be doing together the will of our Father, who is not a God of any one part, of any one nation, or of any one race.

Open our eyes that we may discern what God is doing, and our ears that we may hear what God is saying. And then, O God, give us all we need to take due notice and to govern ourselves accordingly. We ask these things in the strong name of Jesus Christ our Lord. Amen.

MONDAY, FEBRUARY 17, 1947

O LORD of our life, we would know Thee better, that we might love Thee more, and thus be more useful to our fellow men. Make us hungry for Thy spirit and Thy power. Let Thy grace come upon us that the will of our God may be known to us and done through us.

Let us not break faith with any of yesterday's promises nor leave unrepaired any of yesterday's wrongs. Show us what we can do to make this world a better place for men to live in, that the down payment made by 300,000 of our men may not have been made in vain.

May the urgency of the world's need remind us that promises do not feed the hungry nor resolutions give them shelter. May we be willing to act when Thou shalt show us what to do. We join our hearts in this prayer for Thy guidance. In the name of Jesus Christ our Lord. Amen.

WEDNESDAY, FEBRUARY 19, 1947

Oᵁᴿ Father in heaven, we pray for the Members of this body in their several responsibilities. Help them in their offices, in committees, and above all, as they meet here in legislative session.

May they never forget that what is said and done here is not done in a corner, but always under Thy scrutiny. May they feel the weight of their responsibility before Thee, and remember the influence of a good example, that all who come to this place may have a stronger faith in government of the people, by the people, for the people.

May the Senators so speak and act that all who wait upon them may be inspired, rather than disillusioned by what they see and hear and are asked to do. Lord Jesus, make Thyself real to these men, that each may feel Thee sitting beside him, and hear Thy voice, and win Thine approval in all things. So help them, God, for Jesus' sake. Amen.

FRIDAY, FEBRUARY 21, 1947

This was the World Day of Prayer, first observed in the year 1887.

Wᴇ recognize, our Father, as George Washington saw so clearly, that "no people can be bound to acknowledge and adore the Invisible Hand which conducts the affairs of men more than those of the United States. Every step by which they have advanced to the character of an independent nation seems to have been distinguished by some token of providential agency."

Believing that the Hand that hath brought us thus far will

not forsake us now, but if we are willing will lead us on into further inspiration and service to all mankind, we would join our prayers this day with those of Christian women all over the world in this day of prayer.

With so many souls united in intercession for our own beloved country and for all mankind, may there come an outpouring of Thy Spirit into our hearts and minds that we shall feel it and all men may know it. "Lift us above unrighteous anger and mistrust, into faith and hope and charity, by a simple and steadfast reliance on Thy sure will."

We pray for some evidence in what is said and done here that Thou hast been permitted a vote, and that these men have yielded their lives to Thee. In Jesus' name. Amen.

MONDAY, FEBRUARY 24, 1947

OUR Father in heaven, we know that Thou canst see the hidden things in every heart. If our intentions are good, help us to make them live in good deeds. If what we intend or desire makes us uncomfortable in Thy presence, take it from us, and give us the spirit we ought to have that we may do what we ought to do. For Jesus' sake. Amen.

WEDNESDAY, FEBRUARY 26, 1947

WITH all the resources of an infinite God available to them that ask Thee, forgive us, O Lord, for our lack of faith that begs for pennies when we could write checks for millions, that strikes a match when we could have the sun.

Give to us the faith to believe that there is no problem before us that Thy wisdom cannot solve. As Thou hast guided men in the past, so guide these men today. At every desk may there be a whisper of Thy counsel. Help our leaders to weigh their words, that their words may carry weight and, what is more, the echo of Thy will, for Jesus' sake. Amen.

FRIDAY, FEBRUARY 28, 1947

Give to us open minds, O God, minds ready to receive and to welcome such new light of knowledge as it is Thy will to reveal. Let not the past ever be so dear to us as to set a limit to the future. Give us the courage to change our minds when that is needed. Let us be tolerant of the thoughts of others, for we never know in what voice Thou wilt speak.

Wilt Thou keep our ears open to Thy voice and make us a little more deaf to whispers of men who would persuade us from our duty, for we know in our hearts that only in Thy will is our peace and the prosperity of our land. We pray in the lovely name of Jesus. Amen.

MONDAY, MARCH 3, 1947

". . . . help us to share what Thou hast given. . . ."

Much of Europe was facing starvation. Critics of the Adminis-tration thought that the program of exporting $3 billion worth of food (10 per cent of our food stocks, 33⅓ per cent of our total wheat production) would impoverish us.

But Peter Marshall felt that the 10 per cent was merely a "tithe" of our food riches, and that God would abundantly bless the nation for this sharing. So it proved to be. We had a bumper wheat crop that year.

Lord God of Heaven, who hath so lavishly blessed this our beloved land, keep us humble. Forgive our boasting and our pride, and help us to share what Thou hast given. Impress us with a sense of responsibility, and remind us, lest we become filled with conceit, that one day a reckoning will be required of us.

Sanctify our love of country, that our boasting may be turned into humility and our pride into a ministry to all men everywhere. Make America Thy servant, Thy chosen channel of blessing to all lands, lest we be cast out and our place be given to another. Make this God's own country by making us willing to live like God's people. We ask these things in the name of Jesus Christ our Lord. Amen.

WEDNESDAY, MARCH 5, 1947

Gen. George C. Marshall, then Secretary of State, was about to leave for Moscow to attend the Conference on Peace Treaties with Germany and Austria.

OUR Father, we know that we, by ourselves, are not sufficient for these days and for problems greater than the measure of our best wisdom.

We pray that Thou wilt grant safe journey to our Secretary of State as he carries the hopes and the prayers of this Nation to the conference across the sea. A soldier himself, may he remember the price that was paid by millions for this opportunity, and may we, who pray for the success of the mission, be willing to pay the price for peace.

We believe, O Lord, that Thou wilt be present, with the marks of the nails in Thy hands, to lead them, and bless them, if they will receive Thy Spirit.

May the ministers be aware of the Unseen Delegate. May Thy Spirit move them, that there may be concession without coercion and conciliation without compromise. May they, who represent us, represent Thee and, in Thy Spirit, be courageous enough to begin anew, fearless enough to admit mistakes, and loving enough to forgive others. May we have the courage to apply what we applaud, to the end that we may help to establish Thy way of life for the people of the world. So may we all do the best we can, by Thy help, and be willing to leave the issue in Thy hands, through Jesus Christ our Lord. Amen.

FRIDAY, MARCH 7, 1947

O THOU Holy Spirit, who hast promised to lead us into all truth, prepare our hearts and minds for the business of this day, that we may behave with true courtesy and honor.

Compel us to be just and honest in our dealings.

Let our motives be above suspicion.

Let our word be our bond.

Save us from the fallacy of depending upon our personality, or ingenuity, or position to solve our problems.

Since Thou hast the answers, make us willing to listen to Thee, that we may vote on God's side, and that God's will may be done in us. Through Jesus Christ our Lord. Amen.

MONDAY, MARCH 10, 1947

Mrs. Alben W. Barkley, wife of Senator Barkley (Kentucky), Minority Leader, had died in Washington.

OUR Father, as we come into Thy presence this morning, we are saddened by the announcement of the great loss and bereavement sustained by one of the most distinguished Members of this body. Our sympathy goes out to him, deep and tender, as we stand at his side sharing his sorrow as far as friends may, and joining our prayers that he may feel even now the Everlasting Arms upholding him and Thy grace and Thy love sustaining him in this dark hour.

We give Thee thanks for his constant devotion, for the courage and the fidelity to duty that has marked these last years when he was called upon by Thy strange and mysterious providence to walk a hard road; and we give Thee thanks for the beauty and inspiration that his helpmeet provided in the difficult experiences they shared together.

We thank Thee for her charm and for the winsome beauty of her life and spirit, and we pray that Thy grace may be sufficient now for him who was her partner and for the members of the family who mourn her going.

We thank Thee for the hope Thou hast given us that there will come a day when the lost chords of life may be found again in that happy land, and all that is dark and mysterious now shall be revealed and its purposes made plain.

We pray that in this great sorrow, shared by each Member of this body, we may be drawn closer to each other in true comradeship and fellowship. May sympathy unite our hearts to each other and bind us to Thee, who dost mark our tears and hast promised to wipe them away.

So may Thy blessing be upon our brother now and upon all who are with him in the fraternity of sorrow, that their faith may be strengthened and their hope made bright and triumphant. Through Jesus Christ our Lord. Amen.

WEDNESDAY, MARCH 12, 1947

ALMIGHTY Father of the universe, we come to Thee, conscious of our own shortcomings but with confidence and composure, knowing that, having put our trust in Thee, our faith is well founded.

May we tolerate nothing in our personal living which, if multiplied, would weaken our Nation. Teach us that our country is no better than its citizens and no stronger than those in whom it puts its trust.

So may we see ourselves as Thou dost see us, that being ashamed we may seek forgiveness, and knowing our weaknesses may accept Thy strength. With Thy blessing upon us, we need not fear decisions nor hesitate to act. So use us, guide us, and act through us, we ask in Jesus' name and for His sake. Amen.

FRIDAY, MARCH 14, 1947

God of our fathers and our God, in the gloom of this troubled hour, disclose the brightness of Thy presence and revive within us the hope of our faith.

Deliver us from discouragement, and when we feel most helpless, make us turn to Thee for the answers Thou hast for every question. Enable us to see issues clearly, before crisis clouds them, and help us to choose the good course, lest relying upon our own wisdom we have to choose between evils.

Give us the boldness of a faith that has conviction as well as sentiment, and take from us all fear save that of failing to do Thy will. We ask in the name of Him who died for all men, even Jesus Christ our Lord. Amen.

MONDAY, MARCH 17, 1947

Lord Jesus, we turn in confidence unto Thee, since Thou wast tempted in all points like as we are, and yet without sin. Help us, that we may obtain victory over our temptations. We feel ashamed that we have so little power in our lives and so often fall at the same old hurdles. Sometimes we grow discouraged and filled with doubts when we see so little evidence of growth in grace, in faith, and in spiritual perception.

We know that we are not what we ought to be; and we know that we are not yet what we will be; but we thank Thee that we are not what we once were. For whatever progress Thou hast made with us we give Thee thanks, and by Thy grace we are kept from despair. Help us to remember that they that wait upon the Lord shall renew their strength. May we wait and be made strong. Through Jesus Christ our Lord. Amen.

TUESDAY, MARCH 18, 1947

Our Father in heaven, who dost know every secret of our hearts—all that we fear, all that we hope, and all of which we are ashamed—in this moment of confusion, as each man looks into his own heart and mind, have mercy upon us all, and make us clean inside, that in all we do today we may behave with true courtesy and honor. Let us be kind in our criticism of others, and slow to judge, knowing that we ourselves must one day be judged.

We pray for a new spirit to come upon us that we may be able to do more and better work. Through Jesus Christ our Lord. Amen.

WEDNESDAY, MARCH 19, 1947

Lord Jesus, Thou who art the way, the truth, and the life, hear us as we pray for the truth that shall make men free. Teach us that liberty is not only to be loved but also to be lived.

Liberty is too precious a thing to be buried in books. It cost too much to be hoarded.

Make us to see that our liberty is not the right to do as we please but the opportunity to please to do what is right.

So may America, through Thy servants, the Members of this body, do what is right, that Thy blessing can rest upon their labors and give them good conscience. Through Jesus Christ our Lord. Amen.

THURSDAY, MARCH 20, 1947

". . . . Teach us economy in speech. . . ."

A long, windy debate was going on over the budget. The Senate wished to cut the budget by $4.5 billion. Many sharp words were being spoken. Finally at the suggestion of Senator Knowland (Cali-

fornia), is was decided to reduce the national debt rather than taxes.

O THOU who hast the words of eternal life, help us to cultivate proper speech. Surrounded as we are in this city with noble inscriptions of the plain, stirring words of wise men, may we say what we mean and mean what we say. And may it be worth saying. Teach us economy in speech that neither wounds nor offends, that affords light without generating heat. Bridle our tongues lest they stampede us into utterances of which, later, we shall be ashamed. This we ask in Jesus' name. Amen.

FRIDAY, MARCH 21, 1947

> ". . . . Help us to stand up for the inalienable rights of mankind and the principles of democratic government. . . ."

Britain, completely sapped by the war, was no longer economically able to continue to be the world champion of democratic principles. Greece and Turkey needed to be defended against communist encroachment. The question was: would the United States now take over this world leadership? Because of the leadership of Senator Vandenberg and Secretary of State Marshall, we did accept that leadership.

O LORD our God, in the midst of the troubles that surround us, when compromises come home to roost and expediencies return to plague us, keep us from adding to the mistakes of the past.

Save us from accepting a little of what we know to be wrong in order to get a little of what we imagine to be right.

Help us to stand up for the inalienable rights of mankind and the principles of democratic government consistently and with courage, knowing that Thy power and Thy blessing will be upon us only when we are in the right. May we so speak, and vote, and live, as to merit Thy blessing. Through Jesus Christ our Lord. Amen.

MONDAY, MARCH 24, 1947

". . . . the blatant voices of aggressive pressure groups. . . ."

Seeing Capitol Hill at close range, Peter Marshall was appalled at the number and persistency of minority pressure groups. He sympathized with the Senators in the dilemma into which this constantly plunged them.

LORD God of hosts, Thou who art concerned about two billions of Thy creatures all over the earth, and yet who art concerned about each of us here as if we were an only child, Thou dost understand how hard it is for these Thy servants to keep in mind the millions of their fellow citizens for whom they must legislate.

Thou knowest the clamor of voices in their ears, the constant tugging at their sleeves, forever trying to influence them; the small voices of the little men without money or names; the blatant voices of aggressive pressure groups; the big voices of selfish men and those working for personal gain; even the whispering inner voices of personal ambition, those insinuating voices holding out the lure of unmerited reward.

Amid all the din of voices, give these Thy servants the willingness to take time to listen to Thy voice, knowing that if they follow the still small voice within, all Thy people will be served fairly and all groups will get what they deserve. For Jesus' sake. Amen.

TUESDAY, MARCH 25, 1947

OUR Father in heaven, as we pray for Thy guidance and help, we know that Thou dost not intend prayer to be a substitute for work.

We know that we are expected to do our part, for Thou hast made us, not puppets, but persons with minds to think and wills to resolve. Make us willing to think, and think hard, clearly, and honestly, guided by Thy voice within us, and in accordance with the light Thou hast given us.

May we never fail to do the very best we can. Help us to pray in the knowledge that it all depends on Thee. Help us then to work as if it all depended on us, that together we may do that which is well pleasing in Thy sight. For Jesus' sake. Amen.

WEDNESDAY, MARCH 26, 1947

In the name of Jesus Christ, who was never in a hurry, we pray, O God, that Thou wilt slow us down, for we know that we live too fast. If we are to burn ourselves out, may it be in causes worth dying for.

With all of eternity before us, make us take time to live— time to get acquainted with Thee, time to enjoy Thy blessings, and time to know each other. Deliver us from wasting time and teach us how to use it wisely and well. We ask these things in the lovely name of Jesus. Amen.

THURSDAY, MARCH 27, 1947

". . . . our great need of Thy guidance. . . ."

*The question of whether to end sugar rationing was being de-
bated. The Senators were harried by thousands of letters from
housewives begging that controls not be continued.*

*On this day one of the Senators approached Peter at the close
of his prayer. "I've been listening pretty closely to your prayers,"
he said. "You seem to think a man can get specific guidance from
God about his work. Tell me now, do you really think God could
tell someone like me how to vote on the Sugar Bill?"*

Peter felt that this was sincere seeking, and it heartened him to know that his prayers were pointing the men to the real source of the wisdom they constantly needed.

Our Father, we stand to join our hearts in prayer in our acknowledgment of our great need of Thy guidance. We know that by ourselves we are not sufficient for these days or for problems beyond the measure of our best wisdom.

We are finding out that government of the people by the people is not good enough. We pray for government of the people by God.

As this Nation was founded under God, so we confess that our freedom, too, must be under God. Then, and only then, shall we achieve the peace we seek and the righteousness which alone exalteth a nation.

Hear our prayer, O God, and grant unto the Members of this body Thy guidance, we humbly beseech Thee in Jesus' name. Amen.

FRIDAY, MARCH 28, 1947

> ". . . . Thy solutions to the questions that perplex us. . . ."

For ten weeks the Senate had been debating the appointment of David E. Lilienthal as a member of the Atomic Energy Commission.

This procrastination was finally ended by a masterly speech by Arthur Vandenberg, President pro tem of the Senate.

Though Peter usually left immediately after his prayer, on those occasions when Vandenberg turned the Chair over to someone else and took the floor, Peter always stayed to hear him speak.

Lord Jesus, who didst promise that by faith Thy disciples might remove mountains, increase our faith till we no longer are awed by difficulties and frightened by problems. Hold us by Thy mighty hand until doubts shall cease and we begin to believe. Then shall we find all things possible, even Thy solutions to the questions that perplex us. For this we do pray. Amen.

MONDAY, MARCH 31, 1947

Our Father, as we seek Thy blessing, remind us that we cannot deceive ourselves.

We dare not devise our own plans and draft our own schemes and then have the nerve to ask Thee to bless them, for we know that there are some things Thou wilt not and cannot bless.

And unless Thy blessing accompanies what we do here, we waste our time. So guide us in what we propose, so that Thou canst bless us in what we produce. Through Jesus Christ our Lord. Amen.

TUESDAY, APRIL 1, 1947

When we are honestly perplexed and have to do something, and are not sure what to do, we need Thy help, O God. In our choices let us not ask, "Will it work?" but rather, "Is is right?" In this prayer we reach up to Thee. May we find that Thou art reaching down to us, and may we believe that when we are willing to listen, Thou wilt speak. We wait upon Thee, O God. Through Jesus Christ our Lord. Amen.

WEDNESDAY, APRIL 2, 1947

O god, who didst love us all so much that Thou didst send us Jesus Christ for the illumination of our darkness and the salvation of our souls, give us wisdom to profit by the words He spoke, faith to accept the salvation He offers, and grace to follow in His steps.

As Christ said: "When ye stand praying, forgive, if ye have aught against any." O God, give us grace now so to do.

As Christ said: "It is more blessed to give than to receive." O God, give us grace today to think not of what we can get but of what we can give.

As Christ said: "Judge not, that ye be not judged." O God, give us grace this day first to cast out the beam out of our own eyes before we regard the mote that is in our brother's eyes.

And when we find it hard to be humble, hard to forgive, O Lord, remind us how much harder it was to hang on the Cross. Amen.

THURSDAY, APRIL 3, 1947

On the night of April 2 the Senate was in session until midnight. * *There had been a steady four hours of debate, climaxing ten weeks of discussion over the appointment of David E. Lilienthal as chairman of the Atomic Energy Commission.*

The Senators were exhausted; Senatorial tempers were raw. At almost midnight, Senator Morse wanted the floor; Senator Wherry moved to recess and refused to yield the floor to Morse. The motion to recess carried. Immediately afterward there were a few sharp words between Wherry and Morse.

The Washington papers the next morning exaggerated the incident into a near fist fight. Peter had not seen the papers and knew nothing of the incident when he wrote or delivered the prayer which follows.

But the prayer spoke to Senator Wherry's heart. He thought his minister was praying right at him. After the prayer, he followed Peter into the corridor. "Parson," he said, "I guess you know God pretty well. You know the Catholics believe in having a father-confessor. Will you be mine? I'm awfully sorry for what happened last night. . . ."

This incident gave Peter a great lift. Obviously, the Spirit of God was at work in the United States Senate.

* See pages 228 to 230 of *A Man Called Peter.*

GRACIOUS Father, we, Thy children, so often confused, live at cross-purposes in our central aims, and hence we are at cross-purposes with each other. Take us by the hand and help us to see things from Thy viewpoint, that we may see them as they really are. We come to choices and decisions with a prayer upon our lips, for our wisdom fails us. Give us Thine, that we may do Thy will. In Jesus' name. Amen.

MONDAY, APRIL 7, 1947

WE KNOW, our Father, that there is a time to speak and a time to keep silence. Help us to tell the one from the other. When we should speak, give us the courage of our convictions. When we should keep silence, restrain us from speaking, lest, in our desire to appear wise, we give ourselves away.

Teach us the sacraments of silence that we may use them to know ourselves and, above us, to know Thee. Then shall we be wise. Through Jesus Christ our Lord. Amen.

TUESDAY, APRIL 8, 1947

ALMIGHTY and eternal God, Thou who alone knowest what liest before us this day, grant that in every hour of it we may stay close to Thee. Let us today embark on no undertaking that is not in line with Thy will for us here, for our country and our world.

Bestow Thy grace upon the Presiding Officer, the Members, and the servants of this body. Illumine our minds and direct our thinking, that our thoughts and our actions may merit Thy blessing. For our Lord Christ's sake. Amen.

WEDNESDAY, APRIL 9, 1947

Our fathers' God, to Thee, who art the author of our liberty, and under whom we have our freedom, we make our prayer.

Make us ever mindful of the price that was paid to obtain that freedom and the cost that must be met to keep it. Help us in this Nation so to live it that other men shall desire and seek after it. Believing in it, give us the backbone to stand up for it. Loving it, may we be willing to defend it. In the strong name of Him who said, "If ye continue in My word, ye shall know the truth, and the truth shall make you free." Amen.

THURSDAY, APRIL 10, 1947

Our Father in heaven, we give Thee thanks for good weather and the lovely promises of spring. We thank Thee for good health, good friends, and all the things we so often take for granted.

We thank Thee for the keen challenges of this hour, for work to do that demands the best we have and still finds us inadequate.

Then may we seek Thy help, knowing that in partnership with Thee, in applying Thy will to our problems, there shall be no dull moments and no problems beyond solution. God bless us all and help us to be right and to do right. Through Jesus Christ our Lord. Amen.

FRIDAY, APRIL 11, 1947

We come in prayer to Thee, Lord Jesus, who never had to take back anything spoken, to correct anything said, or to apologize for any statement. Wilt Thou have pity upon our frailties and deliver us from pitying ourselves.

Bless the Members of this body as they think together and

work together in this Chamber, in the committee rooms, and in their offices. Help them to stand up under the strains and the tensions of problems and decisions, of meetings and conferences, and the endless demands made upon them. Teach them how to relax and to take time to turn to Thee for guidance and for grace, and thus discover the secret of power. In Thy name we ask it. Amen.

WEDNESDAY, APRIL 16, 1947

O LORD our God, in the face of life's mysteries and its vast imponderables, give us faith to believe that Thou makest all things to work together for good to them that love Thee.

Strengthen our conviction that Thy hand is upon us, to lead us and to use us in working out Thy purposes in the world. Even though we may not see the distant scene, let us be willing to take one step at a time and trust Thee for the rest. Through Jesus Christ. Amen.

THURSDAY, APRIL 17, 1947

O GOD, our Father, in whom is our trust, Thou alone dost know the end from the beginning, and we, Thy children, must needs walk by faith.

We are anxious about the consequences of what we do. May that concern restrain us in our private lives as it does in our public duty.

In our troubled minds there is confusion and honest perplexity. But we know there is no confusion with Thee. Wilt Thou guide us, that we may do what is right; and if we suffer for it, we shall be blessed. This we ask in Christ's name, who was crucified, having done nothing amiss. Amen.

FRIDAY, APRIL 18, 1947

Our Father, we yearn for a better understanding of spiritual things that we may know surely what Thy will is for us and for our Nation. Give to us clear vision that we may know where to stand and what to stand for—because "unless we stand for something, we shall fall for anything."

Remind us, O God, that Thou hast not resigned. Harassed and troubled by the difficulties and uncertainties of the hour, we rest our minds on Thee, who dost not change. May it ever be in our minds as upon our coins that in God we trust. For Jesus' sake. Amen.

MONDAY, APRIL 21, 1947

Lord Jesus, help us to see clearly that the pace at which we are living these days shuts Thee out of our minds and hearts, and leave us, even with good intentions, to wander in the misty land of half-truth and compromise.

Deliver us, O God, from the God-helps-those-who-help-themselves philosophy, which is really a cloak for sheer unbelief in Thy ability and willingness to take care of us and our affairs.

Give to us a passion for that which is in principle excellent rather than in politics expedient, for that which is morally right rather than socially correct. These things we ask in Jesus' name. Amen.

TUESDAY, APRIL 22, 1947

The Senators were hurried and under constant time pressure. Their chaplain understood the problem of busy men making "time their servant and not their master."

Lord Jesus, who didst fill three short years with the revelation of all eternity, in life, precept, and promise, that we have not yet learned and can never forget, help us to make every minute count, making time our servant and not our master. Thou didst never ask for time to prepare Thine answers but always had the word of Truth for every occasion. Reveal to us now Thy word for today. Amen.

WEDNESDAY, APRIL 23, 1947

". . . when we say 'No' to Thee, we are denying our own best interest. . . ."

Increased exports to meet the economic need in Europe might well send prices up in the United States. The question was whether this danger was worse than the collapse of the rest of the world. In general the Senate did proceed to act in a responsible manner concerning the needs of the world.

OUR Father, help us to understand that when we try to live without Thee, we are unable to live with ourselves; and when we say "No" to Thee, we are denying our own best interest. Whatever other rewards or punishments Thou hast ordained, we are finding out that we cannot do wrong and feel right, for there is a law within Thy universe that acts around us and in us.

Give to each of us, we pray, that intelligent self-interest that shall persuade us to do Thy will. Teach us that obeying Thee and Thy will is a forced option—like eating. We do not have to eat, but if we do not, we cannot live. We are not forced to obey Thee, but if we do not, we hurt ourselves. Convict of us of the folly of walking against Thy lights, that we may live longer and better. By the grace and mercy of Jesus Christ our Lord. Amen.

THURSDAY, APRIL 24, 1947

> ".... May we confess our part in creating our dilemmas. ..."

Sometimes the Congress made shortsighted decisions. It was little wonder! Overworked Senators were having to make dozens of decisions for conquered and liberated countries.

To cite one example, the United States and her Allies were busy destroying Germany's capacity to manufacture fertilizers by destroying her nitrogen and phosphoric acid plants. This was meant to circumvent any conversion to future munitions manufacture, but it wasn't helping agriculture in starving Europe. A dilemma indeed!

Our Father, we in this place are weighed down by the problems of our Nation and of our world. Convict us of our share of personal responsibility for the situation in which we find ourselves. May we confess our part in creating our dilemmas, lest we feel no obligation to solve them.

Help us to quit waiting for the other fellow to change his attitude and his ways, lest we never give Thee the chance for which Thou hast been waiting, to change us. This we ask in the lovely name of Him who came to change us all, even Jesus Christ our Lord. Amen.

FRIDAY, APRIL 25, 1947

Our Father which art in heaven, we pray for all the people of our country, that they may learn to appreciate more the goodly heritage that is ours.

We need to learn, in these challenging days, that to every right there is attached a duty and to every privilege an obligation. We believe that, in the eternal order of things, Thou hast so ordained it, and what Thou hast joined together, let us not try to put asunder.

Teach us what freedom is. May we all learn the lesson that

it is not the right to do as we please but the opportunity to please to do what is right.

Above all, may we discover that wherever the Spirit of the Lord is, there is freedom. May we have that freedom now, in His presence here, to lead us and to help us keep this Nation free. This we ask in Jesus' name. Amen.

MONDAY, APRIL 28, 1947

WE UNITE our hearts, O God, in this prayer that Thou wilt teach us how to trust in Thee as a Heavenly Father who loves us and who is concerned about what we do and what we are.

Forgive us that there are times when we find it hard, when it ought to be easy. It is not that we have no faith, but that we seem so reluctant to put our faith in Thee.

Men have proved to be untrustworthy, yet we trust each other. Banks have failed, still we write our checks. Depressions have upset our economy, still we carry on business in faith. Blizzards have made the winter drear, yet with the coming of spring we plant our seeds. Hurricanes have screamed across the land, yet we build our windmills.

Give to us the faith to put our trust in Thee who dost hold in the hollow of Thy hand all things living. May we learn, before we blunder, that Thou art willing to lead us, to show us what to do, and that it is possible for us to know Thy will and to be partners with Thee in doing what is right. This we ask in the name of Christ, who never made a mistake. Amen.

TUESDAY, APRIL 29, 1947

GIVE us open eyes, our Father, to see the beauty all around us and to see it in Thy handiwork. Let all lovely things fill us with gladness and let them lift up our hearts in true worship.

Give us this day, O Lord, a strong and vivid sense that Thou art by our side. By Thy grace, let us go nowhere this day where Thou canst not come nor court any companionship that would rob us of Thine. Through Jesus Christ our Lord. Amen.

WEDNESDAY, APRIL 30, 1947

"... the little progress of the conference just concluded across the seas. . . ."

The Moscow Conference was over. The United States and the U.S.S.R. had been at odds over every major question. We were unwilling to have puppet states made of Germany and Austria.

Our Father in heaven, who dost love the whole world, save us from despair and fear as we ponder the little progress of the conference just concluded across the seas. Help us to see that there is gain in our statement of faith while others voice their fears, and that nothing is lost when our convictions and principles are expressed boldly and honestly in the midst of intrigue and suspicion.

Keep us ever resolute in striving for the things for which so many of our men gave their lives in battle. Let us not throw away their sacrifice.

Since we seek unity and harmony in the world and in our own land, help us to achieve it in this place. If we, Thy servants, who pray together, who speak the same language, who share the same basic ideals, cannot work as a team, what hope have we that the leaders of other nations, with different languages, who do not pray together, whose ideals are so different, can achieve agreement?

Help us, a hundred men, to find the secret agreement, that we may show it to our own Nation and lead it into teamwork between management and labor, between every group and faction, that our Nation may be one.

As we express our own ideas and listen to the ideas of those who differ with us, may we be humble enough to think about the third idea—Thine—and be persuaded by Thy Holy Spirit to embrace it, and thus discover the secret of harmony. In the name of Jesus Christ, who was always right. Amen.

THURSDAY, MAY 1, 1947

The prayer which follows is a good example of Dr. Marshall's down-to-earth approach.

Our Father, we would not weary Thee in always asking for something. This morning we would pray that Thou wouldst take something from us. Take out of our hearts any bitterness that lies there, any resentment that curdles and corrodes our peace.

Take away the stubborn pride that keeps us from apology and confessing fault and makes us unwilling to open our hearts to one another. For if our hearts are closed to our colleagues, they are not open to Thee. We ask Thy mercy in Jesus' name. Amen.

FRIDAY, MAY 2, 1947

O Lord, Thou dost know the secrets that will remake Thy world, for Thou art the way. Help us to see that the forces that threaten the freedoms for which we fought cannot be argued down, nor can they be shot down. They must be lived down. Give to the leaders of our Nation the inspired ideas that shall lead this country into making the American dream come true. Through Jesus Christ our Lord. Amen.

MONDAY, MAY 5, 1947

Most gracious God, facing the activities and the opportunities of another week, may we be eager and not reluctant. Keep us ever alert to the need for change and open as channels for divine power. Help us to keep keen the edges of our minds, to keep our thinking straight and true.

Give us the will to keep our passions in control and the common sense to keep our bodies fit and healthy, that we may be able to do what Thou hast called us to do. Through Jesus Christ our Lord. Amen.

TUESDAY, MAY 6, 1947

FORGIVE us, O God, that in this land so richly blessed by Thee, we, Thy people, have been wasteful. We have wasted the treasures of the earth, stolen the virtues of the soil, in failing to restore after we had received.

But we have been wasteful of ourselves. We have wasted our strength in enterprises not inspired of Thee. We have wasted our talents in unworthy causes, wasted our love in loving the unlovely. We have wasted our money for that which satisfieth not. We have wasted our time in activities that profited nothing.

Forgive us all wherein we have been prodigal, and like the younger son, help us to come to ourselves that we may come to Thee to be forgiven and restored. This we ask in Jesus' name. Amen.

WEDNESDAY, MAY 7, 1947

". . . . the pressures that drive us and the tensions that break us down. . . ."

Two days earlier, Representative Charles Gerlach (Pennsylvania), aged fifty-one, had died of a heart attack. Peter was acutely aware of the tension under which the Representatives and Senators worked. . . .

O GOD, our Father, who hast given us life and made our earth so fair, reveal to us this day Thy heart of infinite tenderness yearning for our love.

Make us to feel Thy Spirit brooding over us, longing to help us in our decisions, to save us from the pressures that drive us and the tensions that break us down.

How strange it is, O Lover of our souls, that Thou who art love, who dost give love to hungry human hearts, shouldst Thyself be the great unloved. Give us love to love Thee for Thy love, and to love Him who first loved us and gave Himself for us. Loving Thee, we shall love one another, and loving one another, we shall do Thy will, and doing Thy will, we shall always do right. We make our prayer in the lovely name of Jesus. Amen.

THURSDAY, MAY 8, 1947

Before going into the Vice President's office to meet Senator Vandenberg, Peter often had an informal chat with Mr. John D. Rhodes in the office of the Reporters of Senate Debate.

On this particular day he read his prayer to Mr. Rhodes. "I want your opinion about it," he said. Mr. Rhodes was mildly shocked. "I don't know what to say, Peter. It's pretty daring—"

But the prayer was used just as it stood. The Associated Press picked it up, and it subsequently received very wide publicity.

WE OPEN our hearts unto Thee, our Father, and pray that Thy spirit may indwell each one of us and give us poise and power. We believe in Thee, O God. Give us the faith to believe what Thou has said. We trust in Thee, O God. Give us the faith to trust Thee for guidance in the decisions we have to make.

Help us to do our very best this day and be content with today's troubles, so that we shall not borrow the troubles of tomorrow. Save us from the sin of worrying, lest stomach ulcers be the badge of our lack of faith. Amen.

MONDAY, MAY 12, 1947

IN THIS, the day that the Lord hath made, help us, O God, to appreciate its beauty and to use aright its opportunities.

Deliver us, we pray Thee, from the tyranny of trifles. May we give our best thought and attention to what is important, that we may accomplish something worthwhile. Teach us how to listen to the prompting of Thy Spirit, and save us from floundering in indecision that wastes time, subtracts from our peace, divides our efficiency, and multiplies our troubles. In the name of Christ Jesus our Lord. Amen.

TUESDAY, MAY 13, 1947

". . . the will to work together as a team for the welfare of all our people. . . ."

Discussion of the Taft-Hartley Bill was raging. Many thought it was needlessly vengeful to labor. Teamwork was sorely needed.

OUR Father, give us the faith to believe that the words now spoken, and the yearnings of the hearts now open before Thee, are heard and understood in Thy presence.

We, the Members and officers and servants of this body, unite our petitions for Thy blessing, Thy guidance, and Thy help, that we faithfully may do what is best for the people and what is right in Thy sight, O God. Give to these, Thy servants, the representatives of the people in different parts of our land, the will to work together as a team for the welfare of all our people.

Give them courage to withstand the pressure of the selfish, and give to the people the vision to see that sacrifice must be shared by all, that there is no substitute for hard work and no joy in unmerited reward.

May we fear nothing, save that, knowing what is right, we fail to do it. So help us God, in Jesus' name. Amen.

WEDNESDAY, MAY 14, 1947

FORBID it, Lord, that "we should walk through Thy beautiful world with unseeing eyes." Forgive us, our Father, for taking our good things for granted, so that we are in danger of losing the fine art of appreciation. With such dire need in every other part of the world, make us so grateful for the bounties we enjoy that we shall try, by Thy help, to deserve them more.

Where we are wrong, make us willing to change, and where we are right, make us easy to live with. For Jesus' sake. Amen.

FRIDAY, MAY 16, 1947

LORD Jesus, when we get sick of ourselves, ashamed of our littleness, our selfishness, and the petty things that irritate us, then let it be the beginning of spiritual health by making us willing to have Thee create in us clean hearts and renew right spirits within us.

Hold us steady lest we lose our poise. Blunt our speech lest by cutting words and careless deeds we hurt our colleagues and the cause for which we speak.

Where we differ in approaches to a problem, may we ever be open to consider another and a better way, guided not by whether it be popular, or expedient, or practical, but always whether it be right. Hear our prayer, O Lord, and help us, through Jesus Christ. Amen.

THURSDAY, MAY 22, 1947

GOD of our fathers, give unto us, Thy servants, a true appreciation of our heritage, of great men and great deeds in the past, but let us not be intimidated by feelings of our own inadequacy for this troubled hour.

Remind us that the God they worshiped and by whose help they laid the foundations of our Nation, is still able to help us uphold what they bequeathed and to give it new meanings.

Remind us that we are not called to fill the places of those who have gone, but to fill our own places, to do the work Thou hast laid before us, to do the right as Thou hast given us to see the right, always to do the very best we can, and to leave the rest to Thee. Amen.

FRIDAY, MAY 23, 1947

O LORD our God, shed the light of Thy Holy Spirit within the minds and hearts of Thy servants in this place of responsibility and decision, that all who sincerely seek the truth may find it, and finding it may follow it, whatever the cost, knowing that it is the truth that makes men free.

When we have the truth, let us not hit each other over the head with it, but rather use it as a lamp to lighten dark places, in order that we may see where we are going. This we ask in the name of Jesus Christ our Lord. Amen.

MONDAY, MAY 26, 1947

WE THANK Thee, our Father in heaven, for this sacred moment when our hearts may be united in prayer, and when forgetting all else save our need of Thy guidance and help, we may reach up to Thee as Thou art reaching down to us.

Let not the beauty of this day, or the glow of good health, or the present prosperity of our undertakings deceive us into a false reliance upon our own strength. Thou hast given us every good thing. Thou hast given us life itself with whatever talents we possess and the time and the opportunity to use them. May we use them wisely, lest they be curtailed or taken away.

Deliver us from the error of asking and expecting Thy blessing and Thy guidance in our public lives while closing the doors to Thee in our private living. Thou knowest what we are wherever we are. Help us to be the best we can be. We ask in the name of Jesus Christ our Lord. Amen.

WEDNESDAY, MAY 28, 1947

IF THOU, O Lord, shouldst mark iniquities, who among us could stand unafraid before Thee? For there is much bad in the best of us, and so much good in the worst of us, that we dare not criticize each other. But Thou canst reprove us all.

Ere we begin our duties, cleanse Thou our minds and hearts. What no proper shame kept us from committing, let no false shame keep us from confessing. In this moment may we find grace to seek Thy pardon and find the joy of the Gospel of making a new beginning. In the power of Christ our Lord and Master. Amen.

MONDAY, JUNE 2, 1947

"The long week end" was Memorial Day week end, which was marked by a series of tragic air accidents. In Japan an Army C-54 rammed into a mountain; in Iceland a DC-3 crashed; at LaGuardia Field, New York, a DC-4 crashed; before June 2d was over, another DC-4 fell into a Maryland bog. Total casualties—160.

ONCE again, our Father, the long week end that brings rest and refreshment to so many of our people has brought disaster and sorrow to some, and our Nation is sobered in the reflection that death is in the midst of life. Since we know not at what moment the slender thread may be broken for us, teach us to number our days that we may apply our hearts unto wisdom. And may we be compassionate, remembering the hearts that are sore and our brethren who languish in sorrow and affliction.

Take from us the selfishness that is unwilling to bear the burdens of others while expecting that others shall help us with ours. Make us so disgusted with our big professions and our little deeds, our fine words and our shabby thoughts, our friendly faces and our cold hearts, that we shall pray sincerely this morning for a new spirit and new attitudes. Then shall our prayers mean something, not alone to ourselves but to our Nation. In the name of Jesus Christ our Lord. Amen.

TUESDAY, JUNE 3, 1947

WE PRAY, O God, that Thou wilt fill this sacred minute with meaning, and make it an oasis for the refreshment of our souls, a window cleaning for our vision, and a recharging of the batteries of our spirits. Let us have less talking and more thinking, less work and more worship, less pressure and more praying. For if we are too busy to pray, we are far busier than we have any right to be.

Speak to us, O Lord, and make us listen to Thy broadcasting station that never goes off the air. Through Thy Holy Spirit, who is waiting to lead us into all truth. Amen.

WEDNESDAY, JUNE 4, 1947

O LORD our God, as we seek Thy guidance this day we do not ask to see the distant scene, knowing that we can take only one step at a time. Make that first step plain to us, that we may see where our duty lies, but give us a push, that we may start in the right direction. Through Jesus Christ our Lord. Amen.

THURSDAY, JUNE 5, 1947

> ". . . . if it be Thy will that America should assume world leadership. . . ."

On this day, the Secretary of State, Gen. George C. Marshall gave a speech at Harvard urging an economically integrated Europe. He wanted United States help to be a Europe-wide, not nation-by-nation basis. This speech was the Nation's introduction to the Marshall Plan for aid to Europe.

OUR Heavenly Father, if it be Thy will that America should assume world leadership, as history demands and the hopes of so many nations desire, make us good enough to undertake it.

We consider our resources in money and in men, yet forget the spiritual resources without which we dare not and cannot lead the world.

Forgive us all for our indifference to the means of grace Thou hast appointed. Thy Word, the best seller of all books, remains among us the great unread, the great unbelieved, the great ignored.

Turn our thoughts again to that Book which alone reveals what man is to believe concerning God and what duty God requires of man.

Thus informed, thus directed, we shall understand the spiritual laws by which alone peace can be secured, and learn what is the righteousness that alone exalteth a nation. For the sake of the world's peace and our own salvation, we pray in the name of Christ, Thy revelation. Amen.

FRIDAY, JUNE 6, 1947

> ". . . . In spite of present difficulties. . . ."

The Communists had just seized Hungary, and the people of the United States were outraged at this violation of the Yalta Agreement.

O GOD, our Heavenly Father, restore our faith in the ultimate triumph of Thy plan for the world Thou hast made. In spite of present difficulties, our disappointments, and our fears, reassure us that Thou art still in control.

When we become frustrated and give up, remind us that Thou art still holding things together, waiting and working and watching. When we make mistakes, help us to remember that Thou dost not give up on us.

Forbid it, Lord, that we should give up on Thee and forget that all things work together for good to them that love Thee. Through Jesus Christ our Lord. Amen.

MONDAY, JUNE 9, 1947

FORGIVE us, O God, that we are so anxious in all we say and do, to have the approval of men, forgetting that it is Thy approval that brings us peace of mind and clear conscience. Make us aware of the record Thou art writing—the record that one day will be read by the Judge of all the universe. We need to remember that there is no party in integrity, no politics in goodness. We pray for Thy grace and Thy help to do better and to be better. Through Jesus Christ. Amen.

TUESDAY, JUNE 10, 1947

O LORD of our lives, wilt Thou teach us true discrimination, that we may be able to discern the difference between faith and fatalism, between activity and accomplishment, between humility and an inferiority complex, between a passing salute to God and a real prayer that seeks to find out God's will?

We can stand criticism. We can stand a certain amount of pressure. But we cannot stand, O God, the necessity of making grave decisions with nothing but our own poor human wisdom. Our heads are not enough and our hearts fail us.

Cabbages have heads, but they have no souls. We, who are created in the image of God, are restless and unhappy until we know that we are doing Thy will by Thy help. This is what we pray for, through Jesus Christ our Lord. Amen.

WEDNESDAY, JUNE 11, 1947

Our Father in heaven, as we unite in prayer for Thy blessings upon the Members of this body, we know that Thou art lovingly concerned about the way we live and how we wear ourselves out, taking less care of ourselves than we do of our cars.

Bless Thy servants, the Senators, with good health, and the good sense to preserve it. Bless the members of their families. May they commit them all to Thy care, that no leaden anxiety shall keep any man from doing his best work.

We feel that we have to do so many things that we would rather not do, as we plead that we have no time to do some things we know very well we should do. Help us to make wise choices and proper use of our time. We wait upon Thee for the continual answer to our prayers. In the name of Christ, Thy Son. Amen.

FRIDAY, JUNE 13, 1947

God of our fathers, in whose name this Republic was born, we pray that by Thy help we may be worthy to receive Thy blessings upon our labors.

In the troubled and uneasy travail before the birth of lasting peace, when men have made deceit a habit, lying an art, and cruelty a science, help us to show the moral superiority of the way of life we cherish. Here may men see truth upheld, honesty loved, and kindness practiced.

In our dealings with each other, may we be gentle, understanding, and kind, with our tempers under control.

In our dealings with other nations, may we be firm without obstinacy, generous without extravagance, and right without compromise. We do not pray that other nations may love us, but that they may know that we stand for what is right, unafraid, with the courage of our convictions.

May our private lives and our public actions be consistent with our prayers. Through Jesus Christ our Lord. Amen.

MONDAY, JUNE 16, 1947

WE CONFESS, our Father, that we know in our hearts how much we need Thee, yet our swelled heads and our stubborn wills keep us trying to do without Thee.

Forgive us for making so many mountains out of molehills and for exaggerating both our own importance and the problems that confront us.

Make us willing to let Thee show us what a difference Thou couldst make in our work, increasing our success and diminishing our failures. Give us the faith to believe that if we give Thee a hearing Thou wilt give us the answers we cannot find by ourselves. In Jesus' name. Amen.

TUESDAY, JUNE 17, 1947

THOU must be grieved, O Lord, that, after nineteen hundred years, mankind nevere seems to learn how to live by faith, and still prefers worry to trust in God. We know what worry does to us, yet are all too reluctant to discover what faith could do.

Since we strain at gnats and swallow camels, give us a new standard of values and the ability to know a trifle when we see it and to deal with it as such. Let us not waste the time Thou hast given us. So help us, God. Amen.

WEDNESDAY, JUNE 18, 1947

ONCE again, our Father, we come to Thee in prayer, on the same old terms, because of our need of Thy help, and our faith that Thou dost govern in the affairs of men and wilt hear our prayer in the name of Christ, Thy Son.

Thou hast given us the inner voice of conscience, and Thy Holy Spirit enables us to distinguish good from evil. But where we are to choose between two courses when both are good and commendable, then we need the crystal clarity of Thy guidance, that we may see one to be better than the other. Help us, O God, at the point of our uncertainty, for there is no uncertainty with Thee. Thou hast a plan. We would clasp Thy hand. That shall be to us "better than light and safer than a known way." Through Jesus Christ our Lord. Amen.

THURSDAY, JUNE 19, 1947

The Senate pageboys liked the "straight-shooting" of a prayer like the one which follows—and told Peter so.

O GOD, our Father, while we pride ourselves that we learn something every day, we seem to make little progress in spiritual things.

Nowhere is our ignorance more tragic. So long have we been riding on the balloon tires of conceit, for our own good we may have to be deflated, that on the rims of humility we may discover the spiritual laws that govern our growth in grace.

If our pride has to be punctured, Lord, make it soon, before we gain too much speed. For the salvation of our souls and the good of our country. In Jesus' name. Amen.

MONDAY, JUNE 23, 1947

WE THANK Thee, O Lord, that this land is still governed by the people's representatives. Let democratic processes be seen at their best in this time of testing.

As these chosen men discharge their duties, guide them, O God, in the decisions they must make today. Give them the grace of humility, and shed now Thy guiding light into every mind. Break down every will that is stubbornly set against Thine or that has ignored Thee.

May what is done be so clearly right that it needs no incendiary justification. Soothe our still-smoldering hearts and minds with the spirit of forgiveness. Let us be swayed not by emotion or ambition but by calm conviction. This we ask in Jesus' name. Amen.

TUESDAY, JUNE 24, 1947

OUR Father, when we become satisfied with ourselves, hold ever before us Thy demands for perfection.

Lest we become content with a good batting average, let us see the absolutes of honesty, of love, and of obedience to Thy will Thy dost require of us. Seeing them, may we strive after them by Thy help. Through Jesus Christ our Lord. Amen.

THURSDAY, JUNE 26, 1947

OUR Father, we are beginning to understand at last that the things that are wrong with our world are the sum total of all the things that are wrong with us as individuals. Thou hast made us after Thine image, and our hearts can find no rest until they rest in Thee.

We are too Christian really to enjoy sinning and too fond of sinning really to enjoy Christianity. Most of us know perfectly well what we ought to do; our trouble is that we do not want to do it. Thy help is our only hope. Make us want to do what is right, and give us the ability to do it. In the name of Christ our Lord. Amen.

FRIDAY, JUNE 27, 1947

Teach us, O Lord, the disciplines of patience, for we find that to wait is often harder than to work.

When we wait upon Thee, we shall not be ashamed, but shall renew our strength.

May we be willing to stop our feverish activities and listen to what Thou hast to say, that our prayers shall not be the sending of night letters, but conversations with God. This we ask in Jesus' name. Amen.

MONDAY, JUNE 30, 1947

Lord Jesus, we know of no better way to begin the work of another week than by rededicating our lives to Thee, resolving to trust Thee and to obey Thee, and to do our very best to serve Thee by serving our fellowmen.

In these days that call for understanding, for mercy, for the salvation of men's souls and the healing of their bodies, may we have Thy Spirit that we may work to that end, for Thou art the Saviour of the world, and we have no hope apart from Thee. Hear our prayer for Thy mercy's sake. Amen.

TUESDAY, JULY 1, 1947

Teach us, our Father, how to look at the things we see, and to look at them without bias or prejudice. We may not know how much of our troubles are caused by refusing to look at the facts or by viewing them so differently.

We are all too familiar with "dirty looks," "scornful looks," "unbelieving looks," "black looks." Give to us discerning and understanding looks. With the truth waiting to be looked at, discovered, and applied, forgive us when we refuse to look at it or to welcome it.

If Thou wilt help us to cast the mote of prejudice and pride out of our eyes, then shall we see clearly. We pray for good sight and good sense, in the name of Jesus Christ. Amen.

WEDNESDAY, JULY 2, 1947

LORD of our lives, we pray that Thou wilt fill with new meanings this sacred moment of prayer. Help us to feel and to believe that we are talking with God. In this interlude of intercession, may we forget all else save our deep need of Thy guidance and Thy help.

In our hearts are fears and frustrations, and we cannot view the future of our world without misgivings. If there is a way for this God-believing Nation to live at peace with nations that deny Thee, Thou wilt have to reveal it to us, for we have not found it yet.

The disappointments and indecisions in our own lives teach us that we, ourselves, are not in tune with Thy will for us. God help us, and save us, and tell us what to do.

May the Great Physician minister to our brethren in sickness, and the sympathizing Jesus be near to those in trouble, and the Holy Spirit be in our hearts and minds this day, we ask in Jesus' name. Amen.

THURSDAY, JULY 3, 1947

GOD of our fathers, whose Almighty hand hath made and preserved our Nation, grant that our people may understand what it is they celebrate tomorrow.

May they remember how bitterly our freedom was won, the down payment that was made for it, the installments that

have been made since this Republic was born, and the price
that must yet be paid for our liberty.

May freedom be seen not as the right to do as we please but
as the opportunity to please to do what is right.

May it ever be understoood that our liberty is under God
and can be found nowhere else.

May our faith be something that is not merely stamped
upon our coins, but expressed in our lives.

Let us, as a nation, not be afraid of standing alone for the
rights of men, since we were born that way, as the only nation
on earth that came into being "for the glory of God and the
advancement of the Christian faith."

We know that we shall be true to the Pilgrim dream when
we are true to the God they worshiped.

To the extent that America honors Thee, wilt Thou bless
America, and keep her true as Thou hast kept her free, and
make her good as Thou hast made her rich. Amen.

MONDAY, NOVEMBER 17, 1947

". . . hunger that knows no politics and want that will
not wait. . . ." ". . . what Thy plan is. . . ."

*Congress was called back into session by President Truman,
who asked for sweeping peacetime controls over our economy, to
head off rising inflation.*

*Western Europe was running a deficit of $5 billion a year in
fuel, grain, oils, and basic commodities. Secretary of State Marshall
warned the Nation that a crisis was imminent. If European civilization collapsed, the receiver would be Russia.*

*It was characteristic of Peter Marshall that, while others on
Capitol Hill were, during this period, talking about the Truman
Plan, the Marshall Plan, the European Recovery Plan, he was un-
abashedly talking about God's plan.*

O GOD, our Father, we pray for Thy wisdom and Thy guidance for the Members of this body as they meet in this
troubled hour to consider what this Nation should do about

hunger that knows no politics and want that will not wait.

We cannot escape history: that we have found out. May we also discover that we cannot evade responsibility. By Thy Holy Spirit awaken the conscience of America, that our people may be willing to put humanity first.

Give to our leaders the highest motives and the courage to propose that which will be worthy of Thy blessing, lest we do the right things for the wrong reasons.

Help our Senators to see what Thy plan is, in the name of Jesus Christ, who, being rich, for our sakes became poor. Amen.

MONDAY, NOVEMBER 24, 1947

GOD of our fathers and our God, give us the faith to believe in the ultimate triumph of righteousness, no matter how dark and uncertain are the skies of today.

We pray for the bifocals of faith—that see the despair and the need of the hour but also see, further on, the patience of our God working out His plan in the world He has made.

So help Thy servants to interpret for our time the meaning of the motto inscribed on our coins.

Make our faith honest by helping us this day to do one thing because Thou hast said, "Do it," or to abstain because Thou hast said, "Thou shalt not."

How can we say we believe in Thee, or even want to believe in Thee, when we do not anything Thou dost tell us?

May our faith be seen in our works. Through Jesus Christ our Lord. Amen.

TUESDAY, NOVEMBER 25, 1947

O LORD, keep strong our faith in the efficacy of prayer as we unite our petitions in this sacred moment.

We have asked for Thy guidance in difficult decisions many times, yet it has not always come when we thought it should come. Many of the situations and relationships which we have asked Thee to change have remained the same.

Forgive us for thinking, therefore, that Thou art unwilling to help us in our dilemmas, or that there is nothing Thou canst do.

Remind us, our Father, that when we plug in an electric iron and it fails to work, we do not conclude that electricity has lost its power, nor do we plead with the iron. We look at once to the wiring to find what has broken or blocked connection with the source of power.

May we do the same with ourselves, that Thou mayest work through us to do Thy will. This we ask in Jesus' name. Amen.

WEDNESDAY, NOVEMBER 26, 1947

"... there exists ... and indescribable union ... between duty and advantage. ..."

A Thanksgiving Day Prayer. After seven months of debate, the world's greatest trading nations, led by the United States, took a long step toward unclogging the world's trade channels. Tariffs were much reduced. We pegged tariff rates to the then-present level on 20 per cent of dutiable imports, cut from 25 per cent to 50 per cent on the rest.

The Geneva conference also worked out the basic principle that all negotiators would have to benefit from any tariff cuts granted.

Peter Marshall saw all this as heartening progress toward "One World"—the Kingdom of God on earth.

Our Father in heaven, if ever we had cause to offer unto Thee our fervent thanks, surely it is now, on the eve of our Thanksgiving Day, when we, the people of this Nation, are comfortable, well-fed, well-clad, and blessed with good things beyond our deserving. May gratitude, the rarest of all virtues, be the spirit of our observance.

Let not feasting, football, and festivity end in forgetfulness of God.

May the desperate need of the rest of the world, and our own glorious heritage, remind us of the God who led our fathers every step of the way by which they advanced to the character of an independent nation.

May the faith and conviction of George Washington be renewed in us as we remember his words: ". . . there is no truth more thoroughly established than that there exists in the economy and course of nature an indissoluble union between virtue and happiness; between duty and advantage; between the genuine maxims of an honest and magnanimous policy and the solid rewards of public prosperity and felicity; since we ought to be no less persuaded that the propitious smiles of Heaven can never be expected on a nation that disregards the eternal rules of order and right which Heaven itself has ordained. . . ."

For if we do not have the grace to thank Thee for all that we have and enjoy, how can we have the effrontery to seek Thy further blessings? God, give us grateful hearts. For Jesus' sake. Amen.

FRIDAY, NOVEMBER 28, 1947

". . . . instead of indicting other philosophies, we shall inspire our own. . . ."

Congressmen coming back from European jaunts were beginning to see the absolute necessity of exporting some of our democratic ideas and ideals along with financial aid. They were therefore ready to restore some of the 40 per cent that had been cut from appropriations for the Voice of America.

"The "band wagon" was much in evidence, since the 1948 elections were in the offing.

O LORD, lift from our hearts all the discouragement, the cynicism, and the distrust of one another that destroy our faith in the little people who make up this Republic and eat at the very foundations of our democracy.

Give to our leaders faith in our way of life, so that, instead of indicting other philosophies, we shall inspire our own. Give them faith in the people, in their deep desire to do whatever is for the good of all, in their willingness to make personal sacrifices for a good cause.

May we have courageous leadership, based on faith and not on fear—leadership that goes out in front and is not forever running to catch up with a band wagon. Lord, increase our faith, through Jesus Christ our Lord. Amen.

MONDAY, DECEMBER, 1, 1947

". . . . before we reach any decisions, make us willing to ask 'What would Jesus do?' . . ."

An Interim Aid Bill authorizing European aid up to $397 million was proposed. Senator Vandenberg opened the debate on this with a speech which urged a bipartisan foreign policy and swift passage of the bill out of "a self interest which knows . . . we cannot definitely prosper in a broken world."

The Interim Aid Bill was finally passed 83–6.

As we come together in prayer, O God, we know that there is nothing in our hearts, in our minds, or in our past that we can hide from Thee, for our lives are all of one piece in Thy sight—not partitioned as we like to think.

Therefore deliver us from the error of seeking and expecting Thy guidance in our public lives while we close the door to Thee in our private living.

Help us to be good men, that we may become good leaders. For this day, before we reach any decisions, make us willing to ask, "What would Jesus do?" Then give us courage and the grace so to act. We ask it in His lovely name. Amen.

MONDAY, DECEMBER 8, 1947

THOU, O God, art our Father, and to our Father we come in this prayer. Reassure us that we have, each one, a place in Thy heart and are precious in Thy sight.

We know that we have offended Thee by some of the things we have done. We know that Thou canst not bless all that we undertake and dost not approve of all our attitudes. But we would hold on to that love Thou hast for each one of us —the love that wilt not let us go and wilt not let us off.

When we are overwhelmed by our sense of littleness in the world, may we remember that Thou hast made us all different, hast given to each of us life for a purpose, and if we fail it will never be fulfilled.

As our Lord preached some of His greatest sermons to audiences of one, may He now whisper to each one of us, as we wait upon Him, yielded and still. Amen.

WEDNESDAY, DECEMBER 10, 1947

IT IS good, O Lord, that it is not custom that brings us again into this sacred moment of prayer, but our deep sense of need.

Forgive us all that we talk too much and think too little. Forgive us all that we worry so often and pray so seldom. Most of all, O Lord, forgive us that, so helpless without Thee, we are yet so unwilling to seek Thy help.

Give us grace to seek Thee with the whole heart, that seeking Thee we may find Thee, and finding Thee may love Thee, and loving Thee may keep Thy commandments and do Thy will. Through Jesus Christ our Lord. Amen.

FRIDAY, DECEMBER 12, 1947

OUR Father in heaven, be gracious unto Thy servants, the Senators of the United States. Give them strength for the tasks of this day and guide them in their labors.

When they are tempted to wonder if a righteous peace is not an impossible dream, remind them that Thou are not senile, or asleep, or defeated. "A different world cannot be built by indifferent people." Let us never give up hope of the possibility of change.

When we feel the pressure of crisis, remind us that Thou hast plenty of time. We have to remember that Thou are never in a hurry and wilt not be rushed by the deadlines of impatient men or by the violence of the wicked.

Give us the grace to wait upon Thee, for "they that wait upon the Lord shall renew their strength; they shall mount up with wings as eagles; they shall run, and not be weary; and they shall walk, and not faint."

Grant these mercies unto Thy servants, through Jesus Christ our Lord. Amen.

MONDAY, DECEMBER 15, 1947

OUR Father, as our heads are bowed in prayer, may our hearts be open to Thy Spirit, lest we say words with our hearts not in them and make Thee yawn at the emptiness of our petition, or make Thee angry at the insincerity of what we do.

Give us faith to believe in prayer, and in Thy willingness to work in us that Thy will may be done among the nations and in our own land. We ask this in Jesus' name. Amen.

TUESDAY, DECEMBER 16, 1947

LORD Jesus, in the hush of this moment we pray that Thy tender Spirit may steal into our hearts and reveal to us how near and how dear Thou art.

There are times when Thou are not real to us, and we know why. It is not because Thou hast withdrawn from us, but because we have wandered away from Thee; not because Thou art not speaking, but because we are not listening; not because Thy love for us has cooled, but because we have fallen in love with things instead of persons.

O Lord, melt the coldness of our hearts that we may again fall in love with Thee who didst love us. Amen.

WEDNESDAY, DECEMBER 17, 1947

LET us now rejoice, most gracious God, in the love Thou hast shown toward us, opening up to us a way whereby we might be delivered from our sin and foolishness.

We have found out that we cannot do wrong and feel right. By our tolerance of some wrongs, we have come close to being intolerant of the right.

Make us bold enough to confront the face of evil and of wrong, even when it bears our own image. May we see that in every choice we make we are for Thee or against Thee. God, help us to keep our moral voting record straight. Through Jesus Christ our Lord. Amen.

THURSDAY, DECEMBER 18, 1947

Peter Marshall felt himself to be a possible channel of God's love and help to the Senators. The depth of his belief in prayer is clearly shown by his concern lest he be a clogged channel.

OUR Father, let not my unworthiness stand between Thee and the Members of this body as we join in prayer.

Hear not the voice that speaks, but listen to the yearnings of the hearts now open before Thee in this moment when each one of us is alone with Thee.

May the love of God, which is broader than the measure of man's mind; the grace of our Lord Jesus Christ, which is sufficient for all our needs; and the fellowship of the Holy Spirit, who shall lead us into all truth, be with us all this day. Amen.

FRIDAY, DECEMBER 19, 1947

WE THANK Thee, O.God, for the return of the wondrous spell of this Christmas season that brings its own sweet joy into our jaded and troubled hearts.

Forbid it, Lord, that we should celebrate without understanding what we celebrate, or, like our counterparts so long ago, fail to see the star or to hear the song of glorious promise.

As our hearts yield to the spirit of Christmas, may we discover that it is Thy Holy Spirit who comes—not a sentiment, but a power—to remind us of the only way by which there may be peace on the earth and good will among men.

May we not spend Christmas, but keep it, that we may be kept in its hope, through Him who emptied Himself in coming to us that we might be filled with peace and joy in returning to God. Amen.

TUESDAY, JANUARY 6, 1948

The prayer which follows is probably the shortest prayer ever prayed in the Senate. Often at the close of the prayer Senator Vandenberg would whisper some comment to Peter. On this day Vandenberg smilingly commented, "Now I know just how a condemned man feels."

OUR Father, who art Lord of heaven and of all the earth, Thou knowest the difficulties these men have to face and the grave decisions they must make. Have mercy upon them, for Jesus' sake. Amen.

WEDNESDAY, JANUARY 7, 1948

O SAVIOUR of the world, Thou who hast a plan for peace and a program for all the nations, make it plain, and make us see it clearly, that we may find that which will work and will have Thy blessing.

Save us from hotheads that would lead us to act foolishly, and from cold feet that would keep us from acting at all.

May Thy Holy Spirit work among us to lead us into all truth. Through Jesus Christ our Lord. Amen.

FRIDAY, JANUARY 9, 1948

". . . . Without Thee, we shall discuss more and more and settle less and less. . . ."

There was plenty for the 80th Congress to discuss and settle— the Marshall Plan for European Recovery, Universal Military Training, extended price supports and crop insurance, unemployment compensation, the admission to the United States of displaced persons, etc.

LORD, Thou wilt still be here after this prayer is said, and we would have it so, for we know deep down in our hearts that without Thy help we can do nothing abiding.

Without Thee we shall discuss more and more and settle less and less.

Unite, we pray Thee, the leaders of our Nation behind the right way to achieve a just and lasting peace in our land and in all the world, that we may win it together, lest we lose it apart. Amen.

MONDAY, JANUARY 12, 1948

LORD Jesus, we need Thy power, obtained through prayer, to solve problems, decide issues, and to do Thy will. But let us not imagine that this formal prayer can take the place of private petition. May there arise from every desk the silent prayer that seeks to know Thy will.

We long for such guidance that when a thing is right, we shall all know it; and when it is wrong, it will not be proposed.

We would not run away from truth, but find a refuge in it.

We would not avoid the discipline of hard thinking, but deliver us, O Lord, from wrong thinking that leads to wrong conclusions. Guide us this day, for Thy mercy's sake. Amen.

WEDNESDAY, JANUARY 14, 1948

WE ARE glad, our Father, that troubles are cannibals—the big ones eat up the little ones.

But may it not be so with our duties and responsibilities. Help our Senators to keep a sane perspective, lest the big issues overshadow the lesser ones, and they fail to do Thy will with them. In all things, big and little, reveal to us Thy wisdom and Thy love. Through Jesus Christ our Lord. Amen.

FRIDAY, JANUARY 16, 1948

OUR Father, we turn to Thee because we are sore vexed with our own thoughts. Our minds plague us with questionings we cannot answer, and history confronts us with responsibilities we cannot evade. Who among us is sufficient for these things?

We are humbled by our experience of failure and driven by pressure to act before we are sure what Thou wouldst have us do. Thou knowest our deadlines as Thou knowest our need. We cannot push Thee, for Thou wilt not be hurried. But only Thou canst keep us from being pushed.

Give us, therefore, the unhurried mind and the untroubled heart, by the mercies of Christ our Lord. Amen.

MONDAY, JANUARY 19, 1948

O GOD, we turn to Thee in the faith that Thou dost understand and art very merciful.

Some of us are not sure concerning Thee; not sure how

Thou dost reveal Thy will to us; not sure that it is possible for us to know, in every decision, just what Thou desirest Thy servants to do. But if we could say, "This is what God wants us to do," none would vote against it, and how much time and temper and money would be saved.

Make each one of us willing to yield himself to Thee in prayer and obedience. Come and deliver us, O Holy Spirit, for we have no hope in ourselves. Amen.

WEDNESDAY, JANUARY 21, 1948

O LORD most high and very near, to whose mind the past and the future meet in this very day, hear us, we pray.

The great questions that stand unanswered before us defy our best wisdom. Though our ignorance is great, at least we know we do not know. When we do not know what to say, keep us quiet.

When we do not know what to do, let us ask of Thee, that we may find out. We dare to ask for light upon only one step at a time. We would rather walk with Thee than jump by ourselves. We ask this in the name of Jesus Christ, who promised to send us a guide into all truth. Amen.

MONDAY, JANUARY 26, 1948

O GOD, our Father, we pray that the people of America, who have made such progress in material things, may now seek to grow in spiritual understanding.

For we have improved means, but now improved ends. We have better ways of getting there, but we have no better places to go. We can save more time, but are not making any better use of the time we save.

We need Thy help to do something about the world's true problems—the problem of lying, which is called propaganda; the problem of selfishness, which is called self-interest; the problem of greed, which is often called profit; the problem of license, disguising itself as liberty; the problem of lust, masquerading as love; the problem of materialism, the hook which is baited with security.

Hear our prayers, O Lord, for the spiritual understanding which is better than political wisdom, that we may see our problems for what they are. This we ask in Jesus' name. Amen.

WEDNESDAY, JANUARY 28, 1948

Our Father, it seems hard to care for those we find it far easier to hate, to love those whom we regard as unlovely, to spend our lives for those who are so ungrateful.

If we are to learn, Thou must be our teacher. Since we will be criticized, let it be for doing too much or too little rather than for doing nothing.

Teach us to trust not to cleverness or learning but to that inward faith which can never be denied. Lead us out of confusion to simplicity. In the name of Jesus Christ. Amen.

FRIDAY, JANUARY 30, 1948

O Lord, our God, even at this moment as we come blundering into Thy presence in prayer, we are haunted by memories of duties unperformed, promptings disobeyed, and beckonings ignored.

Opportunities to be kind knocked on the door of our hearts and went weeping away. We are ashamed, O Lord, and tired of failure.

If Thou art drawing close to us now, come nearer still, till selfishness is burned out within us and our wills lose all their weakness in union with Thine own. Amen.

MONDAY, FEBRUARY 2, 1948

LORD, we are finding that without Thee we can do nothing. Let not foolish pride or stubborn will keep us from confessing it.

Help us, O Lord, when we want to do the right thing but know not what it is. But help us most when we know perfectly well what we ought to do and do not want to do it. Have mercy upon us, Lord, and help us for Jesus' sake. Amen.

THURSDAY, FEBRUARY 5, 1948

WE CONFESS, O Lord, that we think too much of ourselves, for ourselves, and about ourselves.

If our Lord had thought about Himself, we would not now be bowed in prayer, nor have the liberty in which and for which to pray.

If the great men whom we honor for their part in building our Nation had thought about themselves, we would have no free Republic today.

Help us to see, O Lord, that "I" is in the middle of sin, and let no man among us think more highly of himself than he ought to think, to the end that we may be used of Thee in Thy service for the good of all mankind. Through Jesus Christ our Lord. Amen.

MONDAY, FEBRUARY 9, 1948

". . . . less freedom in the world than there was before. . . ."

In January 1948 another European country—Romania—went behind the Iron Curtain. On January 30 Gandhi had been murdered. His death dramatized the sense of frustration that pervaded the non-communist world.

Most merciful Father, strengthen our faith, we pray, and save us from discouragement. Let not our hearts fail us when, after a war to set peoples free, there is less freedom in the world than there was before.

Setting up standards of right and justice, we have seen them betrayed for money and mocked by selfishness. We have tried to forgive our enemies; we have humbled ourselves before haughty and cruel men, but we have not changed their hearts. Only Thou canst do that. But it takes faith to wait.

So we are tempted to despair of our world. Remind us, O Lord, that Thou hast been facing the same thing in all the world since time began.

But let not our hearts become hard or our spirits bitter. Keep our souls in faith and in hope. Through Jesus Christ our Lord. Amen.

WEDNESDAY, FEBRUARY 11, 1948

> ". . . . Give to the people of America, and to their leaders . . . old-fashioned love of country that seeks to give rather than get. . . ."

Candidates for the coming Presidential campaign seemed to be everywhere on the landscape—Harry Truman, Henry Wallace, Thomas Dewey, Stassen, MacArthur. In New Hampshire, an "Eisenhower for President" club was formed. "A Vandenberg-for-President" fever was growing in Michigan.

Our Father, as we remember the great men who by their trust in Thee helped to give this Nation its glorious heritage, remind us that we honor them best when we follow their good example.

Give to the people of America, and to their leaders, the old-fashioned love of country that seeks to give rather than to get.

Help us to acknowledge our dependence upon the patience

that forgives our failures, the truth that indicts our compromise and our hypocrisy.

We ask Thee not for tasks more suited to our strength, but for strength more suited to our tasks. May we so live that the sacrifices that have been made for our liberty shall not have been in vain. This we ask in the name of Thy dear Son, our Lord and Master, Jesus Christ. Amen.

FRIDAY, FEBRUARY 13, 1948

Our Father, on this World Day of Prayer, we join the ten million women in our own country and their sisters in many other lands in this their petition for Christian fellowship and world brotherhood.

"Father of all mankind, we come in deep humility, giving Thee our thanks and praise. Here and now we confess our sins. Forgive us our mistakes and transgressions.

"Grant us faith to look with fearless eyes beyond the chaos of our world and time, knowing that out of this shall rise, lifted by Thy grace, peace with justice and a time of brotherhood.

"Vouchsafe unto us the will to work together. Create within us the unselfish purpose of Thy Son, who gave His life for all peoples, and may our deeds reflect the mind of Christ. Remove from us greed and suspicion.

"Lift us above pettiness and destroy the hate that is the great destroyer. Throughout the earth, may that which we profess come alive in human relations.

"May we serve Thee better and love Thee more, that Thy kingdom may come on earth as it is in heaven. Through Jesus Christ Thy Son, our Lord." Amen.

TUESDAY, FEBRUARY 17, 1948

OUR Heavenly Father, save us from a worship of the lips while our hearts are far away.

In the battle now being fought in the realm of ideas, where deadly attacks are made upon our greatest treasure, our belief in God and the Gospel of Christ, deliver us from the peril of indifference, for we know that trust will crumble a metal when hammer blows will only harden it.

May this minute of prayer find each one of us, in his own way, reaching out for Thy help and guidance. Hear our prayers and be with us this day. We ask in Jesus' name. Amen.

FRIDAY, FEBRUARY 20, 1948

O GOD, be merciful when we pray with half our heart or listen with half our mind, and pity us that we are torn as we are and bedeviled with compromises. Vainly we long for life without such difficult decisions, yet we know that we have only ourselves to blame for the tensions in which we live.

We need to pray that our own eyes be opened to the truth. Deliver us from the reservations that would pray: "Thy kingdom come—but not yet; Thy will be done on earth—by other people." Help each one of us to see that if Thy Holy Spirit is to lead America, He must be permitted to lead us. If Thy will is to be done, we must do it.

O God, most merciful, consider not our cowardice, but forgive our failings.

Harken to those prayers of our hearts which come to us in high moments when we forget ourselves and think of Thee. Amen.

TUESDAY, MARCH 2, 1948

O GOD, forgive the poverty and the pettiness of our prayers.
Listen not to our words but to the yearnings of our hearts.
Hear beneath our petitions the crying of our need.

Thou gavest men life and at the same time gavest them
liberty, and Thou must help us who love liberty to keep it in
these days when it is stolen and destroyed. Help us to see that
when other men lose their freedom our own freedom is threatened.

And may we meet the threats of this hour with courage and
with boldness. Through Him whose truth makes us free indeed. Amen.

FRIDAY, MARCH 5, 1948

*Vandenberg's European Recovery Program was unanimously
passed in the Foreign Relations Committee and sent to the floor.
During the days that followed, Vandenberg bravely and effectively
defended the plan on the floor of the Senate against those Senators
who were not quite ready to give up their isolationism.*

*Peter watched, with great interest, this day-by-day sparring.
He felt that the Marshall Plan was right. This is reflected in such
fervent petitions as . . . "May no cowardice or callous selfishness
make us reluctant to assume the responsibilities of leadership in
a world hungry for hope. . . ."*

*The European Recovery Program finally passed the Senate
69–17.*

GRANT, O Lord, that this assembly of freemen, chosen to lead
a nation that loves and lives its freedom, may give hope and
help to all those who, loving liberty, long to live in it.

May no cowardice or callous selfishness make us reluctant
to assume the responsibilities of leadership in a world hungry
for hope. This we ask in the name of Jesus Christ, who is the
hope of our salvation. Amen.

MONDAY, MARCH 8, 1948

Eternal God and our loving Father, we come to Thee this day in the name of Jesus Christ, who is the lover of our souls and the Saviour of all mankind.

May we feel His love and respond to it. May His Spirit shine into lives that are darkened by worry, doubt, or fear. Strengthen and guide all those who are sincerely trying to do what is right, and make it plain.

Make us more mindful of the needs of our fellow men and less absorbed in selfish concerns, that Christ may approve and bless what we do here this day. We ask these things in His name. Amen.

TUESDAY, MARCH 9, 1948

".... the war is not really ended...."

The communist coup in Czechoslovakia had gone off as expected, and one more of freedom's lights was extinguished. Another coup was expected almost daily in Finland. In Italy, communist strength was growing ominously.

Our Father, to whom all mankind is dear, if we feel frustrated in efforts to achieve a just and lasting peace, how must Thou feel that men so long and so willfully refuse to heed Thy laws and live in Thy love.

We have found that peace does not come when the guns are silenced, for the war is not really ended. The job is not done when the fire engines drive away.

So deliver us from the blasphemy of optimism that is mere wishful thinking.

Save us from the delusion of health, that we may find the cure for our sickness. Teach us, O God, that what is needed is not new things but new spirits.

Give us the uplifted face and the flashing eye that express a purpose in life, that will make sacrifice a joy and discipline our peace. Through Jesus Christ our Lord. Amen.

WEDNESDAY, MARCH 10, 1948

O GOD, our Father, let us not be content to wait and see what will happen, but give us the determination to make the right things happen.

While time is running out, save us from patience which is akin to cowardice. Give us the courage to be either hot or cold, "to stand for something, lest we fall for anything." In Jesus' name. Amen.

THURSDAY, MARCH 11, 1948

". . . . May we trust, not in bombs, however powerful, but in Thee . . . in Thy plan. . . ."

Lilienthal, chairman of the Atomic Energy Commission, was pleading about this time that the temporary respite bought for us by the A-bomb must be used to spread understanding—not fear.

O CHRIST, who givest peace to every believing heart, bestow that gift upon us now, for we are troubled and uneasy. Events in our world take away our hope and shatter our peace. We need to be reassured that peace is still possible and that God's will shall yet be done upon the earth.

We believe that God's judgments are sure and altogether right, but we do wonder how long Thou wilt suffer godless men to defy Thee and to destroy the dreams Thou hast planted in human hearts. May we trust not in bombs, however powerful, but in Thee, in Thy might, in Thy love, in Thy plan, and in our secret weapon, the prayers of them that love Thee. Through Jesus Christ our Lord. Amen.

FRIDAY, MARCH 12, 1948

Our Father, when we long for life without trials and work without difficulties, remind us that oaks grow strong in contrary winds and diamonds are made under pressure. With stout hearts may we see in every calamity an opportunity, and not give way to the pessimism that sees in every opportunity a calamity.

Knowing that Thou art still upon the throne, let us get on with the job on hand, doing the best we can and leaving the rest to Thee. Help us to show ourselves to be good workmen who need not be ashamed, rightly dividing the word of truth. This we ask in Jesus' name. Amen.

SATURDAY, MARCH 13, 1948

O LORD, direct our hearts into the patience of Christ. Make strong our faith that God's will, though it may be hindered for a time and obstructed by human blindness and folly and sin, must in the end be triumphant.

May all that we do be in accordance with that victory of our God. Graciously minister to Thy servants, the Members of this body, according to their needs. Through Jesus Christ our Lord. Amen.

MONDAY, MARCH 15, 1948

O SPIRIT of the Living God, breathe upon this assembled company Thy gracious power. As the coming of spring rouses Nature from winter sleep, so may Thy Spirit revive us, giving us new hope and a livlier faith. If we have never before been conscious of our need, make our souls hungry for Thee, O God, that we may no longer be content to be half alive, which is half dead.

Give us fullness of life, set free from fear and doubt, that we may find new joy in our labors. Through Jesus Christ our Lord. Amen.

TUESDAY, MARCH 16, 1948

WE PRAY unto Thee, O God, and call Thee our Father. Since Thou art our Father, we are Thy children; and if Thy children, we need never despair, no matter how dark and troubled our horizons.

Teach us not to despise the life we are called to live, since it was given us by Thee.

Teach us not to neglect the task of today because we cannot see its eternal effect.

Teach us not to neglect the little duties which are training us for a great stewardship.

Help us to give a good account of this day for Jesus' sake. Amen.

WEDNESDAY, MARCH 17, 1948

WE PRAY, O God, in this uncertain hour, that Thou wilt reveal Thyself and Thy will to the leaders of our Nation.

Help them to see the right way to preserve the things so dearly bought and to resolve the difficulties that seem so great.

Inspire their thoughts by the mind of Christ coming into their minds and the courage to challenge America to accept the moral responsibilities of the spiritual leadership of the world.

May we not be afraid to face facts, however unpleasant. Take away the acrophobia of our souls that we may breathe the pure air of high ideals and lofty purpose without becoming lightheaded.

For the sake of the world, for the sake of peace, for the sake of America, for conscience' sake, for God's sake, help us to do the right thing. Amen.

THURSDAY, MARCH 18, 1948

Our Father in Heaven, save us from the conceit which refuses to believe that God knows more about government than we do, and deliver us from the stubborness that will not seek God's help.

Today we claim Thy promise: "If any man lack wisdom, let him ask God, who giveth to all men liberally . . . and it shall be given him." Thou knowest, Lord, how much we need it. Make us willing to ask for it and eager to have it. In Jesus' name we pray. Amen.

FRIDAY, MARCH 19, 1948

O god, our Father, as a battery is recharged without sound or motion, so wilt Thou, in this moment so precious, send Thy spirit into the hearts and minds of Thy servants, the Senators of the United States.

With newness of life, with spiritual power, vision, and lively faith, enable them to meet all the demands of this day with glad anticipation, and give them peace. Through Jesus Christ our Lord. Amen.

MONDAY, MARCH 22, 1948

". . . . in the midst of the dangerous opportunity that we call crisis. . . ."

President Truman called a joint session of the Congress and reported that hopes for peace were badly shaken. Jan Masaryk of Czechoslovakia had died either by suicide or by Communist hands.

Oᴜʀ Father, give us the faith to believe that it is possible for us to live victoriously even in the midst of dangerous opportunity that we call crisis. Help us to see that there is something better than patient endurance or keeping a stiff upper lip, and that whistling in the dark is not really bravery.

Trusting in Thee, may we have the faith that goes singing in the rain, knowing that all things work together for good to them that love Thee. Through Jesus Christ our Lord. Amen.

TUESDAY, MARCH 23, 1948

This was Easter week.

Lᴏʀᴅ Jesus, in the days of this holy week of solemn remembrance, bring to our minds again Thy new commandment that we love one another.

With loving concern in our hearts, may we cherish each other and be willing to put the welfare of others ahead of our own. In loving other people we shall best express our love for Thee. So help us to love that we may be loved. For Thy name's sake, Amen.

WEDNESDAY, MARCH 24, 1948

Gᴏᴅ of mercy and compassion, Thou knowest out nature and readest our secret thoughts, and we can hide nothing from Thee.

Help us, then, to lay aside every disguise we wear before the face of man and find rest and peace in being what we are and nothing more. Enable us to put off all sham and pretense, so that from now on we may live a life of freedom and sincerity.

It is not dangerous to be honest, but help each one of us to be true to himself at his best, and make us the best we can be, for the sake of Him who died for us all. Amen.

THURSDAY, MARCH 25, 1948

LORD Jesus, Saviour of the world, in Thy holy name we join our hearts in prayer. This week, as we remember all Thou didst endure for us, we may be sure Thou hast not forgotten. For we will not let Thee forget.

With every sin of ours, we renew the pain Thy heart did know. Every time we ignore Thee, forget Thee, and heed not Thy way, we revive for Thee the loneliness Thou didst feel and the spiritual blindness that broke Thy heart.

O Lord, give us Thy grace that we may not crucify Thee afresh but, loving Thee, keep Thy commandments.

With steady faith that Thy kingdom will yet be established upon the earth, help us to hasten its coming by letting Thee work in us and through us to do Thy will. Amen.

MONDAY, MARCH 29, 1948

OUR hearts still singing with the beauty and joy of Easter, we pray to Thee, O Christ, to keep us under the spell of immortality.

May we never again think and act as if Thou wert dead. Let us more and more come to know Thee as a living Lord who hath promised to them that believe: "Because I live, ye shall live also."

Help us to remember that we are praying to the Conqueror of Death, that we may no longer be afraid nor be dismayed by the world's problems and threats, since Thou hast overcome the world. In Thy strong name, we ask for Thy living presence and Thy victorious power. Amen.

THURSDAY, APRIL 1, 1948

HEAR, O God, our Father, the earnest supplications of the Senators gathered for this sacred moment of prayer and deepen our feelings of unity and fellowship as we pray with them and for them.

Give us wisdom to see that no good life comes without right discipline. Give us the grace to impose it upon ourselves, lest others do it for us.

Help us to discipline our speech, that we may seek clarity rather than cleverness and sincerity instead of sarcasm.

Help us to discipline our thinking and our actions, that in this place the world may see democracy at its best and us at our best for democracy and for Thee to use us. In the name of Jesus Christ, Thy Son, our Lord. Amen.

FRIDAY, APRIL 2, 1948

". . . . Together we pray for . . . their loved ones concerning whom they are anxious. . . ."

One of the individuals whom Peter had in mind here was Mrs. Arthur Vandenberg. One day, shortly before this, Senator Vandenberg had, in conversation with Peter, revealed his deep concern for her health. Peter had replied, "Catherine and I are going to pray definitely for her." Vandenberg merely gripped Peter's hands, tears in his eyes, and turned away, unable to say anything.

OUR Father, let us never be ashamed to come to Thee in prayer, for we are Thy children, Thou art our Father.

Together we pray for the Members of this body who need

the healing ministry of the Great Physician and for their loved
ones concerning whom they are anxious.

O Christ, our Saviour, Thou art still the sympathizing Jesus.
Be near this day to those whose names we whisper in our
hearts and minister to them according to their needs and Thy
loving kindness.

Help those who are in trouble. Give Thy consolation to
those who sorrow and Thy love to us all. In Thy name we
pray. Amen.

TUESDAY, APRIL 6, 1948

*Peter usually assiduously avoided mentioning specific political
issues in his prayers. This prayer was, therefore, an exception,
since it is most specific.*

*Italy seemed to be trembling on the brink of communism and
civil war. Red boss Togliatti had bitterly denounced the Marshall
Plan. The candidate for the Christian Democrats was De Gasperi.*

*These Italian elections were most important to the free world
and to America in particular. American-Italians were urged to
write relatives in Italy urging them to vote anti-communist.*

*The elections were decisive. Ninety per cent of Italy's voters
turned out. The Christian Democrats piled up 48.7 per cent of
the popular vote—Chamber of Deputies: 307 out of 575 seats;
Senate: 151 out of 350 seats. Counting all parties, there was a land-
slide anti-communist vote of 18 million.*

O GOD, who hast made of one blood all the nations of mankind, so that all are kinsmen, forgive the selfishness that ignores the ties which Thou hast established.

We pray today for the people of Italy that they may be
guided in the grave decisions they shortly must make. May
Thy will be done in that ancient land. Save Thy people there
from intimidation and coercion, and give them the courage
of true faith in democracy that they may be free.

May we in this free land esteem more highly our liberties,

in the light of the price others are called upon to pay. For Jesus' sake. Amen.

WEDNESDAY, APRIL 7, 1948

O GOD, our Father, history and experience have given us so many evidences of Thy guidance to nations and to individuals that we should not doubt Thy power or Thy willingness to direct us.

Give us the faith to believe that when God wants us to do or not to do any particular thing, God finds a way of letting us know it.

May we not make it more difficult for Thee to guide us, but be willing to be led of Thee, that Thy will may be done in us and through us for the good of America and all mankind. This we ask in Jesus' name. Amen.

THURSDAY, APRIL 8, 1948

OUR Father, in times of confusion, when men doubt their beliefs and believe their doubts and are victims of ideologies that seek to divide and conquer, give to the people of this Nation a true appreciation of the great affirmations we hold in common.

Let us appreciate our agreements and have the courage and conviction to stand up for them, that we may stand united and fearless before the world.

Direct our government that it may ever make it as hard as possible to do wrong and as easy as possible to do right. To that end, incline our leaders to the eternal truths Thou hast revealed in the Bible and in Thy Son, Jesus Christ, our Lord. Amen.

MONDAY, APRIL 12, 1948

Our Eternal Father, whose kindness is loving and whose patience is infinite, hear us again as we pray, not because of what we say but because of the deep need that drives us to Thee.

We rest in the thought that Thy love knows no change, else it would not love us long. We are burdened by things that do not matter, bewildered by problems of our own creation.

Thou hast made us heirs of a great heritage and trustees of priceless things, yet we forget the price that was paid for them and the eternal vigilance required to preserve them. Make us strong, O God, in conviction, with insight for our times and courage for our testing. Through Jesus Christ our Lord. Amen.

TUESDAY, APRIL 13, 1948

O Christ, our living Lord, Thou hast brought us to this new day and further opportunity.

Help us to work with Thee that it may be a good day with good things done. We know that a "different world cannot be built by indifferent people." May there be no apathy in this place, no lukewarmness when we should be hot.

Abide with us, O Christ, that our hearts may burn within us and our imaginations be fired with Thy passion to do God's will. Amen.

WEDNESDAY, APRIL 14, 1948

Our Heavenly Father, in this moment of prayer, when there is silence in this Senate Chamber, may there not be silence in Thy presence. May our prayers be heard.

May no short circuits be made by our lack of faith, our high professions joined to low attainments, our fine words hiding shabby thoughts, or friendly faces masking cold hearts.

Out of the same old needs, conscious of the same old faults, we pray on the same old terms for new mercies and new blessings. In the name of Jesus Christ our Lord. Amen.

THURSDAY, APRIL 15, 1948

IF THESE moments, O Christ, can be spent in honest heart-to-heart communion with Thee, and Thou wilt give us Thy Spirit, then will our whole day be changed for us, and we shall be changed for the day. Our moods will become right, and we shall be sensitized.

Use these moments, O Lord, to make every thought and feeling what they ought to be, that we may be able to do things for Thy sake that we would not have done for our own or the sake of anyone else. Amen.

MONDAY, APRIL 26, 1948

IT IS not our brothers or our friends, but it is we, O Lord, who are standing in the need of prayer. Much as we would like to see this great company engaged in fervent supplication, we remember that Thou hast promised: "If any two are agreed, I will do it."

Let us not be staggered by statistics but rather by the implications of the prayers here uttered by a few. When they really move us, they can move our Nation. Let us not be the stumbling blocks. We ask in Jesus' name. Amen.

FRIDAY, APRIL 30, 1948

O GOD of grace and God of glory, when we resent having so many choices to make, may we remember that good character is the habit of choosing right from wrong.

Help us as a nation to see that our strongest defense lies

back in home and school and church, where is built the character that gives free people the power to win their freedom and to hold it. May we never forget that it is only under God that this Nation or any nation can be free.

And when we have learned well this lesson, then shall we have for export more than money, even the faith and idealism for which all who love liberty will be willing to live. Amen.

WEDNESDAY, MAY 5, 1948

O GOD, our Father, come nearer to us than we have ever known and stay with us through the deliberations of this day, lest we give way to selfishness.

We pray for our country, thrust by world events into high responsibility. May she be willing to grow up and, with adult maturity, looking unto Thee for guidance and wisdom and courage, assume her role of leader among the nations.

So may her statesmen act and her people think that Thou canst bless her and use her. In Jesus' name we pray. Amen.

THURSDAY, MAY 6, 1948

". . . . to disagree without being disagreeable. . . ."

At this time, there was much open disagreement between the Joint Chiefs of Staff, as well as a Navy–Air Force fight. Service rivalries were chiefly to blame.

HEAR us, our Father, as we pray for a freshness of spirit to renew our faith and to brighten our hopes.

Create new warmth and love between the Member of the Senate and those who work with them, that they may go at their work not head first but heart first. May they be able to disagree without being disagreeable and to differ without being difficult.

In an atmosphere of team spirit, give them freedom to be honest without tension and frank without offense, that Thy spirit will not be driven from their midst. This we ask in Jesus' name. Amen.

MONDAY, MAY 10, 1948

FORGIVE us, Lord Jesus, for doing the things that make us uncomfortable and guilty when we pray.

> We say that we believe in God, and yet we doubt God's promises.
>
> We say that in God we trust, yet we worry and try to manage our own affairs.
>
> We say that we love Thee, O Lord, and yet do not obey Thee.
>
> We believe that Thou hast the answers to all our problems, and yet we do not consult Thee.

Forgive us, Lord, for our lack of faith and the willful pride that ignores the way, the truth, and the life. Wilt Thou reach down and change the gears within us that we may go forward with Thee. Amen.

TUESDAY, MAY 11, 1948

O GOD, our Father, be real to each one of us today, that we may become aware how near Thou art and how practical Thy help may be. Deliver us from going through the motions as though waiting for a catastrophe.

Save us from the inertia of futility. Revive our spirit of adventuresome faith. Give us nerve again and zest for living, with courage for the difficulties of peace. Through Jesus Christ our Lord. Amen.

WEDNESDAY, MAY 12, 1948

OUR Heavenly Father, when we have prayed for guidance and it comes, let us not think it strange if it be something we would not have thought of, for Thy thoughts are not our thoughts and our way is not Thine.

Make us eager to know Thy will and Thy way of dealing with situations, rather than devising our own plans and asking Thee to bless them.

Then shall we discover how much better is Thy way and how happy they are who walk in it. Through Jesus Christ our Lord. Amen.

THURSDAY, MAY 13, 1948

O LORD our God, refresh us with Thy Spirit to quicken our thinking and make us sensitive to Thy will.

We may be unconscious of our deepest needs, accustomed to things as they are, ceasing to desire any changes. We may be unwilling to pay the price of better things.

Show us, Thy servants, the things that must be changed, that we hinder Thee no more. Amen.

FRIDAY, MAY 14, 1948

The death mentioned was that of Senator John Holmes Overton of Louisiana.

OUR Father in Heaven, humbly we bow in prayer this day, feeling the deep loss of our Nation and the Senate in the call that has summoned our brother into that life where "age shall not weary nor the years condemn."

Knowing in whom he placed his trust, we know that his faith was well founded.

We pray for those who loved him best and will miss him

most. May they have the comforting ministry of Him who shall wipe away all tears from their eyes and is able to bind up broken hearts.

So teach us to number our days that we may apply our hearts unto wisdom.

May our sympathies be warm and real, and in our great loss may we learn better how to love one another, through Him who has promised: "Whosoever liveth and believeth in Me shall never die. Because I live, ye shall live also." Amen.

MONDAY, MAY 17, 1948

O GOD, at this moment the Senators and the Representatives of the people of this Nation humbly implore Thy help and guidance. Make it a sacred moment, a moment when men are aware of their need of God, a moment when answers come and guidance is given.

Often we pray for that which is already ours, neglected and unused. Sometimes we pray for that which can never be ours, and sometimes for that which we must do for ourselves.

How many times we never pray at all, and then work ourselves to death to earn something that is ours for the asking.

Help us to understand that "faith without works is dead," and that works without faith can never live. Amen.

TUESDAY, MAY 18, 1948

O LORD, in the midst of great activity today we ask Thee to remind us often of Thine invisible presence,

   that out of confused issues may come simplicity of plan,
   out of fear may come confidence,
   out of hurry may come the willingness to wait,
   out of frustration, rest and power.
This we ask in Thine own name. Amen.

THURSDAY, MAY 20, 1948

O LORD, our God, while dealing honestly with thing as they are, keep alive our hope that things may yet be better than they are.

"Earth shall be fair and all her people one:
Not till that hour shall God's whole will be done."

Give us faith to believe in the possibility of change, that, each in his own place, we may do all we can to change from bad to good, and from good to better, until Thou art satisfied with our labors. In the name of Jesus Christ our Lord. Amen.

MONDAY, MAY 24, 1948

OUR Father in heaven, today we pray for Thy gift of contentment, that we may not waste our time desiring more, but learn to use and enjoy what we have.

We may not know everything, but we may know Thee and Thy will. We need not be rich to be generous, nor have all wisdom to be understanding. Our influence may not be great, but it can be good. Our speech may not be eloquent, but it can be truthful and sincere. We cannot all have good looks, but we can have good conscience, and having that, we shall have peace of mind and need fear no man.

May we be kind one to another, tender-hearted, forgiving one another, even as Thou, for Christ's sake, hast forgiven us. Amen.

TUESDAY, MAY 25, 1948

". . . the difference between what we say and what we do. . . ."

The prayer which follows was exceedingly plain-spoken. The House of Representatives—in the face of previous commitments

*by both chambers of Congress—lopped off more than $2 billion
from funds already authorized for the European Recovery Program and other foreign aid. The point of this Congressional "economy" was apparently, as Peter said, along the line of "winning
votes in America." This altered the European program from one
of intelligent reconstruction to one of mere relief. Such a cut for
the Economic Cooperation Administration would brand United
States policies abroad as "capricious, unreliable, and impotent,"
and would make it harder to restore the prestige of our Nation
abroad.*

*The Senate Appropriations Committee was later to save the
day by unanimously approving restoration of all but $245 million
of ECA funds.*

Our Father, sometimes we are discouraged and disappointed
in the government of this Nation; and the common people of
other lands, hungry for peace, cannot understand the difference between what we say and what we do.

We have an uneasy feeling that we have not been right or
consistent and have risked the peace of the world for lesser
gains at home. Only if Thy Spirit guide our spokesmen and
shape our policies can this Nation regain the respect of the
world and merit Thy blessing. Winning peace in the world
must become more important than winning votes in America.

God, direct our Senators to do what is right for Jesus' sake
and the sake of peace and good conscience. Amen.

WEDNESDAY, MAY 26, 1948

O Lord, our God, have pity upon us, who have so little pity in
our hearts.

We give, but not in kindness. We give because the sound of
crying disturbs us, and we want to be free to look after the
things that concern ourselves.

We want peace without pain and security without sacrifice.
We had to accept the responsibilities of war, but we do not
want to accept the responsibilities of peace.

O Lord, be patient with us.

Give us yet more time to learn what love is, and how love should act, and how love can change us as individuals and as a Nation. We pray in the name of Him who loves us all. Amen.

THURSDAY, MAY 27, 1948

LORD Jesus, as Thou dost move among people and see what men are doing today, how sore must be Thy heart.

Thou whose head was cradled in straw must often reflect that straw was not as coarse as man's selfishness.

Thou whose hands were spread upon a Cross and fastened with nails must often reflect that nails were never so sharp as man's ingratitude.

Hear us as we pray for this poor blundering world, in which the nations never seem to learn how to live as brothers. They resort again and again to methods that produce only more bitter tears, methods that only add to misery and subtract nothing from problems.

Heal them that need healing, make strong the wavering, guide the perplexed, befriend the lonely, give new faith and courage to those whose spirits are low.

Lift up our heads, put a new light in our eyes and a new song in our hearts, and we will do better and be better for the sake of Thy love. Amen.

TUESDAY, JUNE 1, 1948

On May 30, in Canada, the Fraser River had overflowed Fraser Valley, British Columbia. Vancouver was isolated. Air Force and civilians evacuated hundreds from the valley. Within three days, 2,000 were forced to flee their homes. Damage was estimated at $15 to $20 million.

Spirit of God, come into our hearts and make us sensitive to the sufferings of other people. We think of the victims of flood and mishap and all those who have heavy hearts today. May we so grow in grace that the sympathy we feel for friends may also be felt for strangers.

Cultivate with us
> the grace of thankful, uncomplaining hearts;
> the grace of boldness in standing for what is right;
> the grace of self-discipline;
> the grace to treat others as we would have others treat us;
> the grace of silence, that we may refrain from hasty speech;
> the grace of kindness, that wherever we go we may take something of the love of God.

Be with our Senators this day and bless them. We ask in Jesus' name. Amen.

WEDNESDAY, JUNE 2, 1948

O Lord, let us never be afraid of a new idea or unreceptive to a new thought, lest we pull down the shades of our minds and exclude Thy holy light. When confronted by mystery, help us to remember that we do not have to explain all we know or understand all we believe. But give us the grace of humility and the spirit of the open mind, the courage to persist in face of difficulties, and a steady confidence in the power of truth.

Help us all to learn something this day, that we shall be wise at its close and more ready for our eternal home when we are one step nearer. Through Jesus Christ our Lord. Amen.

THURSDAY, JUNE 3, 1948

". . . . those in the gallery . . . the youth of America. . . ."

During April, May, and June in Washington there is a con-
stant procession of buses filled with American high-school students.
Most of them visit the Senate to see it in action. Peter was aware
of their fresh eagerness and impressionability.

Oᴜʀ Father in Heaven, as we pray for Thy blessings upon
the Members of the Senate, we are not unmindful of those
in the gallery who join us in this prayer.

We give Thee thanks for the youth of America, the leaders of tomorrow, the young people who shall someday take
our places. We thank Thee for their faith in America, and we
pray that nothing done or said in this place shall cause them
to think any less of the institutions we cherish.

Challenge them, we pray Thee, with the vision of good
citizenship and a love for all that is good in America and a
desire to make it even better, that this land that we love may
become a truth and in fact God's own country. Amen.

FRIDAY, JUNE 4, 1948

Lᴏʀᴅ, we are ashamed that money and position speak to us
more loudly than does the simple compassion of the human
heart. Help us to care, as Thou dost care, for the little people
who have no lobbyists, for the minority groups who sorely
need justice. May it be the glory of our government that not
only the strong are heard, but also the weak; not only the
powerful, but the helpless; not only those with influence, but
also those who have nothing but a case and an appeal.

May we put our hearts into our work, that our work may get
into our hearts. Amen.

TUESDAY, JUNE 8, 1948

O LORD, our God, deliver us from the fear of what might happen and give us the grace to enjoy what now is and to keep striving after what ought to be. Through Jesus Christ our Lord. Amen.

WEDNESDAY, JUNE 9, 1948

O GOD, the light of those who seek Thee, grant to our minds that illumination without which we walk in darkness and know not whither we go.

Remember those who feel no need of Thee, who seem content with a careless unexamined life, whose heart are unvisited by desires of better things. Leave them not to themselves, lest they go down to destruction.

Remember us, O Lord, who do not always remember Thee, and help us to accomplish our tasks without tension or strain, that we may do good work and merit Thy blessing. For Jesus' sake. Amen.

THURSDAY, JUNE 10, 1948

". . . . we are reminded how fragile is the thread of our lives. . . ."

Three days earlier Representative Thomas L. Owens (Illinois) had died of a heart attack. He was only fifty.

OUR Father in heaven, every day we are reminded how fragile is the thread of our lives and how suddenly we may be summoned away from the things that engross us here.

May the uncertainty of life make us the more anxious to do good while we have opportunity, for the sake of the record that has eternal implications far beyond the next election.

Since we shall be judged for every idle word, let us speak carefully, with a deep respect for the truth than cannot be twisted.

Bless each Member of this body, as Thou seest their needs—those who are prevented by duty elsewhere from joining in this prayer, and those who appear to be so adequate for their tasks, but who need Thy help like the rest of us.

Reveal Thy love to all of us and grant us Thy peace. Through Jesus Christ our Lord. Amen.

FRIDAY, JUNE 11, 1948

HELP us, our Father, to show other nations an America to imitate—not the America of loud jazz music, self-seeking indulgence, and love of money, but the America that loves fair play, honest dealing, straight talk, real freedom, and faith in God.

Make us to see that it cannot be done as long as we are content to be coupon clippers on the original investment made by our forefathers.

Give us faith in God and love for our fellow men, that we may have something to deposit, on which the young people of today can draw interest tomorrow.

By Thy grace, let us this day increase the moral capital of this country. Amen.

SATURDAY, JUNE 12, 1948

LORD Jesus, as we pray for the Members of this body, its officers, and all those who share in its labors, we remember that Thou wert never in a hurry and never lost Thine inner peace when under pressure greater than we shall ever know.

But we are only human.

We grow tired.

We feel the strain of meeting deadlines, and we chafe
under frustration.

We need poise and peace of mind, and only Thou canst
supply the deepest needs of tired bodies, jaded spirits,
and frayed nerves.

Give to us Thy peace and refresh us in our weariness, that
this may be a good day with much done and done well, that
we may say with Thy servant Paul: "I can do all things
through Christ, who gives me strength." Amen.

MONDAY, JUNE 14, 1948

ETERNAL God, who hast made us and designed us for companionship with Thee, who hast called us to walk with Thee
and be not afraid, forgive us, we pray Thee, if fear, unworthy thought, or hidden sin has prompted us to hide from
Thee.

Save us, we pray, from all sins of intellect, not only from
the error and ignorance which belong to our frailty but from
the pride that would make us think ourselves sufficient for
our tasks.

Forgive us for thinking of prayer as a waste of time, and
help us to see that without it our labors are a waste of effort.

O God, help us, guide us, and use us for Thy glory and our
good. Through Jesus Christ our Lord. Amen.

FRIDAY, JUNE 18, 1948

". . . . Thou knowest whether we have been voices or
merely echoes, whether we have done Thy will or our
own. . . ."

*The last prayer before the summer adjournment of the Eight-
ieth Congress.*

O GOD, our Father, in these days when men freely judge and condemn each other, remind us all of the Great Assize before which we must all someday appear.

Thou knowest whether we have been voices or merely echoes, whether we have done Thy will or our own, or worse still, have done neither.

Teach us, O Lord, that only Thy "Well done" will afford peace and everlasting happiness.

May we strive for that rather than the approval of men, which is but for a little while. In Jesus' name we pray. Amen.

FRIDAY, DECEMBER 31, 1948

O GOD, our Father, may the year that is past teach us and not torment. Help us to be realistic about ourselves.

May we not steal credit for success, nor deny blame for failure. Give us the grace to take things as they are, and to resolve, by Thy help, to make them what they ought to be, in the strong name of Jesus Christ our Lord. Amen.

"Our Father which art in heaven, hallowed be Thy name. Thy kingdom come. Thy will be done in earth as it is in heaven. Give us this day our daily bread. And forgive us our debts as we forgive our debtors. And lead us not into temptation, but deliver us from evil: for Thine is the kingdom, and the power, and the glory, for ever." Amen.

Eighty-first Congress

WEDNESDAY, JANUARY 5, 1949

Our Father in heaven, give us the long view of our work and our world.

Help us to see that it is better to fail in a cause that will ultimately succeed than to succeed in a cause that will ultimately fail.

Guide us how to work and then teach us how to wait. O Lord, we pray in the name of Jesus, who was never in a hurry. Amen.

THURSDAY, JANUARY 6, 1949

In this prayer, O God, we come to Thee as children to a loving Father. We pray that Thou wilt help our Senators to face the problems that confront them, not alone by giving them wisdom greater than their own but also by relieving their minds of all other anxieties.

May they now turn over to Thee loved ones who need the healing touch of the Great Physician, with every confidence that Thou wilt hear our prayers of intercession, and as we do the work that is before us, Thou wilt do Thy work of healing in those whom we love. May Thy help be so plain and practical in our family affairs that we shall come to believe strongly in the help Thou dost offer in our national affairs.

Deliver Thy servants from personal worries, that they may be able to give themselves wholly to the challenges of this hour. In Jesus' name we ask it. Amen.

MONDAY, JANUARY 10, 1949

Our Father, since we cannot always do what we like, grant that we may like what we must do, knowing that truth will one day be vindicated and right in the end must prevail.

Bless thy servants this day and keep them all in Thy peace. Amen.

THURSDAY, JANUARY 13, 1949

Stop us, O God, for a minute of prayer.

Stop our anxious minds from wandering, and our hearts from desiring anything but to know Thy will.

Let us stand at attention before Thee and hear what Thou hast to say to us.

We believe that Thou canst tell us not only what to do, but also how to do it.

If it needs making up our minds, Thou who didst make our minds canst show us how to make them up.

If it needs changing our minds, Thou canst work that miracle, too. Speak, O Lord, and make us hear, for Jesus' sake. Amen.

MONDAY, JANUARY 17, 1949

Help us, O God, to treat every human heart as if it were breaking, and to consider the feeling of others as we do our own.

Help us to be gentle, and to control our tempers that we may learn to love one another.

Give us the grace so to live this day, in the name of Jesus, who loves us all. Amen.

TUESDAY, JANUARY 18, 1949

Our Father in heaven, once again we offer unto Thee our grateful thanks for Thy mercy that cared for us during the night and brought us safely to this hour.

Today is the tomorrow we worried about yesterday, and we see how foolish our anxiety was.

Teach us to trust Thee more completely and to seek Thy help in all that we have to do, through Jesus Christ, our Lord. Amen.

THURSDAY, JANUARY 20, 1949

This was Inauguration Day. Peter opened the Senate with prayer, as it convened briefly, before the Senators went out to take their places on the platform in front of the Capitol close by the Presidential stand.

GOD of our fathers, in whom we trust, and by whose guidance and grace this Nation was born, bless the Senators of these United States at this important time in history and give them all things needful to the faithful discharge of their responsibilities.

We pray especially today for our President, and also for him who will preside over this Chamber.

Give to them good health for the physical strains of their office, good judgment for the decisions they must make, wisdom beyond their own, and clear understanding for the problems of this difficult hour.

We thank Thee for their humble reliance upon Thee. May they go often to the thone of grace, as we commend them both to Thy loving care and Thy guiding hand. Through Jesus Christ our Saviour. Amen.

MONDAY, JANUARY 24, 1949

".... Thy servant who, in his new capacity...."

Vice President Alben W. Barkley now took Senator Arthur Vanderberg's place in presiding over the Senate.

Peter certainly had no intimation that this was to be his last prayer in the Senate. On this day, at the conclusion of the prayer, Mr. John D. Rhodes walked to the elevator with him. Peter was in fine spirits and seemed to be in good health as he grasped Mr. Rhodes' hand. "See you Thursday," he said.

This last paragraph of this last prayer could not more effectively summarize the ideal which Peter had consistently held up before the Senators.

TODAY, O Lord, as the Members of the Senate pause in this moment of prayer, we unite our petitions for Thy blessing upon Thy servant who, in his new capacity, presides over this body. We thank Thee for his long years of devoted public service, for the testimony of his life and the inspiration of his example.

May he never feel lonely in this chair, but always be aware of Thy hand upon him and Thy spirit with him.

When differences arise, as they will, may Thy servants be not disturbed at being misunderstood, but rather be disturbed at not understanding.

May Thy will be done here, and may Thy program be carried out, above party and personality, beyond time and circumstance, for the good of America and the peace of the world. Through Jesus Christ our Lord. Amen.

THURSDAY, JANUARY 27, 1949

Early on the morning of Tuesday, the twenty-fifth, Peter awakened with severe pains in his chest and arms. It very soon became apparent that his condition was serious, and that he would have to be taken to the hospital.

One of his lasts requests before the ambulance came was that I ask "Cranny"—Dr. Clarence Cranford, of Washington's Calvary Baptist Church—to take the Senate prayer for Thursday.

Peter died at 8:15—on the morning of the twenty-fifth. On the twenty-seventh, Dr. Cranford read Dr. Marshall's prayer which he had already prepared for that morning.

DELIVER us, our Father, from futile hopes and from clinging to lost causes, that we may move into ever-growing calm and ever-widening horizons.

Where we cannot convince, let us be willing to persuade, for small deeds done are better than great deeds planned.

We know that we cannot do everything. But help us to do something. For Jesus' sake. Amen.

John Doe, Disciple

SERMONS FOR THE YOUNG IN SPIRIT

by Peter Marshall

Edited and with Introductions by
Catherine Marshall

Preface by Peter John Marshall

GUIDEPOSTS ASSOCIATES, INC.
Carmel, New York

ACKNOWLEDGMENTS

It is never possible to complete a book manuscript without the encouragement, the advice, and the help of many people. I am grateful to Miss Patricia Harris, my secretary, who for many months went far beyond the call of duty in typing and retyping this manuscript; to my husband, Leonard Earl LeSourd, who first conceived the idea for this book, whose enthusiasm for Peter Marshall's material is unflagging, and whose editorial knowledge has been invaluable; to my son, Peter John Marshall, who has made many valuable suggestions; to friends who have been generous in permitting me to use some of their reminiscences of Dr. Marshall; Miss Jean Tucker, the Reverend Mr. J. David Simpson, Mr. David Kerr, Mr. Willard Daughtry, Marguerite Barze (Mrs. Roland Barze).

CONTENTS

PREFACE

It has been fourteen years since the death of my father, and now I am preparing at Princeton Seminary to go into the ministry. I am being guided to carry out Christ's ministry to men not so much to follow in my father's footsteps as to follow in the footsteps of the Lord he served.

Because one of my greatest hopes for this book is that the youth of America will read it, and because I am myself only recently out of my teen-age and college years, it is perhaps fitting that I briefly give you my perspective on these dozen sermons of my father.

I have always had difficulty separating what I remember about my father from what I have been told about him. Like most PKs (preachers' kids), I didn't see as much of my father as I would have desired. Since he died when I was only nine, my recollections of him are somewhat hazy. This meant that I didn't really begin to appreciate my father's ministry and his relationship with his "Chief" until I had embarked on my own relationship with this same Lord.

Young people in postwar America have grown up in the disillusioning knowledge that the world is no longer "safe for democracy," or for that matter safe for much of anything. It is not hard to see the reason for this when we are being honest with ourselves—man has never, cannot now, and will not be able in the future to control completely his own destiny. This knowledge tends these days to make young people cynical. Why? Because all children grow up with their hearts full of ideals, but the youth of postwar America have also grown up with their eyes full of the chaos of the society that adults are handing on to them to manage. This combination has produced cynicism in young people, for cynics are really those who have become disillusioned by the seeming impossibility of their idealism.

America has become fascinated lately with an introspective psychoanalysis of the problems of youth in our society. Americans have decided that today's teen-ager is really the victim of the anxieties of the Bomb and the Cold War, not unlike his parents. It is true that the mores of today's teen-ager are in reality only an emulation of those of his parents expressed in a slightly more exuberant manner. However, to decide that the problems of today's youth are also the problems of the world in which we live is to solve nothing. This merely dissipates the guilt by making it collective. The fact of the matter is that every person, whether youngster or parent, you or I, is responsible before God for his own conduct.

I suppose I rebelled against the Christian faith of my parents more than most children raised in a Christian home, probably because as Peter Marshall's son I was somewhat in the spotlight. However, when I had finished college and rebellion had soured, I found that I could see no purpose or direction for my life. It was at this time that I realized my youthful cynicism was not the fault of my parents, or the society of which I was a part, but solely a result of my refusal to accept the love of Christ and God's plan for my life. The seeds planted in me by my parents' faith had begun to sprout.

At this same time I saw what father was trying to say to all of us, or—perhaps better—what Christ was trying to say to all of us through father. One aspect of his sermons has always stood out in my mind, and I think it applies emphatically to the sermons in this book. His sermons are timeless. They have an eternal significance that not only strides back to the blowing sands of man's past, but also rockets forward into the starlit void of man's future. Why? Why does the work of Peter Marshall continue to stir the soul of man?

There are two answers, I think. First, because the questions he asks here out of his concern for youth are the perpetual ones of human existence—love and marriage, freedom and responsibility, honesty and deception, faith and hope, adventure and destiny—in short, the meaning of life and death. Second, because he answered these eternal questions with the only eternal response—God's abiding Word to man, the burning light that Christ's love for man sheds into a world of darkness.

Only Christ's love can free us from the necessity of clutching at material possessions. A marriage, a beautiful home, a good job, and two cars in the garage do not make happiness! But God's love can convert the disillusioned into disciples of the Idealist whose ideals come true in the lives of men. This is the message of these sermons to all men, especially to youth.

My father had a great love for this country, which I share. Now it seems as though America has sold its ancient Puritan birthright—the possibility of a nation that is great because of its relationship to its Lord—for cocktail parties and expense-account lunches. How long are we going to watch ourselves become, in T. S. Eliot's words,

> . . . the hollow men
> . . . the stuffed men
> Leaning together
> Headpiece filled with straw. Alas!

Our problem is not really communism, nor is it bigness in government, nor any of the other issues that fill the headlines. It is ourselves and our love of self. There is only one answer for us, and it is an answer for each individual heart. Only when we accept Christ's love for us, and enter into a daily relationship with Him, can we be freed from the chains of selfishness that bind us.

I hope that you will find, as I have, that the only Reality in life starts with the Reality that is Jesus Christ. This is the good

news Peter Marshall proclaimed in every sermon—the Risen
Christ.

Peter John Marshall

Princeton, N.J.
June 1963

*Editor's Note: Since writing this, Peter John Marshall has gradu-
ated from Princeton Theological Seminary and is now serving as
Assistant Pastor to the Westminster Presbyterian Church in West
Hartford, Connecticut.*

INTRODUCTION

Why should there be another book of Peter Marshall's sermons?

Mr. Jones, Meet the Master, which came out in the autumn of 1949, nine months after Peter's death, used only twelve sermons out of six hundred complete manuscripts. In *A Man Called Peter* other sermons were referred to, with brief excerpts from fourteen quoted. And in *The First Easter*, Peter's Easter material was collected and edited into a sermon-narrative of the last days of Christ on this earth. Apparently these books only served to arouse greater and greater interest in Dr. Marshall's ministry, for, through the years, there has been a never-ceasing stream of requests for more. Many of these requests have come from teen-agers:

I am wondering if I could have copies of the four sermons listed below? I ask you this because I have read small passages from them, and I long to see the rest.
I know this is an awful lot to ask . . . I am a freshman in college. . . . I was so far away from God, but because of what Peter Marshall has taught me about the joy of the Christian life, I am happy to tell you that this is no longer the case. . . .

While the sermons in this book should be of special interest to the young, the book is not directed exclusively to them. It could not be—because Peter Marshall never segregated young people, never talked down to them or patronized them. He expected the most of the younger members of his congregations and he got it—by paying them the compliment of treating them as adults. Conversely, he made the old people in his congregations feel young in spirit, and they loved him for it.

The hunger in young people today for answers (implicit in letters like the one above) is something to remember as we read our newspapers and periodicals so full of the "teen-age problem." That there is a problem, a deep and serious one, few thoughtful persons would question. Yet my experience has been that many of these young people are seriously seeking resolutions to the puzzles in their lives and are scorning saccharine or superficial answers. Something about the temper of our time has given them an eleventh-hour consciousness. They want the truth—even when it hurts.

The truth was what Peter Marshall always gave them. Perhaps that is one reason why during his lifetime and afterward when his sermons and prayers were published, the young in heart have clamored for more of the man, his ideas, his wisdom. This book's title, *John Doe, Disciple,* is taken from one of his sermons. It is meant to challenge: would you, John Doe, be a disciple today were Christ to reappear? Would you have the courage? Would you make the sacrifices?

My initial impressions of Peter Marshall come from my own teen-age years. It was during the autumn of my sophomore year at Agnes Scott in Decatur, Georgia, that the name Peter Marshall kept cropping up in dormitory talkfests. It was obvious that the young bachelor Scotsman had captured the imagination of the college girls.

Finally, my curiosity aroused, I went with a group of them to the Westminster Presbyterian Church in Atlanta to hear him. I still remember what a production it was to get there— a minimum of forty-five minutes each way by slow streetcar.

But it was worth the effort. My friends had not exaggerated. He was young, with unruly curly hair, the build of a football player under his Geneva gown, and a strong Scots burr. More important, Peter Marshall preached to us of a red-blooded living Lord. I had never heard preaching quite like that, and I—along with hundreds of other young people from Atlanta's five major colleges and universities—was drawn back again and again.

I was aware of intriguing contrasts in this young minister: intense earnestness, and an irrepressible sense of humor; rugged manliness alongside a poetic sensitivity; idealism with touches of earthiness. We college students felt that he spoke our language. Yet he could also lift the King's English to a dignity and beauty at times lyrical, sometimes Shakesperian . . . at moments (for me, anyway) Churchillian. Outside the church he could exhibit exuberant playfulness, but in the pulpit a mantle of power and dignity fell upon him.

After Peter and I were married, I soon found that there was a sense in which he was younger than I, though chronologically he was twelve years older. Peter would still be fresh at 1 or 2 A.M., long after I had wilted. He could outdance me, outplay me, exhibit a bounding physical vitality I never had. Nor did this change through the years. He was bowling on the night before his first heart attack. He was out for an evening of recreation with three men friends on the night before he died.

In Washington during the second world war, some of the old-timers at the New York Avenue Presbyterian Church were afraid that the staid and historic church with its dignified pulpit was turning into a youth center. Girls had poured into the nation's capital from every section of the country for government jobs. There were always servicemen, WAVES, and WACS in the city on leave. A steady procession of all these young people came through the church. There were 125 young voices in Charlie Beaschler's chorus-choir. There was a canteen. There was a Sunday-school class which Peter Marshall taught for many years. There was a Sunday-evening youth service. Busloads of girls from private schools came to the regular Sunday-morning service. It must have seemed to the old-timer that the foyers, the Lecture Room, the Lincoln Room were overrun with noisy youngsters.

Peter gloried in this. He felt that he knew how mothers and fathers in little towns in Ohio, Iowa, or Kansas would feel about their sons and daughters having found a home away from home centered in the encircling arms of the church.

His hold on these young people was not just that of a speaker to whom they enjoyed listening. He bowled with them on one of the church's four teams in a city-wide league. A group usually went with him to a small newsreel theatre near the church after the informal midweek service. Of a Sunday evening—after a day of speaking three times, sometimes four —he always felt the need to unwind. Usually at the close of the service, a group would be patiently waiting to help him relax. He kept a supply of games—Parchesi, Rook, Chess, Sorry, Yacht—in his church office. Even after such a grueling day, he could outlast any of his youthful opponents.

His relationship with young people was characterized by familiarity, but never disrespect. They could call their minister "Peter" if they wanted to, but never "Doc" or "Pete"—both of which he disliked. There were no off-color jokes told in his presence. He held them to their highest and they loved him for it.

After his death, one young man wrote me, "I used to look forward to our Sunday evenings last year. I enjoyed the chess games, but I especially prized the chance for informal conversations and sociability with Peter."

Another reminisced, "He lived what he believed, but never with long-faced piety. He did everything from fishing or going to baseball games to preaching with such delight and devotion that he made it seem like a high adventure. You enjoyed things with Peter by proxy. . . . I received Peter's preaching with all the eagerness of a hungry man for a square meal. His powerful messages burned deep into my soul and became the very foundation for what I believe today.

"Yet my friendship with him had another, equally wonderful side: Helping him do the wiring and the layout for an elaborate electric train. . . . Sharing with him the making of an amateur movie travelogue of Washington. . . . A trip with him and two other men to New York where we had a dizzy round of radio shows, musical comedies, the opera, and numerous restaurants. Perhaps it was because he took Christ into his recreation that it was such fun to be with him."

A reporter who came to the New York Avenue Church for an interview-story one day, pointing out the roomful of young people in the downstairs church office, said to Peter Marshall, "We are hearing a lot about the godlessness of modern youth. Do you think these kids will get into heaven?"

Peter's answer was decisive. "All I know is—if they *don't* get to heaven, then I want to be where they go."

Catherine Marshall

June 1, 1963

• I •

If ever a man felt himself guided by direct communication with his Lord, that man was Peter Marshall. To me he seemed Exhibit A of God's ability to guide His children in our day quite as well as He did in centuries long gone.

"Look at me," Peter's presence in the pulpit said; "If God had not led me, I might still be an engineer in Stewart and Lloyds Imperial Tube Works in Scotland."

It was a long way that God led him, with His hand apparent time after time. At twenty-one, Peter had volunteered to the London Missionary Society for service in China. That door was shut firmly. The way led not to the Orient but to the United States.

New Jersey—was that the place? Peter was miserable there. Within four months he knew that the next sealed order read Birmingham, Alabama.

Two months after Peter's arrival in the Southern city he was writing to a relative:

I have found happiness at last. It is not a happiness of my job in the Circulation Department of the *Birmingham News*, though I like that very well. It is a deeper joy that has to be with numerous opportunities for service for the Lord. . . .

It is romantic how things are happening. Dr. Mordecai, the minister of the church I have joined, says that he will do all in his power to put me into a theological seminary next fall. He recognizes, as I do, that my vocation in life is clearly the ministry. . . .

1

Indeed I was sent to Birmingham. Everything is great!
I am blessed beyond words. All the unhappiness I had in
New Jersey has only served to make me appreciate this all
the more. . . .

*Dr. Mordecai kept his pledge and Peter entered seminary
the following September. Still there was that continuing sense
of God's hand on his shoulder. After graduation, the little mill
town of Covington, Georgia, was his first pastorate, then
Atlanta. There his happiness and delight in his ministry could
scarcely have been greater.*

*Then in 1936 came the call to Washington, D.C. Peter
could not bear the thought of leaving Atlanta. Surely the time
was not yet, there was still so much to be done. So, flattering
though the offer was, he refused it. Eight months later the call
came again. This time there was no mistaking the by-now
familiar tap on the shoulder: his marching orders from his
Chief said* Washington.

*Through subsequent years there were tempting offers from
important churches in other cities—Baltimore, Pittsburgh,
Dallas, Philadelphia, Tulsa, New York. On occasions the guidance was not easy to get; there were times when he struggled
and strained to hear God's voice. But looking back now, I
know that he was guided aright. When a man intensely desires
to obey God's directions, somehow God manages to get
through to that man.*

*Peter received propositions of other types that tested this
matter of God's guidance. A famous New Orleans attorney,
while a naval commander during the second world war, began
coming to hear Peter Marshall preach. Eventually he made
Peter an astonishing offer: "If you will leave the ministry to
become a criminal lawyer, my firm will pick up all the tabs on
your legal education, provide abundantly for your family, take
you into our firm to plead all important cases, guarantee you
a beginning minimum salary of X dollars." Compared to the
salary of any minister, it was a magnificent amount.*

Peter was as flattered by this as anyone would have been.

For a few days he flirted with the idea. But in this case, the answer was not difficult to hear. It was a clear, resounding "No, you know perfectly well that I called you to preach. You would never for one moment be really happy doing anything else."

The years sped by. On the morning of March 30, 1946, Peter suffered an unexpected and devastating heart attack. It looked as if it might well be the end of the road for him. But that was not God's plan. "I have a surprise for you," the message seemed to be. "Some of your most important work is still ahead." When on January 5, 1947, Peter was made chaplain of the United States Senate, it could scarcely have been more of a surprise. Eleven days later he wrote to a dear friend in typical Peter Marshall style:

> The whole thing came out of the blue. I agreed to accept it, if it came to me as a call from the Chief. So it did—and I could do no other than to accept it. . . .

The Senate Chaplaincy made the nation as a whole aware of Peter Marshall. This was important only in that it provided him with an ever-widening area of service for his Lord.

How wide that ministry would eventually be, Peter himself could never have guessed. For even as he was Exhibit A for the reality of God's guidance during his lifetime, so he would also be a prime example of the glory that can attend our transition into the next life and proof of how there can be no "losses" in God's planning.

I like to think that the next portion of the "sealed orders" came to me. The gist of those orders was: "Peter's ministry is not cut off by his death at all. You will see—"

I saw. I have had proof—glorious corroboration. In the decade after his death millions of people who had never seen Peter Marshall or heard him preach read his sermons and prayers as well as the story of his life.

Of course, God can guide your life and mine. And once you have experienced this direct communication, you will not want to live by any other Guide.

UNDER SEALED ORDERS

I DO not know what picture the phrase *under sealed orders* suggests to you.
To me it recalls very vividly a scene from the first world war, when I was a little boy spending vacations at a Scottish seaport.

I saw a gray destroyer slipping hurriedly from port in response to some urgent commands . . .
I watched the crew hurry their preparations for sailing,
    watched them cast off the mooring hawsers . . .
saw the sleek ship get under way, as she rose to meet the lazy ground swell of a summer evening . . .
Her Morse lamp was winking on the control bridge aft, and I watched her until she was lost in the mists of the North Sea.

She was a mystery vessel.
She had sailed under sealed orders.
Not even her officers knew her destination or the point of rendezvous.
We all start out in life, going—we know not where.
It will be revealed later.
But meanwhile we must go out in faith—
                    under sealed orders.
So, in like manner, all the pioneers of faith have gone out—and all the explorers—
    Abraham of old
        Columbus
            Magellan
                John Smith
                    Peary
                        Lindbergh
                            Byrd.

Abraham stands out among the Old Testament heroes as the leading example of this kind of faith.

In the Epistle to the Hebrews we are told:

"By faith Abraham . . . went out, not knowing whither he went."
Hebrews 11:8

Here was Abraham, a mature and successful man, having established himself in Ur of the Chaldees.

Then God spoke to him:

"Get thee out of thy country, and from thy kindred, and from thy father's house, unto a land that I will shew thee: And I will make of thee a great nation, and I will bless thee, and make thy name great . . . and in thee shall all families of the earth be blessed."
Genesis 12:1–3

Try to imagine what was involved in obeying this guidance.
Abraham had to sever all his business connections,
uproot himself,
procure supplies for a new and strange way of life.
He was giving up the comforts and conveniences of a world he knew to live as a nomad under canvas with no settled abode.

From a commonsense point of view, it was crazy.
Doubtless Abraham had many friends who told him just that.
Where was he going?
Well, he did not know exactly.
What was he going to do?
He was going to found a new nation somewhere else.
Found a new nation?
What was he talking about?

He and his wife did not even have any children, and they were getting on in years.
Abraham himself was seventy-five!
What kind of crazy talk was that?

Nevertheless Abraham carried out his decision.
He left Ur of the Chaldees.
He did it because of a spiritual insight—an insight which for
him had the authority of a direct command from God.

And God kept His part of the bargain.
Abraham was led to Canaan.
In their old age, he and his wife Sarah had a son—Isaac.
  "I will multiply thy seed as the stars of the heaven . . . and
  in thy seed shall all the nations of the earth be blessed,"
  God had promised.

And it came to pass.
For this pioneer of faith became the father of the Hebrew
nation.
And through him, all men everywhere have been blessed—for
Jesus Christ Himself was to be one of Abraham's descendants.

Some people find it difficult to believe that human beings like
us, like Abraham, can get direct guidance from God,
                 can have their lives ordered by Him.
They ask, "But surely you don't believe that
God speaks directly
    specifically
as I am speaking to you now?
You don't mean that God sends telegrams?

Now the Bible always speaks of God saying to His children
this and that . . . "And God said unto Abraham . . ."
                "God said unto Moses. . . ."
Was that just for Bible times?

If you have never had an experience of God's guidance in your
life, you may question how it comes.
No doubt it comes in various ways to different people.
I cannot fully explain it, but I have to believe it, because I
have had many experiences of God's guidance which were for

me just as dramatic and critical as the guidance that came to Abraham.

I was given an opportunity to leave Scotland and come to this country, and I asked God what I should do about it.
I asked God in the only way we have to ask Him—through prayer.
I prayed and waited for the answer.

I believed that the answer would come; I did not know when or how.
For three weeks I waited with some impatience, I must confess, and at the end of that time, the answer came, and God told me to go.

I could not accurately describe what was a subjective experience.
I did not see the answer written in the sky, nor yet upon the wall of my room.
But I knew—positively, definitely, that God had said, "Yes, go."

I remember well the spot where the answer came.
It was on a beautiful Sunday afternoon outside Glasgow.
I was walking down a path lined with rhododendron on the Sholto-Douglas estate when I heard the voice.
Now, whether it sounded like a voice outside of me or inside of me, I cannot tell.
But I knew it was the voice of God.
I was positive that the answer for which I had prayed had come, and I acted upon it immediately by making application for a visa to enter the United States as a quota immigrant.

Well do I remember on the nineteenth of March, 1927, standing on the afterdeck of the *Cameronia*, watching with moist eyes the purple hills of Mull of Kintyre sinking beneath the screw-threshed waters of the Atlantic, when every turn of

the propeller was driving me farther from the land of my birth
—from all I knew and loved.

And then—I walked slowly and wonderingly for'ard until I
was leaning over the prow.
I stood looking into the west,
   wondering what lay beyond that tumbling horizon—
    wondering what the unknown tomorrow held for me.

I, too, was going out in faith, not knowing whither I went.
I was leaving the tube mill, where I had been working in the
machine shop.
I was coming to the United States to enter the ministry, because I believed with all my heart that those were my orders
from my Chief.
But I did not know how,
           or when
           or where.

I could not foresee the wonderful way in which God would
open doors of opportunity.
I could never have imagined the thrilling way in which God
was to arrange my life . . .
               order my ways
             guide my steps
             provide for all my needs
             give me wonderful friends, generous helpers
until, at last, I would achieve His plan for me, and be ordained
a minister of the Gospel.

It is an amazing adventure simply to be born upon this wandering island in the sky, to make a temporary home on this
rolling ball of matter . . .
To go to school
  to make friends
    to marry
      to choose a career and to develop it,
to rear children and assume life's responsibilities;

to face life with its swift changes of circumstances that no man can certainly predict an hour ahead—
These are all adventures.
And it is an adventure to leave it when death calls and "Taps" sounds for you at the close of life's day.

Each new day is like an hitherto unvisited country which we enter—like Abraham leaving Ur for a strange land—
"not knowing whither he went."
And every new year we begin a tour of exploration into twelve months where no man's foot has ever walked before.

If we all love tales of pioneers, it is because from the time we are weaned until the time we die—life is pioneering.
With all his science, with all his new insights and tools for conquering the unknown, man must face each day as Paul faced his journey to Rome—"not knowing the things that shall befall him there."

As you stand peering into the future—you cannot see what tomorrow will bring.
You cannot even tell as you look upon Grandfather Time whether his indistinct features are smiling or frowning . . .
And his hand behind his back—does it hold a bouquet
                                                    or a brickbat?

Is there no way, then, that we can know the future?
Shall we go—you and I—to some wizened old hag, cross her palm with silver, and permit her to spread fanlike before us a deck of cards so that she may tell us what the future holds?
Shall we listen to her as she interprets a fair lady or a dark knave as the message of a deuce or a trey?

Can it be that the drawing of a card will signify
the career we shall follow,
    or the girl we shall marry,
        or the family we shall have?

Nonsense!
There are so many things that even the most educated among
us do not know!
Things that no faculty can teach us . . .
    that no textbooks can contain . . .
        that no man can foresee or prophesy.

I urge you then simply to go out in faith—even as Abraham
                          Columbus
                  or the Pilgrim Fathers
and all the host of pioneers of the centuries.

Yet this is not easy.
Today we must send young people into a changing world
    where old concepts are being discarded,
        old theories exploded,
           where standards are constantly changing—
into this unknown they must go, whether they like it or not.

But then is everything so uncertain, you ask?
Is there nothing on which I can rely?

Yes, there is an assurance that can help you to confidently and
successfully face the unknown vistas of all the tomorrows.
It is an assurance given to us in the old Book:

  "But I trusted in Thee, O Lord:
   I said, Thou art my God.
   My times are in Thy hand."   *Psalm 31:14–15*

If you trust in God, if you are willing to give your life to Him,
then, and only then, will you have no fear.
For no matter where you go, He will be with you.
You can never wander from the pathway, for He will lead you.

Some people speak of *luck* and accord it a great and determin-
ing place in their lives.

They trust to luck,
they count on it, live by it.
They cross their fingers, knock on wood,
look for four-leaf clovers and carry rabbits' feet.
But I would not dare wish you or anyone else "Luck"
because there is no such thing as luck!
Others speak of "accidents"—and make allowance for the happening of accidents—regard certain events as purely accidental.
Yet are there really such things as accidents?

Was the creation of the world an accident?
Are the laws that maintain the universe accidental?
Ask Eddington
　　or Jeans
　　　　or Milliken
　　　　　　or Einstein.

Were the prophecies of the Old Testament accidental?
Was the birth of Jesus Christ an accident?
It was no accident that Judas printed the kiss of betrayal on
the fair cheek of Jesus!
The old Rugged Cross was no accident!
Paul's conversion was not an accident!
The work of Martin Luther was no accident!

Was it an accident that John and Charles Wesley were rescued from a burning house, as they themselves described it,
"like brands from the burning"?

Is this nation of ours an accident?
Were George Washington and the Declaration of Independence,
　　Abraham Lincoln and the Emancipation Proclamation
purely accidental?
Is a rose an accident—merely the coming together of capricious factors in nature?

I shall not soon forget the words of Dr. W. R. Whitney, a past
President of the American Chemical Society,
> Fellow of the American Academy of Arts and Sciences,
>> director of many vast electrical researches, as he made
>> the simplest of all experiments.

Dr. Whitney picked up from his desk a small bar magnet.
He brought this near a steel needle, and the needle leaped to
the magnet.
Why?
Dr. Whitney said:

> "We have worked out elaborate explanations.
>> We speak learnedly of lines of force.
>> We draw a diagram of the magnetic field.

"Yet we know that there are no lines there and the *field* is
just a word to cover our ignorance.
Our explanations are only educated guesses.

"Or consider," Dr. Whitney continued, "the beam of light
that comes speeding from a star, traveling hundreds of years.
Finally it reaches your optic nerve, and you *see* the star.

"How does that happen?
We have our corpuscular theory of light,
> our wave theory,
>> our quantum theory.
But they are all just educated guesses.

"So," explained Dr. Whitney, "after we are all finished with
our theories and our guesses, we are still backed up against
the fact of God—the will of God at work in what we call
'science.'"

Thus an eminent scientist looks beyond science (that some
still think infallible and the source of all answers) for guidance.

Many of our scientific theories and explanations are only educated guesses.
The day before yesterday, the atom was thought of as whirling
particles but that is outmoded now.
Yesterday the atom was described as a wave in space, according to Schrödinger's theory; that too is outmoded.

Today the atom has been split and developed into the greatest
explosive force in the history of mankind.
No, the theory of relativity is not final.
No scientific concept stands still.
All is in motion, because we are forever in the process of dis-
covering more of what God has placed in this world.

But the will of God, the laws we discover
        but cannot always understand
      or explain,
the will of God alone is final.

No there are no accidents.
God is still the ruler of His universe and of our lives,
                    yours and mine.

So, even though you go out, not knowing whither you go,
             you can go confidently, like Abraham,
provided you can say with the Psalmist:
   "My times are in Thy hand."

God knows each one of you, and He has a plan for *you*.
God made one you—and only one.
Nobody who ever lived was quite as you are now.
God gave you life for a purpose, and if you fail to fulfill it, that
purpose will never be realized.

I long for all you young people to know the full fellowship of
the Christian life . . .
   what it is to be guided by the Lord into the very place

where He wants you to be . . .
  to know when you make decisions that you are doing
  what He wants you to do.

Not only ministers can find God's will; so too can clerks
                                     and secretaries
                                   and engineers
                                  and waitresses
                                  and salesmen
                              and bus drivers.

If you only knew the peace that comes with the conviction
that you are in the place where God wants you to be . . . and
that you are doing the thing for which He created you.
What a difference it makes!

To Abraham, God spoke directly and specifically.
Nowadays, since the advent of Jesus Christ, I believe that God
speaks to you and me through the Holy Spirit.
Indeed, we are told in the Scriptures that it is the function
of the Holy Spirit to guide us,
  to lead us into all truth.

So the Holy Spirit is available to guide us in everything:
  A young man into his life work,
    A young woman into the friendship out of which will
    grow love and marriage to the man of God's choice for
    her.
      A family can be led to the city where God wants them
      to live . . .
        A businessman can be guided to make the right
        decisions.

No, that is not silly, it is not fanaticism.
Nor does it do violence to human responsibility.
As soon as you try living this way, you will find that God's
purpose for your life is maximum creativity, achievement, and
responsibility—not less.

Others object to the idea that the Lord of the universe could possibly be concerned with the details of millions of lives. Yet this glorious truth could never have been imagined. Jesus said it was so, and He would never raise false hopes in a human heart.

Jesus' emphasis was always upon the one—the single soul. Consider His parables—the story of the lost coin,
> of the one lost sheep,
> and of the lone lost boy.

". . . the very hairs of your head are all numbered," He said.
Matthew 10:30
" . . . your Heavenly Father knoweth that ye have need of all these *things*." *Matthew 6:32*

In this viewpoint, Jesus was being realistic about human life. The truth is that our lives are made up of the sum of the small decisions
> the little turnings
> the minute choices.
If we do not let God into these everyday details, practically speaking we are not letting Him in at all.

Would you like to have God's guidance for your life? If you would, first you have to believe that He can guide you.

But faith is not belief. Faith is belief plus what you do with that belief.

I might have believed intellectually that God could guide me, indeed, that I had heard His voice that afternoon in the park. But that would have counted for nothing, had I not gone on to act on that belief by applying for my number as a quota immigrant. Belief becomes faith only at the point of action.

First of all, if you want to hear God, you will have to face up squarely to the question,

"Am I willing to follow His plan wherever it may lead?"
"Am I willing to do whatever He tells me to do?"

This is a decision that must be resolved before you can receive any guidance from God
before your Christian adventure can begin.
How hard it is for our proud wills to bow the neck and call Him "Master and Lord"!
Yet bow we must, if we are to understand what life is all about, if we are to take even the first step toward maturity,

or fulfillment,
or greatness.

Understand that this is no craven slavery Christ asks of us:
"Henceforth I call you not servants; for the servant knoweth not what his lord doeth; but I have called you friends . . ."
John 15:15

A friend of Jesus!
No knight of old ever had a greater privilege.
He who bows before This One—joyously to hand over his life and his future—
finds himself raised to knighthood,
received into the inner circle,
immediately heir to all the rights and privileges of the King.

But the move is ours . . .
Are you willing to tell God now that you will follow His plan wherever it may lead?

This is important because God has given us free will, and this He will never violate.
He holds in a more profound respect than any of us could the sanctity of every human personality.
Therefore He requires the consent of our wills before He will enter our hearts and lives.

And it is just at this point that many of us are in the grip of a
terrible conflict:
We want to hear God speaking to us . . .
   but we are afraid of what we might hear.
We want to be made clean . . .
   but there is still a hunger for the husks the swine eat.
We would follow Christ . . .
   but we don't want our friends to think us queer.
We want God's way . . .
   but we also want our own way.

There is an answer to our dilemma . . .
Tell Christ honestly about our divided will . . .
                     our divided self.
Ask Him to take that over and make it whole.
And He will.

It may be that His plan for you will not be revealed for some
time.
You will have to keep close to Him, keep listening for His
signals.
His plan for you may be a gradual development.

There are a thousand ways in which He may use you.
You may have to make some changes in your life,
                  break with some of your present companions,
               change some of your habits . . .
I cannot tell you that—but He can.

He will send His power surging into you,
         to give you power to defeat temptations,
      to chase away your fears,
   to give you a quiet heart,
   to make you joyous and free.

We are living in a hazardous epoch of history.
The wind . . . the earthquake . . . and the fire of old are here,

in fact the threat of more terrible fire than man ever thought possible.

It would be tragedy indeed if the still, small voice of God's wisdom and direction is not heard at such a time.

You are leaving port under sealed orders and in a troubled period.

You cannot know whither you are going or what you are to do. But why not take a Pilot on board who knows the nature of your sealed orders from the outset,

    and who will shape your entire voyage accordingly?

He knows the shoals and the sandbanks,

              the rocks and the reefs.

He will steer you safely into that celestial harbor where your anchor will be cast for eternity.

Let His mighty nail-pierced hands hold the wheel, and you will be safe.

Now is a splendid time to entrust your life to Him, *now, as you begin.*

Give Him your life.

He will treasure it, even as you.

Then, though you may not know what will be your harbor, you will know your Pilot . . .

And all will be well.

•II•

The letter from the young girl read in part:

I smoke, I drink, I enjoy playing cards for money, I pet. I haven't gone the limit yet, but only God knows whether I will. My family does not seem to know that I am bad. Of course, they don't know—or at least don't appear to know —that I do all these things.

But are parents deaf and dumb? You may as well know why I can't take part in church affairs anymore. Maybe I'm a good girl, but I feel bad. I can't pray.

Sometimes after an exceedingly wild party I drop on my knees and say, "Oh God, forgive us all." You understand my crowd is not tough—just the boys and girls of the best families I was brought up with.

What puzzles me is the older people all saying that they have faith in us. . . . You preachers standing around telling us how fine and good we are. Sometime I'd like to kidnap you and take you on one of our parties. I guess your next sermon after that would be about sin. And that's what we need to hear.

Here are some of my questions:

Did my mother do the things I'm doing? Did my older sisters? Am I wrong in thinking that I am a bad girl? Is that the way of the world? Shall we go to heaven or to hell following such acts? Does God care? Do you preachers know that we young people do these things? Please write something to quiet my mind, or I shall go mad.

*It was to answer this letter that Peter Marshall preached
"Heaven Can't Wait."*

HEAVEN CAN'T WAIT

Each one of you has a philosophy of life.
You may not realize it . . .
You may not even know it, but you have one nevertheless.

It may be sound—or it may be false.
It may be positive—or it may be negative.
It may be Christian—or it may be pagan.
Perhaps you could not expound it in so many words,
   but you have one just the same.

It lies back of every decision you make . . .
   it colors every opinion you hold . . .
It suggests every action you take . . .
         and it shows itself in a hundred different ways:
               The type of amusements you seek . . .
               The kind of pictures you prefer . . .
               The magazines and newspapers you read . . .
               The television programs you watch . . .
               The slang you use . . .
               Your favorite songs . . .

All these things are indicative of the tenor of your thinking
and are clues to your philosophy of life.
Such a clue, I believe, is the title of a song of some years ago,
"Heaven Can Wait."
It is indicative of a prevailing idea to which a great many of
us subscribe . . .
"This is paradise enough" is a philosophy which says,
"We're only young once, let us have our fun while we can.

There's plenty of time for responsibility and serious thoughts.
We're not ready to settle down yet . . .
We're out for a good time, so don't be a wet blanket by asking
us to be serious.
This is the time to be gay—so come along, let's dance.
Have another drink . . . you're only young once."

This idea is not new, nor is it modern.
You and your parents and your grandparents have been saying it down through the ages.
Always there have been young people who have fallen victims
to this pagan philosophy and have expressed it in many different ways.

It was this idea that Robert Herrick expressed in the seven-
teenth century when he said:

> "Gather ye rosebuds while ye may,
>   Old Time is still a-flying:
>   And this same flower that smiles to-day,
>   To-morrow will be dying."

You see, there is nothing new about the idea of sloughing off
of responsibilities or duties
    or thoughts of a future life.
There is nothing new here—but there is also nothing good
about it.

I wonder why it is that so many young people are afraid of
that which is high—afraid of high ideals
                of high thoughts
                of high morality.

Is it because so many grew up in homes saturated with cynicism
                                and helplessness
                                and defeatism
now that we have a bomb of such awesome destructiveness?

Some of you grew up in an age when not only big sisters and brothers—but fathers and mothers took to drinking and staying out nights . . .
When young girls were trained to serve liquor in barrooms no better than the old saloon . . .
When American women were persuaded by brilliant advertising that it was fashionable to drink . . .
When Hollywood and Freudian psychology were making us sex-conscious as never before.

It is not surprising, therefore, that many of you young people have lost your moorings . . .
    are confused and bewildered . . .
And have the feeling that no one—not even God—
    cares about you.

Yet behind the "so what" indifference—the cynicism, the boredom, all of you want challenges and jobs.
All of you want to make your own way in life . . .
unless you have been softened and spoiled by parental indulgence.

Most of you want to get married—and deeply and sincerely desire your marriage to be a success . . .

You want to have a home and a family
    and you want to see some light ahead for your children.

You would like to give yourself to something worthwhile,
    perhaps a hospital project . . .
        works with children . . .
            the church.
Inside are stirrings and longings and a hunger for the real meaning of life.
You are in search of happiness but don't know where to find it, or even how to look.

So meanwhile you say, "Let's not worry or think about it.
Turn on the record player, and fill the room with jazz.
Live for today, do what comes naturally . . .
This doesn't take thought,
  or hard work,
   or being different.
  "Heaven can wait."
But will young people, by postponing serious thoughts and
refusing to think of spiritual things, eventually stumble upon
some satisfying beliefs?
Will you one day—without thinking about it—find a satisfying
experience of God?

Will you manage to find the happiness you seek by drifting
along, day by day, "gathering rosebuds while you may"?
Is it true that "Heaven can wait"?
  Does Heaven wait?
 Will Heaven wait?

Youth is the period of the most important decisions of life
for which the Lord's guidance is particularly needed.
It is in youth that we form our basic ideals and philosophies . . .
It is in youth that we come to crossroads where decisions are
made between right and wrong:
  To do homework—or to sneak out the sexy magazine . . .
  To take a low grade—or cheat . . .
  And when caught doing something wrong to tell the truth
  fearlessly—or lie cravenly—
  perhaps even shifting the blame to someone else.

These are the crossroads . . .
Here is where greatness begins its journey
  or weakness and evil take over.

Habits are begun in youth that solidify like concrete:
  Putting off assignments until it is too late . . .

Telling little lies that grow into bigger lies
that trap

enmesh

entwine

imprison . . .

Giving away a priceless treasure a little at a time until it is all
gone, and you are soiled, distraught, bitter,
> and desperately disillusioned that love can turn so
> dirty . . .

Choosing friends that help lift your thinking,
> or lower it by feeding your ego, tempting you to do the
> things that deep inside you know are wrong.

It is in youth that we decide upon a life work.
Either we just drift into something as the only thing we could
get, or we carefully prepare at home and in school for that
niche in life which we feel is specifically ours.
But whether we drift or whether we steer a direct course, we
achieve that place we choose in youth.
It is usually in youth that we select a life partner.
And in this, the most important decision of our whole life,
we need the help and guidance of a Wisdom greater than our
own.

The prophet promised that it was the young who would see
visions . . .
> the old who would dream their dreams.

Joan of Arc was only seventeen when she was riding at the
head of the army that liberated France from the English.

John Calvin was twenty-six when he published his *Institutes.*
John Keats died at twenty-six . . .
Shelley was thirty when he was drowned, leaving English
literature his undying *Odes* . . .

Sir Isaac Newton had largely discovered the workings of the
law of gravitation when he was twenty-three . . .

Henry Clay was sent to the United States Senate at twenty-nine, and was Speaker of the House of Representatives at thirty-four . . .

Raphael painted his most important pictures between twenty-five and thirty—he died at thirty-seven.
Van Dyck had done his best work before he was thirty.

Jesus Christ was not quite thirty-three when He died.
For the most part, His followers were young men.

Those who gathered at Pentecost were young people . . .
The movement that started when the winds of the Holy Spirit blew through the streets of old Jerusalem was essentially a youth movement.
It is for all these reasons, you see, that Heaven can't wait.
The visions that are to be granted are given to youth.
But voices that are unheeded have a way of being heard no more.
And visions that shine through the fogs and above the mists have a way of fading and disappearing as time goes oozing out.

"Heaven Can Wait"?

"Well," you may say, "it sounds fine. I do want to be happy with a lasting kind of happiness.
I do want to get the most out of life.
I want to be successful.
I would like to feel that there is a God who is interested in me and my life.
Of course, I don't want to make any big mistakes that will mar my life—that will mess it all up.

"I would like to believe that it is not simply a lot of sentimental pious nonsense to say that God cares whom I marry . . .
    that marriages are still made in heaven

that somewhere there is a particular person for me
    that I can feel close to God in my daily life
but—let's be practical.

"Suppose I am ready to call your bluff!
Suppose I am willing to give it a trial.
How does God become real to me?
What do I do?"

These are legitimate questions—if asked by an open mind.
All right, let's be specific . . .
If you want anything in this life, you must reach out for it,
                                the right job . . .
                        the ideal marriage partner . . .
                achievement in any area.

Just so, if you desire the treasures in the Christian life, they
will not come to you unless you seek them.
Christ said, "And all things, whatsoever ye shall ask in prayer,
believing ye shall receive."
Notice that the *ask*—which is action on your part—has to
come first of all.
He also said:

    "Ask, and it shall be given you;
        seek, and ye shall find;
            knock, and it shall be opened unto you."   *Matthew 7:7*
The key words here are action words: *ask* . . .
                            seek . . .
                            knock.

Jesus never said that there was plenty of time.
He never said to take it easy now and things would work out.
He never suggested that you can sow your oats while young,
        because there will always be a chance later on
            to straighten out your life.
He never told us "Heaven will wait while you make up your
mind about Me."

Jesus Himself was a Man of action.
He did not want publicity
> praise
> comforts
> success as the world measures it . . .

He wanted lives—all or nothing.
He has never changed.
He wants your life committed to Him
now—not tomorrow.
And you would be surprised at the wonderful changes that can
come into the life of anyone who is willing to say to Jesus
Christ:
> "Yes, I do want to give myself to You today. Here I am.
> Please take over the direction of my life in every area."

That was the case back in the eighteenth century in the life
of the British parliamentarian, William Wilberforce.
I first learned of him in my history textbooks in Scotland.

As a teen-ager, Wilberforce had idled through Pocklington
School, and then through St. John's College, Cambridge.
After that, he had spent several years enjoying London's society life.
Later he was to comment that he "could not look back without
unfeigned remorse" on all the opportunities he had neglected
during those years in school.

Then in 1784, he went to Nice, France, with an old friend,
Isaac Milner. During the trip, Milner talked seriously to Wilberforce about what he was going to do with his life . . .
> Was he going to drift with the tide on London society?
> What did he intend to do about the talents God had
> given him?

The result of this talk was that before he got back to England,
William Wilberforce did hand his life
> his dreams

his future
his potential over to God.

Changes in the young man's life came thick and fast.
Within three years he knew that God had given him a special
assignment . . .
It was a prodigious one, breathtaking:
He was to end forever the vicious slave trade of the then far-
flung British Empire.

How could one man achieve that?
The slave trade cut directly across some of the most powerful
financial interests of the Empire.
Wilberforce knew that since God had given him the assign-
bent, God was in the fight too.
So this young man rolled up his sleeves and soon became a
voice to reckon with in Parliament.
His days of drifting were over.
      Now his life had a goal.
            He was on God's side.
And he found within himself unflagging zeal for a fight on
those terms.

The fight took forty-six years in all, but God and Wilberforce
won it.
By act of Parliament, the British emancipated every slave in
the Empire twenty-two years before we achieved the same end
in this country with the bloodshed of the War Between the
States.

Do changes take place in a life handed over to God? Yes, al-
ways . . .
Adventure? Decidedly . . .
Does a goal emerge and with it an understanding of that goal?
Yes. But it begins for each of us with an act of commitment.

I knew a girl named Jane who came to Washington from a
small town in the Midwest.

She was excited about her nation's capital . . .
    stirred by the monuments to greatness she saw . . .
        awed by the famous names.

She was a wholesome girl—the type you would like to have
for a daughter
    or a sister
        or a friend.
She dreamed of serving her country, of filling a need.
Her story is, in a way, the story of all quiet lonely girls in a new
city.

Jane became a typist in an office with many girls, in a govern-
ment office on Constitution Avenue.
She soon discovered that one can be lonely in the midst of
many.
A shy girl can get lost in a big city . . .
A girl with ideals may not immediately attract men.
Jane became a steady worker, reliable, conscientious.
In a simple, wholesome way she was attractive, and she did
receive invitations to a few parties.

At first she accepted these invitations eagerly.
But when she saw what went on, she felt sick inside . . .
                    the constant drinking
                    the petty gossip
                    the blatant sexuality
                    the lack of sincerity.
It was hard to refuse invitations, because she needed friends.
Yet she felt soiled and unclean when she came home.

There were times when the pressure of it all made her wonder
why she held on to her ideals, when other people seemed to
be having a good time without scruples
    without being bothered by ideals.
After some of these parties, Jane made concessions, com-
promised with her conscience.

It seemed the thing to do.
Yet the memories of what happened made her blush and feel miserable.

She knew she could never be happy that way—not really happy. But Jane was puzzled, because neither was she happy as she was now—in her loneliness.

Then came a sudden new temptation, worse than the others because it devastated her at the center of her greatest need— her loneliness.
She was torn, seared by the desire to do something she knew was completely wrong.

All that she believed, all her ideals stood in her path.
She longed to thrust them ruthlessly aside, to say "Yes" to a young man's proposition.
He liked her; she liked him. Why not?
                    Heaven can wait!

Jane went to her room to think it over.
There the four cold walls of the drab one-room apartment,
        the comfortless furniture,
            her aloneness and confusion overwhelmed her.

She buried her head in her hands, sobbing, "Oh God—
        Why am I so miserable? Oh God—help me!"
And although she heard nothing, something made her look up.
        Jesus was there by her side.

Jane was startled, but she did not feel fear.
Something about His Presence calmed her,
                dried her tears:
                    His compassionate face . . .
                understanding eyes . . .
It was His eyes that seemed to phrase the statement:
        "You called for Me!"

How universal the appeal—man loses the way and cries for his
Maker.

He comes in many ways . . .

Through the gentle illumination of a thought . . .

In the soothing coolness of understanding that dissolves
hot emotion . . .

In the brilliance of light that pierces foul darkness.

And He comes also as a Presence—a living Presence.

Jane found herself pouring out to Him all her unhappiness . . .

Her disappointments

Her loneliness

Her fears

Her temptation.

She was ashamed as she spoke, but the look of love never left
His eyes.

And suddenly she realized that Jesus already knew everything
about her.

But that had not changed His love.

Finally Jane phrased the question: "Why am I so unhappy?"

Quietly came the answer: "He who loseth himself for My sake
will find himself. Follow thou Me."

And then with a smile of amazing tenderness, He said:

"Lo, I will be with you always."

And then suddenly He was gone.

Yet there was still that strange and wonderful warmth in the
room.

The furniture did not seem so drab . . .

Something was different inside her too . . .

She felt new hope . . .

new determination to stand on principle . . .

an inner buoyancy, a zest for life . . .

and a new love for the girls whom she had envied and
even despised.

But most wonderful of all, she knew that never again could she doubt that Jesus cared about her—even her.

There is a place in the heart of God for you too . . .
It is reserved in your name.
Is it empty still?
Then it is empty only because you have not claimed it.

When you do, you will be home.
You will know for yourself His warm and wonderful love,
                 how He will guide you,
            and help you,
                  give you joy you have never had before.

Isn't it worth trying?

    Heaven can wait?

Ah, but when we can have the joy of Heaven now—

    who wants to wait?

• III •

Jean had heard from some of her friends that Peter Marshall was preaching at the Montreat, North Carolina, conference grounds that Sunday night. She had paid no particular attention because in her sixteen-year-old eyes, every preacher was like every other preacher.

But that evening found Jean with nothing more exciting to do, so she wandered into the great auditorium and dropped down in a back seat. What happened after that Jean later put down in a theme the following year at school...[1]

"As soon as the speakers mounted the platform, I thought I recognized Peter Marshall. The big, burly Scotsman must be he. . . . Yet that was the man I had seen wrestling with some young boys on the lawn outside the auditorium. Plainly he showed the effects of the wrestling: his Palm Beach suit was wilted and his curly hair untidy.

"After Dr. Marshall had been introduced, he rose and walked slowly to the pulpit. This was the same man I had seen outside—yet different. Then he had been like an overgrown boy, handling as many as two or three youngsters at a time, laughing boisterously as he threw them.

"Now he was a man—strong, earnest. There was something about a smile that played over his face that suggested that he had been communing with an unseen Power and had gotten some special light on the task before him.

"He stood there in no hurry to begin, his big hands resting on the open Bible, looking into the faces of the people. He seemed to be reading their individual needs. Then slowly and clearly he began to speak in his deep, yet musical voice.

"After the first few sentences, I edged out of my seat and crept much further front. Dr. Marshall's voice had carried perfectly to the back of the auditorium, but I did not want to miss the least change of expression on his face or the slightest motion.

"The sermon built in tempo. Certainly I had heard a lot about Jesus all my life. But Peter Marshall was introducing me to a Christ I had never met before. His voice grew vibrant with feeling. Sometimes to emphasize a point, one huge fist would come crashing down on the pulpit. From time to time he would mop his forehead with a crushed handkerchief and push an unruly lock of damp hair out of his eyes.

"For over an hour I sat spellbound, not moving, forgetting all about time. Then suddenly Dr. Marshall was finished. There was no tapering off, no 'And now in conclusion—' He just sat down. There was almost an audible sigh from the crowd, then a hush. . . .

"The benediction was pronounced. Few people spoke as they left; no one seemed to want to break the spell.

"I slipped out the rear door, hurried back to our cottage, and crawled into bed without a word to anyone. I wanted only one thing: to sense to the fullest—right then—the companionship of that Christ who was so real to Peter Marshall."

The sermon Jean heard that evening was "The Chains of Freedom."

THE CHAINS OF FREEDOM

THE great yearning of youth is for freedom.
To be free . . . to be on your own . . .
    to be your own master.
Does not your blood tingle at the thought of it?

But wait a minute—
If you had the freedom to go where you wanted . . .
If you had the money, and your parents would not stop you . . .
and you could take off tomorrow . . .
Where would you go?
What would you do?

This was exactly the situation confronting a young man whose story I once heard . . .
Robert Duvois wanted his freedom.
He did not like the slow tempo of country life, even though "Twin Oaks" was a large plantation in South Carolina.

He thought his older brother stuffy.
His father, while kind and sympathetic enough, had some old-fashioned ideas.
Only his mother might have understood, but she had died six months before his twenty-first birthday.
I have no freedom here, Robert kept telling himself.
Life seemed a cramped sort of thing,
    always in the same old groove,
        no excitement.
John, the elder son, had inherited his father's business ability and steadfast character.
Gradually his father had let John take over the management of the plantation.

Robert had his mother's artistic, restless temperament.
He wanted to go to Paris to study art.
He wanted to be free to paint—to live, really live.

Finally he could stand it no longer.
"Give me," he said to his father as he sought to get his hands on his inheritance.
"Give me," he said to life, as his young blood tingled with anticipation.
"Give me," he said to the world, and his eyes danced with the excitement of it.

There were entrancing worlds and fascinating people beyond
the discipline of home.
He was of age now, old enough to live his own life.
He had money coming from his mother's estate.
"A man has to do what he has to do," he told his father.

The father recognized that he could no longer hold his younger
son at home.
He would merely chafe, grow resentful, and eventually leave
anyway.

So the father turned over the inheritance to his son.
Some of the money was sent to a Paris bank.
And Robert had his freedom . . .
    He was twenty-one . . .
        with enough money to be his own boss.
What more could anyone ask?

At first, all went well in Paris.
Robert took his art studies seriously.
He wrote his father that several of his oils had been hung in
art exhibits.
Then, gradually, the gay life of the French capital began to
lure him.
He moved to a fine apartment, bought a sports car.

As he experimented with life, soon on all sides he found himself faced with restrictions to his freedom.
For example, as he drove his car along the Rue de Rivoli he
was halted by stop signs and red lights.
Even with Robert's tendency toward self-pity, he knew that
the traffic lights were impersonal
                unfeeling
           playing no favorites.

He was free to drive through a red light . . .
    but he was not free to avoid the subsequent collision.

He was free to eat whatever he liked in his favorite Paris restaurants, but if he ate too much of exotic foods in combination, he was not free of the gastronomical consequences.

In the realm of his art, his freedom was limited by his ability or lack of it.
He would see wraithlike mists rising from the Seine . . .
    gay colors of sidewalk cafés under their awnings,
        cypresses bathed in shimmering light . . .
but he was not free to capture on canvas what he saw because there was a limit to his talent.

He was free, free to be a traditionalist
        or an impressionist
          or to turn to Cubism or Surrealism . . .
yet whatever art he chose was held in bondage by his own limitations.
In order to overcome these limitations, he would have to sit at the feet of those who knew more than he did,
    study techniques,
      paint . . . paint . . . paint, hundreds of hours.
It was easier to neglect his studies for the theater,
          gay parties,
           night life in the cafés.
There was a procession of women upon whom Robert lavished gifts
    jewels
    furs and perfume.
"Monsieur Robert's" name soon became well known, even in Paris, for wealth and extravagance and dissipation.
At last he felt really free.

This was the life, he thought.
And the "substance" which represented years of hard work,
        of sacrifice
          and saving on the part of his parents
was scattered to gratify passing whims, to try to satisfy greedy desires that were fed but never fulfilled.

One morning, the young man woke to the bitter realization
that his money was gone.
He was in debt to his clothier
           his landlord
         his clubs
       his jeweler.
All his creditors were hounding him.

Hurriedly he left Paris for a small town in Normandy.
There he lived for a few months—guiltily—at a small country
inn where he tried to go back to his painting.
But the joy and inspiration had gone out of it.
Besides, he scarcely had enough money even for paint sup-
plies.

Finally his past caught up with him.
All his possessions, even his clothes, were confiscated.
There was nothing for him to do but to seek work with one of
the local farmers.

At first, he was made an overseer for a wealthy landowner, but
he had little business ability, and what he had was drowned in
the unquenchable thirst for drink to which he was now a slave.
Years passed.
He had long since lost touch with his home.
Things went from bad to worse, until finally he ended up a
hired hand, herding the sheep and tending the pigs.
The vestiges of the sensitive, artistic nature that had once
been his recoiled from every sight and smell of the barnyard
and the pigsty.
He loathed his surroundings,
     his work
and most of all—himself.

Then somehow the boy came to himself.
Memories of home came surging back before the jaded and
bloodshot eyes of the playboy turned ragged swineherd.

Something—the wooing of God's spirit in his heart,
    the early training of his father and mother,
       the inherent quality of the boy's nature—
something brought him back to himself.

He thought of "Twin Oaks" and the gracious, orderly life he
had left behind.
Wistfully he compared his days with those of the workers on
his father's plantation.
Nostalgically he remembered Christmas back home.
The roast turkey with chestnut stuffing . . .
    the platters of fried chicken
      the beaten biscuits
        watermelon-rind preserves
          pecan pies
           spoon bread
and cold floating island.

He remembered the look in his father's eyes as he had stood
at the head of the table carving the turkey,
    the look of tender pride as he had surveyed his family.

Once again he could feel his father's strong arms around him. . .
    a big hand laid tenderly on a little boy's head that day his
    puppy had been killed.
Dimly he recalled certain moments of growing up when he
had thought his father stuffy, old-fashioned.
Now everything in him cried out for some of that old-fashioned
love.

That night he crept away from the farm, and on foot made his
way to Cherbourg, where he worked his way back across the
Atlantic on a freighter.
He was going home . . .

Yes, the story does have a familiar ring. You have heard it
before.

It is the old, old story of the Prodigal Son,
                    as old as man's sin,
as new as God's forgiveness for every man who thinks that
freedom means the license to do what he pleases.

All of us have to begin by discovering what freedom is . . .
                    and what it is not.
The first valuable revelation is that freedom is not rebellion,
    not anarchy.
Sometimes the act of rebelling . . .
    throwing off parental restraints,
        flouting accepted conventions of society,
            renouncing old and accepted beliefs,
gives the exciting illusion of freedom.

Thus every country and every generation has its equivalent of
the Latin quarter,
        its Montmartre,
    its Shepherds' Market,
    or its Greenwich Village,
and the hot-blooded radicals who live there.

The problem is that a man cannot live negatively,
    just in terms of what he is *against.*
        The more pertinent question is,
            what is he *for?*
Once all parental restraints are withdrawn, then what?
Around what will the "free" one build his life?

Many of the moralities and proprieties against which the
younger generation of the Roaring Twenties revolted and
against which the young writers and painters crusaded seem
trifling now.
Today as then, the trouble with the nonsense verse and the
abstract paintings which flow out of these apostate hearts is
that once you subtract the rebellion—

no matter how artfully expressed—
you have little or nothing left.

The same mistake of confusing anarchy with freedom is made
over and over by political or racial groups struggling to cast
off shackles.
See the Marquis de La Fayette standing on the balcony of the
Château of Versailles beside Louis XVI and Marie Antoinette
pleading . . . pleading with his rioting fellow countrymen not
to fall into this trap.

But they would not heed; La Fayette could not stem the tide.
    The heady wine of anarchy was already brewed.
So blood flowed in rivers down the gutters of the Place de la
Concorde from La Guillotine.
Liberté . . . Égalité . . . Fraternité . . .

Ah, but in the end, murder,
                    drunken mobs with heads on pikes,
                    lawlessness,
                        frenzied promiscuity,
                        anarchy
turned out to be not freedom—but chaos.

Of course you can see it in such extreme instances.
But in the ordinary course of our lives, each of us has to find
for himself that there is more to this freedom than rebellion.

It is also true that freedom is not planlessness.
I am reminded of the child in kindergarten who grew tired of
having the play period planned and supervised.
He rebelled at having to play group games.

So the teacher finally told him to find his own amusement,
                    do whatever he wanted to do.
It was not long before the rebel was back, grumbling,
"What can I do now? I don't want to do what I want to do."

On a more adult level, a recent spokesman of the school of
self-expression and self-indulgence made the same confession:
"We took what we wanted, and now we find we no longer
want what we took."
There you have the disillusionment that inevitably follows
liberty without restraint or plan.
In genuine freedom the plan comes from inside a man.
In the case of Robert Duvois—given his time to use it as he
chose—what did he choose to do?

He was on the right track, so long as he was attempting to
express his true inner self through his painting.
But as soon as this trailed off into irresponsibility . . .
  "wasting his substance in riotous living . . ."
then this young man had betrayed freedom.

The more irresponsible he became, the less freedom he had,
the more hemmed in he was by poverty,
    the more he was shackled by the tyranny of habits,
      the more he was confined by the laws of man and God
that play no favorites and will step aside for no one.

And then—at a crisis moment—Robert Duvois turned himself
around to take his first good look at what freedom really is.
    True freedom is finding oneself . . . choosing oneself.
Always in that process, one or more false concepts of what
he *thought* he was must die.
That is why Jesus' "For whosoever will save his life shall lose
it . . ." is found today to be an incisively penetrating psycho-
logical insight.

Then, once the self is found, for the first time man accepts
full responsibility for that self . . .
    for the choices he makes,
      the disciplines he imposes upon himself,
        the way he relates to other human beings.

No longer does he interpret freedom as rebellion against realities.

Now he accepts himself, other people, and circumstances *as they are* and uses his freedom to shape his circumstances creatively.

At this point he discovers the paradox at the heart of all truth:
> We want our freedom in order to give our love and our loyalty away to something bigger than ourselves.

Michelangelo wanted to be an artist, but his father objected. He wanted no son of his to be "a stonecutter."

But the passion to create was in Michelangelo's blood, so at age thirteen—over his father's stubborn opposition—the boy left home.

He was free now ... Yet what a bondservant to art Michelangelo became!

Long hours of work ...
     pinching hardship ...
         superhuman labor ...

Two years, three months of grueling toil to complete the statue "David" ...

Over four and a half years to paint the ceiling vault of the Sistine Chapel ...

Free—yet voluntarily bound.

We can watch the same pattern with many a scientist.

See Marie Curie in her laboratory—her fine mind,
                 all her training in physics,
                     every moment she could spare, day or night,
                 utter devotion
given to refining from pitchblende a new substance—radium.

In the end, Marie Curie laid down her life on the altar of science because, during those long days and nights of work, she had been exposed to radium too often.

A free woman, but she had given her love and her loyalty away. Yet we can never doubt that this is real freedom, be-

cause it is the heart's voluntary loyalty,
    the man's or the woman's own choice.
Long centuries before, God's first direct word on behalf of His
chosen people had been the thundering "Let My people go,"
to the pharaoh who held them in bondage.
After that, through the long years of Israel's history
    through wanderings and captivities
        through times of obedience and
            through times of falling away—
God's word never changed—"Let My people go."

Finally, the word came to Jesus.
It is no accident that Jesus Christ is so concerned with freedom.
That day in Nazareth when He stood in the local synagogue to
announce His Messiahship to His astounded relatives and
friends, a major portion of the platform of His Kingdom was
    "deliverance to the captives."

Then He proceeded to live this out episode by episode . . .
    He freed many a one bound by sin.
        Everywhere He went, He released the captives of pain
        and disease.
            With gladness, He threw open the dark dungeons of
            hate to the sunlight of God's love.
                He struck the shackles from tortured minds and per-
                sonality compulsions.
Moreover He went on to more dangerous liberties:
He declared war on the bondage of ossified traditions
                        and man-made dogmas.
Almost every point of the Sermon on the Mount begins with
"It hath been said of them of old time. . . .
    "But I say unto you. . . ."
Tangling with entrenched religious tradition . . .
Dangerous! Of course it was dangerous!
Yet if you read the accounts of Christ for yourself, you will see
that He had no trace of fear of public opinion.

Physical fear seems to have been unknown to Him:
He never hesitated to touch any loathsome leper ...
On more than one occasion He walked through the midst
of a rioting mob ...
He slept through a violent storm on the Sea of Gali-
lee ...
He faced spies and inquisitors, temple authorities,
King Herod, or Pontius Pilate
with an equanimity nothing could shake.

"Fear not them which kill the body," He advised His disciples.
His words were prophetic.
Finally, His was the supreme freedom:
He was free even to go to His Cross.

This point He made over and over, so that no man could mis-
take it:
"I lay down My life. ...
No man taketh it from Me.
I have power to lay it down,
and I have power to take it again."
                    John 10:17, 18

Yes, Christ was the freest Man who ever lived.
Yet—here is the paradox again—He was free because He had
given His love and His loyalty away.
Voluntarily, He had made His Father's will supreme:

"I seek not Mine own will," He said repeatedly,
"but the will of the Father which hath sent Me."
                    John 5:30

Out of such freedom and such loyalty always comes intense
joy.
Just here, we do violence to the New Testament narratives if
we imagine Christ to be a melancholy recluse.
Isaiah prophesied that He would be "a man of sorrows and
acquainted with grief."

Yes, but that was in order that *our* joy might be full.
A Christ who with trembling lower lip and tear-filled eyes
looked wistfully at human joy is a caricature that belies the
records.

On the contrary, the picture of Jesus in the Gospels is of a
radiant, laughter-loving Friend whom everybody loved, save
the cynical . . . the hard . . . the hating, who had lost the art of
loving anybody.

He was a guest at the wedding feast at Cana because He enjoyed human fun and fellowship.
He was criticized because of the company He kept . . .
      sneeringly referred to as "a friend of publicans and sin-
      ners . . ."
      even called "a winebibber."

The humble folk heard Him gladly, indeed idolized Him.
Children flocked to Him eagerly, and children never go to the
austere, stern person sunk in perpetual gloom.

Always Christ's message is that His Father has designed you
and me for freedom and for happiness.
Having counted the word *joy* 191 times in the Scriptures . . .
glad or *gladness* 125 times, at that point I gave up counting.

God is a God of laughter as well as of prayer . . .
      a God of singing as well as of tears.
God is at home in the play of His children . . .
      He loves to hear us laugh.

Every one of Jesus' beatitudes begins with the words
      blessed or *happy*.
He came to give you the secrets of living, He said,
      so that "your joy might be full."

"Your joy no man taketh from you," He insists.   *John 16:22*
Indeed, so much does He cherish our liberty and our joy that
if we will let Him—He will see to it that no one takes it from
us.
He will stand shoulder to shoulder beside us
    and battle for our freedom.
This is the point at which turning to Him can be dangerous
business.
For when we get right down to it, most of us *like* some of our
shackles,
    feel so comfortably secure in some of our prisons that we
    resist final maturity and ultimate responsibility.
But Christ will tolerate no compromise with our liberty.

The tyranny of lust or greed cannot abide His presence.
    The despotism of jealousy flees before Him.
        Always He opens the door to the dungeon of judging.
        He can heal the bindings of painful memories and bit-
        ter remorse.
            He sets Himself against the dictatorship of stan-
            dardization and social conformity.
                He had specific words to speak against parental
                or family domination.

Now will you listen to Christ when He says:
    "The Spirit of the Lord is upon Me because . . .
    He hath sent Me to . . . preach deliverance to the captives"?
                                                    Luke 4:18
The captives are you and me.

Yet with Christ Himself as our example—we, like Him, have
to give our love and our loyalty away.
In the end, there is only One into whose hands we dare entrust
the keys to our personal freedom.

Once we put those keys in Christ's hands, we have a surprise
awaiting us.

We had feared that giving Him our loyalty would cramp us,
that He would give us a long list of forbidden pleasures.

That is not His way.
"Where the Spirit of the Lord is, there is liberty," the apostle
Paul exults.   *II Corinthians 3:17*

All during his ministry, Paul battled "the false brethren who
come to spy out our liberty in Christ Jesus" by setting up
moral and ritualistic restrictions.

Augustine was right:
Christ's way is "Love God, and do as you please."

As you grow to love God, what you "please" will change.
This is where the surprise comes in.
God gives the inner man a new set of goals and passions.
It would be bondage indeed to obey God when we do not want
to; it is delightful freedom to do what we most want to do.
And that is the wonderful way that God works it out for us.

It is at that point that, like Robert Duvois, we come to ourselves, experience for the first time real freedom.
For like Robert Duvois, every one of us has misused the freedom that God gave us.
The story of the Prodigal Son is the story of every man.

And when the sands of the desert grow cold . . .
    when the stars go out one by one . . .
        when the earth is rolled up like a carpet . . .
            and thrown over the high balconies of heaven . . .
                when our clever sciences have been forgotten . . .
when the proud boasts of men have been carried away on the
hurricanes of time,
    this story will still speak to us . . .
Of a boy who lost his way
Of a Father who freely forgave him.

It will still have the power to soften our hard hearts and bring
tears to our eyes.
It will still point the way to the heart's true home,
    still unfold to us the love of God.
For this story that Jesus told contains the most appealing pic-
ture of God ever drawn.
This parable contains the heart of the gospel:
    That God is willing, indeed eager, to forgive
    sinners like you and me,
        that the moment we turn around to take the way back
        home, the Father will come running down the road to
        meet us . . .
That He is the One who alone holds in His hands the keys to
our freedom.

> "Make me a captive, Lord,
>   And then I shall be free;
>   Force me to render up my sword;
>   And I shall conqueror be. . . ."

•IV•

One of Peter Marshall's favorite sermon illustrations—especially in the early years of his ministry—was "the King is in the audience." It was a vivid word picture of a scene typical of the London theater.

He described the waiting audience filing slowly into seats that tipped down with a welcoming clatter. . . . The cheerful conversation that spread from row to row and spilled into the foyer. He spoke of the orchestra, emerging stooping, tuning its instruments; of the scenes backstage—ropes, cables, hoisting gear being tried out. . . . Lights being focused and shutters placed in readiness.

In the dressing room each mirror framed a face being made up. Finally warning lights winked backstage. Silence . . . places. . . . The overture had begun. But in the middle, a phrase was broken off; the orchestra stopped abruptly. There was a moment of deathly stillness—then the stately, thrilling strains of the National Anthem.

In the wings, the stage manager and director ran excitedly from group to group, "Give it all you've got tonight. Play as you've never played before."

Why? Why this commotion? Because . . . The King is in the audience.

For Peter Marshall it was a parable of human life. Often he would tell his congregations, "The King is in this audience —walking these aisles or sitting beside you. You may whisper your prayer to the King now"—and heart-searching silence would follow. You seemed to feel Him there in the quiet sanctuary, to hear the rustling of His robe.

But Peter's message was that the King is not in the audience just for one night, that the King is not confined to the church. He is in His world, all of His world, in the joy of it and also in the heartbreak. He is in the laughter of children, but also with the old people left without affection; in the healthy fun of youth, but also with the wives lonely at home. The King is standing beside the bride with shining eyes, but He is also suffering with the woman on the sickbed or with the men who must live beneath the thunder of the guns and the whine of the shells.

Peter knew that his unique mission in life was to introduce men and women to the King walking among them, to make men aware of Him. Who is the King? Even this Jesus.

The plaque in the foyer of the new building for the New York Avenue Presbyterian Church in Washington bears this inscription:

TO PETER MARSHALL

WHO MADE JESUS CHRIST A LIVING REALITY

TO THE CONGREGATION OF NEW YORK AVENUE.

JOHN DOE, DISCIPLE

THERE are many of you who think of Christ as someone who belongs to history—like Caesar.

> or Washington,
> or Napoleon.

You think of Him as one who lived on earth and passed away. A great man, to be sure, but nothing more.

Perhaps you look on His life as an affecting sacrifice,

> a great inspiration.

He was a Wise Teacher, you say, but beyond that Christ is not
really significant for you.

Or do you have an inner contempt for the mild, suffering Jesus
so often pictured?
It is a curious thing that the artists whose brushes have traced
His form on canvas have largely portrayed His gentleness,
                                        meekness
                                        compassion
                                        suffering . . .
rather than the other, equally true sides of His personality . . .
                                        strength
                                        tireless energy
                                        uncompromising will.

Perhaps it is this one-sided picture of the meek and longsuffer-
ing Christ that you and I *want* to see.
Perhaps it is the picture that more nearly suits our generation
with its broad-mindedness
    its easygoing compromises
        its scorn of hell
            its denial of the reality of sin.

But when we throw away our preconceived ideas and turn to
the New Testament for ourselves, we come away with an altogether different conception.
There is a true picture of Christ in the Gospel of John—
a dramatic scene in the Temple of Jerusalem near the beginning of Jesus' public ministry.
It is His first appearance before His nation as the Messiah.

No one could forget it . . . Jesus walking through the colon-
nade with its marble forest of great Corinthian pillars a hundred feet high, then on into the Court of the Gentiles.

It is early morning, but already the temple court is a bedlam
of activity and noise.

Among the tables of the moneychangers, the cages of doves
and the stalls of cattle, people crowd about
                    chatting with their friends,
              selecting a dove for sacrifice,
or getting their money from Tyre or Persia or Egypt or Greece
changed into the sacred half-shekel of the sanctuary.
It is convenient to buy sacrifices on the spot instead of having
to drag them from a distance.
It is helpful to be able to exchange money bearing upon it the
head of the emperor, a graven image and therefore unaccept-
able in the Temple, for the statutory half-shekel.

And so, convenient for all and profitable to many, the temple
huckstering has become a recognized institution.
Shrill voices bargaining
    swearing angrily
        bickering
the metallic tinkle of coins as they drop into the moneyboxes
on the table . . .
all the signs of greed can be heard just outside the Holy Place.
There is no serenity—no peace.
No one can pray there.

Suddenly there is a lull in the confusion.
Startled at the sudden quiet, we look up to find a strange yet
hauntingly familiar figure standing between two of the gigan-
tic stone columns, His face burning with intensity,
                    His face magnificent in its wrath.
Poor peasants are being bled in the name of God.
Has He not watched His own mother patching clothes,
                        skimping on food
to save one denarius after another for the Temple dues?

As He steps forward with a resolution and firmness born of
the terrible conviction that shines in His face, there is a look
in His eyes before which men break away.
His lips are drawn into a thin line . . .

Stooping, He picks up some binding cords which the mer-
chants have discarded.
Deftly He knots them into a whip.

There is something in His attitude,
                        in His eyes,
                    in His face,
in that ominous silence in which He stands watching,
which makes men look at Him with uneasiness in their eyes.

And then the full fury of His wrath breaks.
In a few long strides He is across the court.
Picking up the boxes filled with money—scornfully and deliberately—He empties them on the stone floor . . . and the
coins spill with a clatter and go rolling in a hundred directions.

The tables too go crashing to the floor, and the moneychangers
rush to gather up their coins from the filth.
In their greed—made all the more frantic because of their fear
—they grovel in the dirt, pouncing upon their money and
screaming in protest as the Man with the whip stands over
them.

And then He drives out the terror-stricken cattle.
The muscles of His arms stand out like cords;
    lights dart from His eyes.

Not a voice is heard in protest . . .
    not a hand is raised against Him.
Even the Temple guards only stand and watch helplessly.
His magnificent figure dominates the scene.

His voice rings out, echoing among the stone pillars, and it
sounds like the voice of doom . . .
    like the voice of God Himself . . .
"It is written, My house shall be called the house of prayer,
but ye have made it a den of thieves."

Who is this Christ?

He is a Man whose impact on people who listened to Him
must have been more like dynamite than dew.
One cannot read the Gospels without reaching the conclusion
that there was something disturbing about the march of the
Galilean through the land.
Everywhere He went there was anything but peace.
   Debates and arguments buzzed around Him.

If men did not come to Him with questions,
He challenged their thinking with questions of His own.
He made men wonder about themselves . . .
look into their hearts and see things they had not seen before.
He made them ponder about life and what it meant.
Who is this Christ?

In talking to young people I have the feeling that there is
confusion about Jesus . . .
To many, He is a dim shadowy figure . . . almost a stranger.

You have heard echoes of His person . . .
   rumors of His movements in the hearts and lives of people
   around you.
But again and again you have missed Him—as though He were
some romantic figure moving about the pitched tents of an
army at night.
You have heard stories of Him whispered around the campfires
before which young people seek to warm their souls.

Yet, always you miss Him and grow weary in the search
until you question in your heart His mysterious person.
The fact is that you really have not met Him face to face.
An introduction may help.
John Doe, I would like you to meet One who means every-
thing to me . . .
John Doe, meet Jesus of Nazareth.

This Christ—whence did He come?

His home was in an obscure village of an occupied Roman province.

He was born in a stable where animals from the inn were kept.

His parents were poor working people.

The only records we have of Him are silent about the greater part of His life.

This remains one of the most intriguing historical mysteries of all time.

There are hints that after Joseph's death He took over the family carpentry shop—first in Nazareth, then in Capernaum.

His formal education was in the local synagogue school, and it stopped when He was twelve.

He left no writings.

Indeed, the only record of His ever having written anything is one of finger tracings in the sand . . . and the eddies of wind that swirled around the pillars of the Temple porch soon covered it up.

He spoke Aramaic, the traditional Hebrew, and probably a smattering of Greek and Latin, for He lived in a trilingual world.

Never did He travel more than a hundred miles from home. Standing on the Mount of Olives He could look over the length and breadth of His country . . . which He never left during His life.

When He began His public ministry and took to preaching, His family tried to talk Him out of it, thinking and saying that He was mad.

His friends were mostly as poor as He was—fisherman and peasants.

See Him mingling with the forgotten men,
        talking to the outcasts,
      knowing no social barriers,

caring nothing for money or material things,
  going about with publicans and sinners
until many of His contemporaries were scandalized.

He attracted great crowds, for He walked among the sick,
                    touching here a blind eye,
                  there a palsied limb,
                here a running sore,
              there a crippled leg.
Even His enemies were later to admit these miracles.

But finally the crowds drifted away, for His counsels were too
difficult; men were not ready to accept this hard way of love.
And so the sands ran out and His three-year ministry drew to
its close.
At one point, He feared that His own followers might also
melt away.
In the end, most of them did flee in fear, caring more for
their own safety than for Him.
He died a criminal's death, reviled and mocked . . .
              tormented and laughed at,
            hanging between two theives.
They buried Him in a borrowed grave.

But the story was not finished.
Suddenly His disciples, the same men who had run away, came
back boldly into the streets of the city which had crucified
Christ, proclaiming that He was not dead at all—
He was alive.

The body with the marks of the nails and the spikes had disappeared.
On this everyone was agreed.
There were many attempted explanations, but somehow none
was adequate.
All that His enemies had to do to silence forever the rumor of
this resurrection was to produce the body—but they could not.

Whatever anyone else in Jerusalem thought, it was obvious
that Christ's disciples were convinced beyond any doubt that
their Master was alive.
For they were different—not the same men at all.
They were no longer afraid.
They spoke boldly.
Threats did not intimidate them.

They said fantastic things—that the Living God had once and
for all, in a brief life on this earth, given a full and final revelation of Himself in Christ.
  In Jesus—God had come!

They said that, within thirty-six hours of Christ's death, the
dead body had become alive,
  had walked out of the grave,
appeared to many human witnesses—to *them*.

Among the pillars of the Temple porch itself, their ringing
assertions echoed and reverberated:

  "This Jesus whom ye crucified is risen from
    the dead and now demands that every man repent."

As you would suppose, such a message was laughed at.
"These men are drunk" was the first popular verdict.
Then "They must be mad."

The wild story traveled fast . . . to Asia Minor . . . to Rome.
There was derisive laughter—"Just another superstitious cult."
Was not the world of that day satiated with cults and bizarre
man-made religions?

But then this Jesus began to be talked about too much and
the Roman Empire tried to stop the story's spreading by force
and threats.
"Don't tell these tales again," the disciples were told, "if you
value your lives."

But they did not stop.
The threats only made them more eloquent and bold.

Thrown into prison, they made the cell a pulpit and the dungeon a choir.
Stoned, they rose from the dust bleeding and bruised, but with a more convincing testimony.
Lashed with whips, they praised God the more.

Nothing could stop them.
The Romans made human torches of believers to light the arenas on their holidays.
Yet in death, these Christian martyrs made converts to their strange preaching.
Hunted and persecuted,
    thrown to the lions,
        tortured and killed,
still the number of those who made the sign of the Cross grew . . .
    and grew.
Rome could not stop Jesus.
Her grandeur toppled and fell; Jesus lived on.
What the Empire had regarded as a ripple on the wide sea of polytheism became a tidal wave sweeping over the world.
Incredibly, in A.D. 325 under the Emperor Constantine,
Christianity won official recognition from the Empire which had once vowed to crush every last follower of the Nazarene.

In all of history, has there ever been such an extraordinary sequence of events?
Who is this Jesus?
What is the explanation of His power?
Etched against the skyline of every city,
    carried in the forefront of every human endeavor,
    the Cross on which He died has become a haunting symbol of a haunting Person.

Christ is an end . . . and a beginning.
All secular history is divided into two great divisions:
> before Christ—after Christ

In an old document, Celsus—a Roman historian—trying to explain the strange power of Christianity in his day, wrote:

> "The importance of Christianity is the excessive value it places on every human soul."

Jesus insisted that God's interest centered on the individual.
His is the power that sets the prisoners free, in whatever bondage they languish.
Testimonies are without number.
Changed lives all ascribe the glory to Him.
It is to Him that credit belongs for the newness of life and the victories that men and women have achieved.

How many are there who will testify to this power?
> The power that saves,
> > that forgives,
> > > that leads and guides through life.

There it is . . . a mystery and a power!

But it is more than the power of an idea or a philosophy; more than the memory of a good and great Man.
He is a Presence now—even now.
"Lo, I am with you always," He once said—and many of us have found it true—gloriously true.
Part of the mystery is this: that He lived nineteen centuries ago, in the faraway little land of Palestine.
He wore Oriental robes and sandals.
Yet His words and His Presence are as real and as relevant as if He had spoken last night on the radio in English
> from New York or San Francisco.

Even in our days of neon signs and penthouses, of skyscrapers and fast air travel, He is authoritative, the last word for us.

There is no shortage of evidence that the ethical teaching of Christ is eternally and everlastingly right.
Our best minds today are willing to admit that a great many things on which we pinned our hopes have failed us miserably.

Man has supposed that his new heaven and his new earth will come through materialism . . .
    having two cars in every garage,
        a television set in every living room,
            an electric dishwasher and clothes drier.
Somehow these have not brought about the desired results.

Nor has secularism made life happier or easier.
We are all becoming aware with a sickness of heart that a civilization whose art ends in surrealism . . .
    whose music ends in discord,
        whose literature ends in the airing of sexual license and sexual deviations,
            whose science ends in the power to destroy civilization. . . .
can never satisfy the soul of the world or the hunger of the human heart.

An assistant of Thomas A. Edison once tried to console the inventor over the failure to achieve in a series of experiments what he had set out to find:
"It's too bad," he said, "to do all that work without results."
"Oh," said Mr. Edison, "we have lots of results. We know seven hundred things that won't work."

By this time we ought to know a good many things that will not work in our world . . .
You and I have even found out one or two philosophies of our own that have not brought us peace or happiness.

Still that haunting Figure stands in our midst.
Read the New Testament for yourself and see if this same

Jesus does not step out of the pages to stand beside you
  with His piercing eyes and His quiet vibrant voice—
                    like the voice of God—
"Follow Me," He says. "Follow Me . . ."
"Whom say *ye* that I am?"

What then are you to reply, John Doe?
Have you answered that question in your own mind?
Has your heart whispered its response?
It is a question you cannot dodge forever.

It is today as it was in His day.
When He walked the trails of Palestine, men tried to be
neutral and found that they could not.
Try as they might to brush Him aside—on whatever pretext,
                    they could not have done with Him.
There has always been a quality about Jesus that was urgent.
It had to be accepted—or rejected.
He forced the issue because of the claims He made for Himself.

Consider those claims . . .
He claimed equality with God . . .
    "I and My Father are one."   *John 10:30*
    "He that hath seen Me hath seen the Father."   *John 14:9*

He claimed to be the fulfillment of Old Testament prophecy.
He stated that before Abraham was born, He had lived . . .
    He said that He had come from God in heaven, and that
    He would return to His Father.

Such talk was not misunderstood by the Jews.
Jesus meant that it should be understood, and it was.
Knowing full well the meaning of what He had claimed,
                    they howled for His death . . .

    "Therefore the Jews sought the more to kill Him, because
    He . . . said also that God was His own Father, making
    Himself equal with God."   *John 5:18*

Christ accepted the worship of men.
He took it as His right, accepted it as His prerogative.
When Simon Peter or Thomas or many another worshiped
Him, He did not say, "Stand up on your feet, for I am like
yourselves."
He took their worship and breathed upon them His benediction.

He affirmed His sinlessness.
The challenge He hurled, "Which one of you accuseth Me of
sin?" found none to speak against Him.
It is the testimony of the friends who knew Him best,
   of the enemies who loved Him least.

"I find no fault in this Man," said Pontius Pilate wonderingly.
"This Man hath done nothing amiss," cried the thief dying
beside Him.

Christ has been under the microscope for twenty centuries.
Philosophers
   scientists,
      reformers,
         poets and statesmen,
            cynics and saints,
have examined Him for blemishes and found in Him no flaw.
He claimed the right to forgive sin—a prerogative of God.
This was no mechanical formula, no hocus-pocus or black
magic, for in every case His pronouncement of pardon was
accompanied by a peace of mind and a cleanness of soul that
expressed itself in a transformed life,
   a changed outlook,
      a fresh beginning.

He claimed to have the right and the authority to tell men how
to get in touch with God.
He told them what to do to find peace and happiness and
eternal life.

He gave them new commandments with the authority of God.
He predicted that later He would judge men everywhere.
He claimed to be doing the will of God.

Now as you read the audacious claims made by this Jesus, you
are forced to a simple conclusion:
    either the claims are true—or this Man was a charlatan.

If they were false, did He hope to convince people simply by
making more stupendous claims than any other human being
had ever made?
Men have laughed at fools before ... have been amused, entertained.
But Christ did not affect them like that.
"Never man spake as this Man," even His enemies admitted.

He placed Himself at the center of His ethic and His message.
He did not come to us to point the way.
He said, "I am the way ... I am the door ... I am the truth."

Calmly He obtruded Himself—yet so convincingly that men
were shocked.
Thus Christianity is more than the religion of Jesus:
                            It is the worship of Christ.

Christ is not only the center; He is also the circumference.
Take Zoroaster out of the religion that bears his name, and
you will still have Zoroastrianism.
Take Mohammed out of Islam, and you will still have the
worshipers of Allah.
But take Jesus Christ out of Christianity, and you have absolutely nothing left.

                    Christianity is Christ.

Now what shall we make of all this?
Either it is sheer nonsense—or it is true.
Either anyone who speaks as Christ did was a mumbling idiot,

a deranged megalomaniac who thinks that he is a teapot
. . . or Joan of Arc's horse . . . or Napoleon—
or else Christ was, and is, who He claims to be.

The alternative that He did not leave us is to believe that
He was merely a great moral teacher.
To say this is to betray our ignorance.
For one who made the claims that Christ did—if they were
fraudulent—could scarcely be a great moral teacher.
He would be a maniac, or at the least a consummate liar.

Yet His sanity has never been questioned, for His life and His
teachings were too obviously normal and sensible and clear-
headed.
In fact, as the relatively new science of psychology is progres-
sively finding out, His teachings of love and selfishness lie at
the heart of an integrated personality.

And the suspicion of fraud has no foundation, for the swin-
dlers always use their ability to fool people to gain wealth or
power.
Jesus asked nothing.
He taught unselfishness and indifference to the treasures of
this world, and His own life is the proof of His sincerity.

Did He then speak the truth?
Was He God come down to earth to show us the loving heart
of the Father?
As a matter of fact, there could be no greater proof of the
truth of His claims than that I—some nineteen hundred years
later—should even be asking the question: "John Doe, what
do you think of Christ?"

Perhaps no one has ever confronted you with the fact that
what you decide about Him will be the most important decision of your life.

You cannot go on dodging the issue.
You must be either for Him—or against Him.
Even if you try to be noncommittal, that is an answer too.
A man in a burning house to whom the firemen throw a rope ladder may have difficulty deciding whether or not to risk using it.
Should he hesitate too long, he *has* decided.
The notice of his death in next day's newspaper will leave little doubt of his decision.

What are you going to do with Jesus?

There are stern facts which Christ Himself asks you to consider before you decide.
Few men have ever recruited disciples on such hard-hitting terms...
He warned that following Him might divide families...
alienate friends.
He said that it would mean a shift in values,
a turning away from materialism.
It would involve sacrifice, because you would no longer be able to put yourself and your own comforts first.
For some, hatred, persecution, and death would follow.

Let us not deceive ourselves that these warnings were just for first-century Christians.
If Christ were to reappear—dressed in a modern business suit —on Main Street or Madison Avenue, would we react any differently than did the inhabitants of Jerusalem in A.D. 33?

Would we have enough dedication and stamina
to accept Him and His audacious claims,
to make known our allegiance to Him
under the pressure of an unpopular cause and ostracism?
The sad truth is that purity and sacrifice are unpopular in every century.

At the moment, we are in a period when church membership is socially acceptable and on the rise.

It is not hard to decide for Christ so long as He stays safely in the pages of the New Testament,

or smiles at us on a Sunday morning from a stained-glass window.

But as materialism and secularism accelerate, our civilization may yet, in our time, go full circle.

In that case, we may see a new conspiracy against God,

a modern version of Christian persecution,

even of Christianity having to go underground.

These are the possibilities you should consider, John Doe.

What then *does* He offer you?

His friendship—the most wonderful friendship in the world.

His strength for your weakness . . .

His forgiveness for your sins . . .

His comfort to your sorrow . . .

His light to your darkness . . .

His guidance for your way.

For, start wherever you will in an honest search to find out this truth about this Christ, sooner or later God in Christ will find you.

And then you will have the final, complete proof of His deity—

in your own experience.

Whenever you look into your own heart, you will find His haunting Presence.

He will show you a love that will never let you go.

"Come after Me," He still calls, asking for recruits,

for disciples.

Are you ready to answer Him, John Doe?

Are you ready to be—John Doe, Disciple?

·V·

If ever there was a nonconformist, Peter Marshall was one. I remember a night in Miami Beach, for instance, when he was there for a preaching mission. It was late, around midnight, and he was hot and thirsty after his labors. The only places still open were night clubs.

We entered one. There were thick carpets, a hushed atmosphere, and the usual exotic dim lighting. I knew that the latter was one of Peter's pet aversions. "Nothing glamorous about it," he muttered, "just nefarious gloom."

As he followed the maître d', Peter put out his hand like a blind man groping his way. The dignified man in tails looked at us disapprovingly, showed us to a table and then left shaking his head.

In the semidarkness a waiter ceremoniously presented the liquor list. Just as ceremoniously Peter struck a match to look at it. Fighting off laughter, I saw perplexity and indecision flitting across the sedate waiter's face. He looked closely at his customer to see if this one was drunk or joking.

"Ginger ale all right, Catherine?"

I nodded.

"And I want a glass of milk—make it a large glass," Peter said.

The waiter, frustrated by this nonalcoholic order, opened his mouth, shut it again. "Sir, we may not have milk."

"Of course you have milk," Peter answered blithely.

The man stared contemptuously at Peter, trying to intimidate him. Peter stared back unblinkingly. Finally the waiter retreated to fumble in the back of the icebox for some milk.

68

Peter was enjoying himself hugely. There was nothing he liked better than pricking balloons of pompous conformity. In fact, a look at any area of his life would reveal this same individuality.

His favorites in literature were Shakespeare, Milton, John Buchan, Robert Burns, F. W. Boreham (the Australian), Leslie Weatherhead, George Buttrick, A. A. Milne, and the King James Bible. He had been known to mix any combination thereof in a sermon. Why not? These were men and books he liked.

Clothes? He was fond of the informal—especially open-necked sport shirts. He disliked wearing a hat. Upon appropriate Scottish occasions, he would wear kilts. It was almost impossible to dress him "correctly" for any given occasion.

His tastes in food and drink were an absurd combination of British heritage with American acquisitions: Tea . . . tea . . . tea . . . made properly, of course. Steak-and-kidney pie . . . and corn on the cob. Scottish shortbread . . . angel-food cake. No flavor of ice cream except vanilla in the best British tradition . . . soft boiled custard.

Of course nonconformity in such peripheral areas could have been merely amusing eccentricity. But in Peter's case, he had a way of seeing many accepted conventions with fresh eyes and the courage to act on his personal appraisal.

There was the matter of corporate worship. I saw him hold up his arms to stop a church congregation in the middle of singing a hymn. "Do you really know what you are singing?" he cried.

"I'll go where you want me to go, dear Lord, . . .
Take my silver and my gold.
Not a mite would I withhold. . . .
Do you mean that? I doubt it! Don't sing these words now unless you mean them!"

Race relations? He was ahead of his times. He gloried in the fact that when Chief Justice Charles Evans Hughes was received into the membership of the Calvary Baptist Church in Washington, a Chinese laundress stood beside him, being received at the same time. "The ground at the foot of the Cross is level," he thundered. "Do the words liberty *and* justice for all *mean anything? Where is liberty? . . . If the Spirit of the Living God be not permitted to operate in American hearts to solve the complicated . . . delicate . . . dangerous question of race relationships in this land of ours, then the stone god of paganism will force upon us a solution that will crush and kill every decent thing."*

To his prayers in the United States Senate Peter Marshall brought his fresh approach. He refused to use words to lull the Senators to sleep, so many of his prayers were less than one hundred words. There is nothing soporific about challenges like these: "If there be any here sulking as children" or "Take away the stubborn pride that keeps us from apology." He spoke of stomach ulcers as the "badge of lack of faith"; of "swelled heads and stubborn wills"; "Help us to keep our moral voting record straight."

The sermon that follows—"Get Out of Step"—reflects Peter Marshall's basic belief in the fresh approaches and the creative nonconformity that the Spirit of God can introduce into our lives whenever we let Him.

GET OUT OF STEP

ONE of the memorable scenes in an English novel of some years ago [2] describes how a little boy named Bron goes to church for the first time with his governess.

He watches with interest every part of the service and then the preacher climbs into the high pulpit and Bron hears him give out a piece of terrible news.

It is about a brave and kind man who was nailed to a cross . . . ferociously hurt a long time ago . . . who feels a dreadful pain

even now, because there was something not done that He
wants them all to do.

Little Bron thinks that the preacher is telling the story because
a lot of people are there and they will do something about it.

Bron is sitting impatiently on the edge of the pew.
He can scarcely wait to see what the first move will be in right-
ing this injustice.
But he sits quietly and decides that after the service someone
will do something about it.

Little Bron weeps . . . but nobody else seems at all upset.
The service is over, the people walk away as if they had not
heard such terrible news,
      as if nothing remarkable had happened.

As Bron leaves the church, he is trembling,
His governess looks at him and says:
      "Bron, don't take it to heart—someone will think you are
      queer."

Queer—to be alive and sensitive in one's spirit!
Queer—to show emotion!
Queer—to listen to what is going on in God's house,
                              really to hear,
                           to respond . . .
Queer—to take Jesus Christ seriously!

What does *queer* mean?
The dictionary says "differing in some odd way from what is
ordinary."

Ought not the Christian, then, to be queer?
He should not be satisfied with the ordinary in life.
Christ was not ordinary, and He did not call His followers to
be ordinary.

Yet so many people who call themselves Christians today are living ordinary lives.

There is nothing about them that makes them any different from others who make no profession of belief, acknowledge no faith, and assume no obligations.

In fact, like Bron's governess, what they fear most in life is being "different."

We are becoming an assembly-line society.

The days of rugged individualism that explored the American frontier have been left far behind.

While this pattern of conformity can be seen in every age group, I want to speak about it especially to you young people, because as you huddle together—
     each of you trying to be like everyone else—
you are not finding the satisfactions you seek.

You are still hungry and thirsty on the inside, you still have problems unsolved, questions unanswered.

I want to tell you where you can find some of the answers you seek.

With many of you, conformity has become a creed.

You are terrified at being set apart.

Your own teen-age definition of sin is to be out of step with your friends.

You must wear clothes like everyone else . . .
    collect and listen to the same records
      learn the same dances
        know the latest teen-age slang.

The desire to look and act like everyone else affects all of life:
          your study habits,
          your dating patterns,
        how you spend your time,
      what you buy with your allowance,

your attitude toward parents . . . your nation . . . God . . . the church.

In order not to be different, you have to be content with a low standard of achievement . . .
    a conformity to mediocrity rather than a desire to excel.

Are you, for example, content with average grades, because to excel would be to be thought "a grind"
                  "a square"
             just plain queer?

Why read for yourself and draw your own conclusions when it is far safer to adopt the philosophy of your friends,
              or favorite columnist,
          or television commentator?
The editorial page of our newspaper is ignored by too many readers who turn to the sports page or the comic strips for their reading, because they do not wish to do any serious thinking.

The teen years are the years for discovering "the real you,"
    the time when you should be shaping your own tastes.
Yet the temptation with all thoughts, activities, and goals is to keep right in step,
    marching along like robots,
        fearful of ridicule . . . criticism . . . isolation . . .
if you should, perchance, get out of step with the crowd.

Take the matter of social drinking.
More and more this is motivated by the desire to satisfy the requirements of sociability—and too many young people are facing the ultimatum:
    "Drink . . . or be left out . . .
      No drink . . .
        no dance . . .
          no date!"

If you decline a drink, you are accused of assuming a "holier-than-thou" attitude,

>you are not a "good sport."
>>you are a wet blanket.

The refusal to drink is often interpreted as a boorish criticism of the occasion and those conducting it.

Social pressure is a dreary fact of our day, and you young people who try to buck it run into embarrasing situations and feel certain tensions that result in strained relationships.

Now it is a natural human desire to be congenial with the group and to act in harmony with prevailing customs,
and the liquor trade is exploiting it to the limit.

It is this social pressure that induces you to begin drinking.
It is not because you are thirsty

>or like the taste of alcohol
>>or the smell of it,

but simply because you lack the conviction that will enable you to be "different."
You don't want people to think that you are "queer."
The drinking which is required by the powerful pressure of an authoritative social code is a type of tyranny.
This tyranny of the crowd is actually a flagrant interference with your personal liberty and a gross repudiation of the democratic principle and spirit.

Why is it that people who want to imbibe alcoholic beverages insist that you take one too, just to be sociable?
But do they likewise insist that you are

>>a spoil-sport,
>>a wet blanket,
>>a prude,

if you decline a cup of coffee or prefer a cup of tea?

I am not suggesting that you isolate yourself from social situations to avoid the embarrassment of refusing a drink.

Not at all! This was not Jesus' viewpoint.
He Himself was criticized because He associated with all
types and manner of people.

No ... instead refuse that drink and then show the others that
you can have as much fun as anyone.
In fact, the nondrinker should have more fun, for alcohol
eventually dulls the brain and acts as a depressant.
I can never understand why the person who acts on principle
should be considered dull.
There is excitement in taking a stand ... in being different.
It brings a sparkle to the eyes.
 The mind is alive.
  The spirit sings.
   True values come into sharper focus.

Yet when one falls into line ... going along with the crowd,
conforming to the group pattern, nothing new is happening!
    There is weary repetition,
   dull compliance
  lack of initiative
  boredom.

And that is exactly what so many of you are feeling
 and why so many of you are dissatisfied with life.
Have you ever stopped to wonder *why* you have not wanted
to be different?
Is it because you have not found yourself ...
   who you are ...
   why you are here ...
  where you are going?

So you think that your protection and security lies in huddling
together with your friends,
 losing your unsure self in the group.

The problem is that by losing yourself in the group, you can

go through your whole life and *never* get the answers to what
you are supposed to do with your life.

Then too, what "everyone else" is doing may be quite wrong.
Many students cheat, but that does not make cheating right.
Remember that it is the *mob* that lynches an innocent man.
Entire nations have swallowed evil propaganda which was all
falsehood.
The fact that millions believed it did not turn falsehood into
truth or avert disaster.
In fact, what governments decide can be—and often has been
—quite wrong.

Henry Thoreau—a rugged New England individualist of the
nineteenth century—once went to jail rather than pay his poll
tax to a state which supported slavery.
During this period he wrote his essay "Civil Disobedience"—
now famous the world over.

Thoreau's good friend, Ralph Waldo Emerson, hurried to visit
him in jail, and peering through the bars exclaimed:
    "Why, Henry, what are you doing in there?"

The uncowed Thoreau replied, "Nay, Ralph, the question is,
what are you doing out there?"
Who is the queer one—Little Bron or his governess?
                    Thoreau in jail—or the rest of us outside?

Thoreau was not a churchman because he thought the
churches of his day too convention-bound—and perhaps he
was right. Yet in his book *Walden* he speaks often of God.
He explains that he went to Walden Pond to live the simple
life because he wanted to get just those answers that you and
I seek:

    "I went to the woods because I wished . . . to front only
    the essential facts of life and see if I could not learn

what it had to teach, and not, when I came to die, discover that I had not lived. . . ."

At another time this amazing man commented:
"If a man does not keep pace with his companions perhaps it is because he hears a different drummer. Let him step to the music which he hears, however measured or far away."

Any man or woman who accomplishes anything worthwhile must have the courage to be different, even to be regarded as queer, because they are marching to the drumbeat of a Different Drummer and they are not afraid to be out of step.

Abraham Lincoln was one who listened to the Different Drummer, and not to the vindictive voices of his advisers.

Stephens, Phillips, and Beecher were among Lincoln's contemporaries who were echoing the cry "Crush the South . . ."
"Stamp out the whole slave-holding aristocracy . . .
Make them pay to the last acre of land,
the last vestige of power,
the last drop of blood."

But the great man upon whose furrowed brow the responsibility rested, heard a Different Drummer . . .

"With malice toward none, with charity for all, let us strive on to finish the work we are in, to bind up the nation's wounds . . .
to do all which may achieve and cherish a just and lasting peace among ourselves and with all nations."

What is the verdict of today?
Whose words are remembered and repeated—
Lincoln's or Stephens'?

Woodrow Wilson was another.
As a son of the manse, he knew how to listen to the voice of
God, and he was not afraid to take a position that other men,
hearing no distant drumbeat, delighted to ridicule.

When Wilson went to Paris after the first world war, his con-
suming passion was to work out a peace on a just and righteous
basis.
Someone sneered that Wilson talked like Jesus Christ.
Could there have been a greater compliment paid to any man?
But it was not intended as a compliment.

In our day—as in Wilson's—there are many who are not at all
certain that they want to be like Christ.
Most of their opinions of Him are formed out of puerile ignorance and a tangle of mistaken conceptions.

Yet Christ Himself would be the first to tell you that this is a
central issue you need to face honestly—
　　　before you dare call yourself a Christian.
Jesus never deceived anyone about the cost of following Him.
Over and over He asserted that what He was offering was
hard,
　　　that a man had better sit down and count the cost before
　　　deciding to become one of His disciples.
He offers a cross—not a cushion.
He recruits men—not weak-kneed boys.

And He would have stern words for the minister who pleads
with people to join his church,
　　　as if they were doing the church a favor . . .
who sets the requirements for church membership so low that
people can fall over the threshold.

Yet Jesus did not ask us to be different just to make life hard.
He was thinking of our happiness when He said:
　　　"Woe unto you, when all men shall speak well of you. . . ."
　　　　　　　　　　　　　　　　　　　　　　　Luke 6:26

Why . . . "Woe unto you?"
Isn't it all right to be thought well of?
Isn't popularity a fine thing?

Yes, popularity is pleasant.
I like it as much as you do.
But the truth is no man can have any convictions
                    or stand for any principles,
                 or stick to any standards at all,
and be liked by everyone.

Jesus put it this way:

> "How on earth can you believe while you are forever
> looking for each other's approval and not for the glory
> that comes from the one God?"   *John 5:44*

It always amazes me the way people come to church, partici-
pate fully in the prayers and rituals, nod in agreement during
a sermon on faith and prayer.

Yet if the same people were sitting socially at home that Sunday evening talking about the problems of our time—and if
someone said impulsively, "Let's pray about this"—there
would be a most uncomfortable silence.
The one who suggested prayer would be considered a little
queer—different.
We preach about having faith and vision—yet when somebody
shares a daring dream with us,
        presents us with an exciting and thrilling vision,
we think he is a bit peculiar.

We hold up certain ideals, and when in society a young man
or a young woman takes a stand for these ideals, even to the
point of making the rest of us uneasy, we think that he or she
is an oddball.

We say that we believe that God can lead people, and that
His guidance is available in everything . . .
Yet when certain people try to seek His guidance in planning
a vacation
    in picking a college
        or in selecting friends,
we conclude that they are queer.

There is another reason why Jesus said

    "Woe unto you when all men speak well of you."

As our fear about others' approval grows, our freedom shrinks.
We can see this at its most extreme in the totalitarian state.
The totalitarian state cannot exist unless it is composed of de-
individualized persons.
There the citizen gives up one of Christianity's most outstand-
ing characteristics: the freedom of choice.

It is literally true that only in God's will do we have the chance
to find ourselves, to be persons.
Therefore only in God's will do we have real freedom.
Today the world has a desperate need of people who are willing to be different.

In Bernard Shaw's play *St. Joan,* some soldiers are talking
about the "Maid of Orleans."
One of them says, "There is something about the girl . . . .
Her words and her ardent faith in God have put fire into me."
His captain replies. "Why, you are almost as mad as she is."
And the soldier stubbornly goes on, "Maybe that's what we
need nowadays—mad people.
See where the sane ones have landed us."

If it is sanity that has brought the world to its present state . . .
    if it is sanity that has produced the social order in which
    we live . . .

then I for one am willing to give madmen a chance.
I believe we need people who are different.

All those who have carried civilization forward have been
angry men—grousing in the public parks and the market
places, nailing denunciations up on public buildings.
They knew they were in a conflict, and they took the wrongs
in society—yes, and the wrongs in the church—
    terribly to heart.

We need such people who will carry their faith into the office
                         into Congress
                     into society
                 into the school
             into the home . . .
people who will be different even if it will cost them their
social popularity
    their economic fortunes,
        or their very lives.

But one does not get that kind of faith except by a personal
friendship with Jesus Christ.
Then He will tell you what to do.
    You will be sure of your ground.
        With His hand on your shoulder, you will have no fear
        of the opinion of other people.
Easy? Of course it is not easy.
I think too much of the youth today to offer you a sugar-
coated Christianity.
That would betray my Lord.
It would also not be worthy of your great potential.

If I can read the signs of the times at all, you are more than a
little satiated with softness,
    with having everything handed to you,
      so that you know the value of nothing.
You have contempt when the church contents itself with glad-
handing.

Deep in your hearts you look with longing toward the heights.
You know that there will be rugged terrain,
                    panting lungs,
                aching legs,
but also the cool, clean upper air and the exhilaration of gain-
ing the summit at last,
        of achieving vision and perspective.

God's marching orders always involve sacrifice and courage.
The drumbeat of the Different Drummer calls for bravery.
It is not for dancing.
It does not appeal to the blood—but to the heart of a person.
It calls for will and sacrifice.
It is a stirring drum, and they who hear it are always in a
minority.

Those who answer it may perchance hear the words of a new
Beatitude . . .

>   "Blessed are they who are thought queer, for they have
>   taken the gospel to heart."

•VI•

It was the summer of 1949. My nine-year-old son, Peter John, and I had been shopping on Princes Street in Edinburgh —not for Braemar sweaters or fine tartans—but for toy soldiers. As we looked over the colorful, carefully wrought figures —the Argyle and Sutherland Highlanders, the Beefeaters, the Black Watch, the Seaforth—I was as fascinated as my son. Of course something was missing from the moment; Big Peter should have been there with us. Such a walking compendium of knowledge about the British regiments he had been! And he had looked forward to this trip, but the final tap on the shoulder had come for him the January before.

Peter John poured out on the counter the money he had been saving. There was enough for three boxes of the soldiers. Proudly he walked out of the store with the package under his arm, and we boarded a trolley car. It was only after we had gotten off at our stop and were walking along the street that Peter John realized that he had left his package on the car. He stood disconsolate, staring in the direction the tram had disappeared. For a little boy, it was a great loss.

"Edinburgh is a large city," I told him. "We'll try to get the soldiers back, but you shouldn't count on it." Silently we walked on.

Minutes later we heard a Scottish voice hallooing us, "Mistress . . . Laddie. . . ." When the breathless man came in sight, we recognized the conductor of the tram car. He must have run several blocks.

"Laddie, we found a parcel. Is it no' yours?" And when he

*saw Peter John's face light up like a skyrocket, "Aye—I ken.
I have a laddie o' my ain_____"*

*And at that moment in memory I was hearing another
Scottish voice explain, "In the town in Scotland in which I
spent the first twenty-five years of my life ... if you lost something on the street or in a tramcar ... the chances were very
good that you would recover it_____"*

*This is Peter Marshall's voice—in the sermon you are about
to read. He would have loved the conductor of that tramcar,
as he loved all honest men.*

WALLS OF STRAW

IF God is not real to you,
> and you want desperately to make Him real ...

If you have never met Christ as a Living Person,
> and there is a deep longing in your heart to know Him
> that way ...

If you want to overcome certain problems in your life,
> but can't seem to achieve any victory ...

If you seek God's will for your future,
> but fail to find His guidance a reality ...

then this sermon is for you.

It may point to the difficulty,
> one of the causes of your failure and mine.

Sin does several things to us.
> It cuts us off from God.

> It shatters our fellowship, not because God leaves us
> but because we have left Him.

> It dulls our sense of what is right and what is
> wrong.

> It produces spiritual and moral blindness.

And it does these things just as effectively whether we are
dealing with what we call big sins or little ones.

In the town in Scotland in which I spent the first twenty-five
years of my life, there was a column each week in our weekly
newspaper listing articles found in trams,
on the street
in public places.

These articles had been turned in to the police station.
Always there was great variety:
    a purse containing money
      a key ring
        a rosary
      cooperative tokens
      eyeglasses
  all sorts of articles handed over by the finders.

If you lost something, the chances were good that you could
recover it by going to the police station.
It was generally expected that if you found something, you
would report your find. That was the philosophy in which I
was brought up.

Suppose you lost your billfold in an American city.
What chance is there that you would ever see it again?
If, in the washroom of a restaurant, you slipped off your rings
while washing your hands, and went off and left them behind,
is it likely that you would recover them?

Would you dare lay down your handbag on the counter of a
department store, if there were other shoppers standing beside
you?
Would you risk leaving your grocery bundles just inside the
store door while you went to get your car?
If you are as trusting as that, let me warn you against it,
for in our family we have lost groceries that way.

I have observed with sinking heart that old-fashioned honesty
is a disappearing virtue.

The prevailing attitude seems to be "Finders keepers" so that if you lose something, you are simply out of luck and can write it off.

This lack of fundamental honesty also comes out in cheating in school, which many of you young people admit is quite widespread.
Many of you who believe in God and are active in church still see little or no connection between religion and honesty.

I am told that athletes accept under-the-table payments
                          cheat in academic work
                     "crib" on examinations.
And then you shrug and comment that it is "done" . . . to be expected.
And even where an Honor System exists, many of you say that you would not report another student—no matter what pledge you have signed.
"None of my business" is your feeling.

Part of what is behind all the cheating in our schools is the conviction that in order to secure a good job, a college degree is necessary—by hook or crook.
It is the utilitarian view of education.

The cheater only cheats himself—out of the solid values of learning, the joy of new ideas, enlarging intellectual horizons,
      the privilege of dipping into the great minds of other times,
            the satisfaction of accumulating knowledge
            and wisdom.

Then there is lying—many forms of lying.
To be sure, as you young people look out on our world, everywhere you see older people setting you a miserable example.

It is a shocking thing to realize that witnesses, after being sworn in, will yet persist in telling lies.

There are the lies many people seem to feel justified
   in order to get a job or Social Security benefits . . .
                 lies about their age,
                 their experience,
                 how long they help the last job.
The temptation to be dishonest, however, seems particularly
strong when we are making out our income tax returns.
This is fast becoming a national disease.

No, you are not guilty of these particular lies, of course.
But before you begin to glow with self-righteousness, let me
ask if we—you and I—would be willing to look with God at
our own lives.

It is not easy to confront ourselves.
Most of us have had long practice in avoiding this at all costs.
We make excuses.
We say, "But what I did is nothing compared to what So-
and-So does all the time."
     We rationalize.
     We blame others.

We insist that we could not help certain situations, when we
did absolutely nothing to prevent these situations from arising.
We mutter something about being unlucky—
     getting all the bad breaks.
     Things are never our own fault.

One reason why so many of us are unhappy and worried is that
we are in a state of civil war.
We are at war with ourselves.
It is an age-old conflict.

As Paul puts it:

   "I cannot understand my own actions;
   I do not act as I want to act;

On the contrary, I do what I detest. . . .
I cannot be good as I want to be,
and I do wrong against my wishes. . . .
Miserable wretch that I am!
Who will rescue me from this body of death?"

Romans 7:15,24

I am preaching this sermon to myself, and to as many of you
as will join me in a confession that we are not honest with
ourselves and, what is worse, we are not honest with God.
God—whether we like it or not—is a moral righteous Being.
We can have His help with our life and affairs only on His
terms.
And His terms are square-dealing,
     absolute honesty.

Our wrong-dealings, small or great, eat into our faith like
acid . . .

"And whatsoever we ask, we receive of Him, because we
keep His commandments and do those things that are
pleasing in His sight."   *I John 3:22*

Ah, that's just our trouble.
So often we know perfectly well that we are not doing things
pleasing to a righteous God, and so we have no faith at all
that He will help us with schoolwork,
               or in our social life,
          or help us find His guidance for a job,
     or overcome habits which are defeating us.

Our trouble, you see, is not intellectual or theological.
It is moral.
The strange thing is that so often, when this is our problem,
we are still fascinated with Christ and His gospel.
We can't give ourselves to Him of course, but we can't quite
let Him go.

So we take comfort in long-winded intellectual discussions about religion.

I have watched this with young people at summer conferences. They adore lengthy bull sessions, about life in general, and religion in particular.
They want to discuss the so-called conflict between science and religion . . .
Comparative religions . . . "What right have we to claim that Christianity is superior to other religions?"
"What about those who have never heard of Christ? Are they lost?" . . .
They want to talk about war and peace and "the bomb"— and about weighty theological matters like predestination, when all the time the real issue is their own personal relationship to Jesus Christ.

I have watched the same thing with some of you who come to my office for personal conferences.
Very rarely is the real trouble what you say it is.
"I can't get along with my mother and father," said one sixteen-year-old girl.
"They're not fair to me."
What was really wrong was that beginning in the fifth grade she had been taking money out of her mother's purse, at first coins, and then bills in larger and larger amounts.
This had weighed on her mind until the guilt was even interrupting her sleep at nights.

"I can't join the church," a college student told me, "because intellectual honesty won't let me subscribe to all the creeds. I want to discuss this with you."
But when we got down to discussing it, the boy's real agony was that he had deliberately lied to a high school girl and led her down the primrose path.
He had had an affair with her by promising her marriage, then had abandoned her to try the same ruthless technique with another girl.

So, you see, the issue in Christianity, in spite of what some people say, is not usually an intellectual one . . .
It lies much deeper than that.
It is moral.

Human nature does not change much from age to age.
Jesus Christ understands human nature—all its foibles and dodges.
He knows our difficulty.
See how He dealt with this problem in a woman of the first century . . .

Jesus was on His way from Judea to Galilee.
He chose the shortest route over the Great North Road,
    a route which took Him through Samaria.

Having walked all morning—a long tiring trip over the Judean hills—Jesus and His disciples were hot and weary.
A place to sit down in the shade, and a drink of cool water would be most welcome, they thought.

In a fork of the road, they came upon just such a place. It was a well—Jacob's Well, tradition has it—
    shaded by a spreading tree.

The disciples went on into the nearest village, Sychar, to buy bread, leaving Christ alone, seated on the coping of the well—alone with His thoughts.

Around Him was country more beautiful than His native Judea.
In the valley were clumps of walnut and olive trees.
The ground was carpeted with red anemones.

In the background, seen through a distant blue haze, were the stony sides of Mount Gerizim with its columned temple on top.

Overhead, the sky was a burnished copper, with the mud houses of the nearby village baking in the shimmering sunlight.

Nobody stirred at that hour, if he could help it.
The village streets were usually deserted.
But Jesus heard footsteps; someone was approaching.
Soon He saw a woman—her waterpot carefully balanced on her head—coming down the road.
It was unusual for anyone to come for water in the middle of the day.
Most women drew water in the morning . .
    or in the cool of the evening.
Could it be that this woman wanted to avoid her neighbors?

At first the woman did not notice Christ sitting on the well-coping in the deep purple shadow.
With a start, she saw Him as she drew nearer,
                hesitated . . .
                  and then came on.
His eyes seemed to burn into her troubled heart and she was strangely uneasy.

"I wonder," He said, "if you would give me a drink?"
That, too, was unusual.
He was a Jew, she a Samaritan.
He was a man, she a woman.
It was all most strange and unconventional.

She expressed her surprise: "You a Jew, ask a drink of me, a Samaritan woman?"
In order to understand the woman's surprise, we have to remember that there had been bitter and violent enmity between the Jews and the Samaritans for some seven hundred years.

Through the years, discontented Jews,
    would-be revolutionaries,

always found sanctuary in Samaria.
The worst insult that Jesus' enemies could hurl at Him was:
"Thou art a Samaritan and hast a devil!"
And when Jesus wanted to illustrate real compassion, which
could overcome the racial and national prejudices of His time,
He told the story of the Good Samaritan.

Also, to understand the woman's surprise, you need to understand that the etiquette of Christ's day would not permit the
orthodox Jew to speak to a woman in a public place, even if
she were his own wife or a relative.

No wonder the woman at the well was surprised when Jesus
spoke to her so openly in such a friendly fashion.
"You a Jew, ask for a drink from me, a Samaritan woman?"

And Jesus answered, "If you only knew about a free gift God
longs to give you, and who it is asking you for a drink, you
would have asked Me instead. Then I would give you living
water."

"What a strange man!" the woman thought.
Before that look in His eyes, she suddenly felt ashamed.
Lowering her gaze, the woman tried to brush aside her em-
barrassment by sarcasm:

> "The well is deep. You haven't a thing to draw water
> with. How on earth could you give me water? Have you
> some magic power? Are you greater than our father
> Jacob who dug this well?"

Now, His own thirst forgotten, Christ probed for the woman's
real problem.
Individuals were, and still are, important to Jesus Christ.
Some of His greatest sermons were preached to audiences of
one.

> "I've heard about how wonderful this water from Jacob's

Well is," said Christ. "I hear that it is 'light' water, noted for its purity and flavor. But I know even more wonderful water. Whoever drinks of this water will be thirsty again.
Whoever drinks of the water which I can give will never thirst again . . ."   *John 4:13–14*

Then the woman indulged in what we would call a wisecrack: "Carrying water to and from the well is no fun. I'd like to have this water of yours so that I would never have to come to the well again."
But it was no use.
Though she evaded looking into the burning eyes, she could not throw off that penetrating glance.
She blushed suddenly when Jesus said:

"Go call thy husband and bring him back with you."

Her voice was almost inaudible as she said:

"I have no husband."

Jesus said: "That's right, you have no husband.
You have had five husbands, and the man you are living with now is not your husband."

It was evident that the shaft had gone home.
To cover her confusion, she tried to change the subject again:

"Sir, I perceive you are a prophet.
But I don't want to be selfish. Let's not talk about me.
Now what about this old argument as to where we should worship?
We Samaritans, you know, hold out for this mountain . . . and you Jews insist it is Jerusalem."

Jesus quietly but firmly answered her question with a few wise words on the nature of worship . . .

"God is spirit. The place we seek to worship Him does
not matter. Real worship is to worship the Father in
Spirit and reality—a communion of spirit with Spirit."

Then having gently answered her question, Christ dismissed
it, and inevitably—like the wheels of judgment—came back to
the first point—the real point, the wrong in her personal life
which was cutting her off from a relationship with God.
Three times the woman had tried to build walls of words,
walls of straw.
Three times Christ had knocked them down.
Now no further evasion was possible.

For a long silent moment, the woman looked into Christ's
eyes.
"I don't understand how you could know about my husbands,"
she said. "I would think that only the Messiah could know
such a thing."

Then Jesus gave to this nameless woman the most thunderous,
the most revealing words
ever caught by human ears.
Probably it was His first clear revelation of His Messiahship.
He said simply,

"I that speak unto thee am He!"   *John 4:26*

At that crucial moment, the disciples arrived back at the well.
They were surprised to find their Master talking to a woman,
especially a woman with a most unsavory reputation in the
village.
But they made no comments—asked no questions.

The woman, forgetting all about her waterpot on the coping
of the well, rushed off toward the village.
Suddenly she was seeing all of life in different colors . . .
in fact, it had had no color for years.

The sun on her face was a golden shower.
The brown earth beneath her feet was warm and laughing.
The beat of a blackbird's wings had a rhythm caught up by
the tossing trees.

She wanted to sing or to shout.
What did she care now for gossip or what people might say!

Bursting into the home of her neighbor, she spilled out her
news in a wild torrent of words.
Bubbling excitedly,
     her eyes shining
          her cheeks flushed,
her whole countenance radiated a new light,
she roused the villagers from their noontime siesta.
Some of them stood in the doorways of their houses, shading
their eyes and looking in the direction of the well.
Others, more curious, hurried after the woman to the well to
see for themselves.

And Jesus, seeing them coming down the road in their white
robes, said to His disciples,

> "Look at them. The fields around here are already whiten-
> ing for the harvest. You and I are going to do some
> harvesting now for eternal life in this village."

I wish we had some description, some word picture, of that
nameless woman whose need gave us this story.
But, even without a description, I am sure we can see her in
our minds.
We know that there must have been a look of peace on her
face, such as most of us do not have.
There must have been a serenity, a joy, that we only glimpse
once in a while, because—just like the woman—we spend our
time and our energies building walls of straw.

We go down the road of evasion.

We travel the road of rationalization,
            of excuse and alibi,
                even of lies and deceit.
We try to fool ourselves, and we think sometimes we succeed
in fooling our enemies—even our friends—but we cannot fool
Him, for He will seek us out.

He wants—not to take away our fun in life—but to end our
inner conflicts, to give us that peace of mind in which alone
we can find real joy.

You have no desire to be plastered with a coat of whitewash or
portrayed as a saint or an angel.
You have no desire to be fitted for a halo, and you have a
horror of growing wings.

Sometimes the word *good* is given unfortunate connota-
tions . . .
"Percy is such a good boy," I have heard indulgent parents
say. "He doesn't drink. He doesn't stay out late at night.
He doesn't go out with girls. He doesn't gamble."

Always I have an insane desire to say, "But Madame, just
what *does* Percy do?"

A healthy young person despises the thought of being "goody-
goody."
I dislike it too—in that sense.
But it is a noble, a splendid thing to be *good*, sincere, clean,
and decent . . .
That is an achievement worth striving for.

There are young people who look upon Christianity as a sort
of harness which confines and restricts,
        as a garment that pinches or a hair shirt . . .
something that cramps their style and imposes severe limitations on their enjoyment of life.

To them enlistment in the ranks of the church means surrender of liberty and adherence to a long list of prohibitions
and negatives.
The Christianity I know is not negative,
                but joyously positive.
What some people do not understand is that those young
people who have truly met Jesus Christ have embarked on a
wonderful adventure . . .
      They have found the reality of His Presence . . .
        They have accepted His advice for their lives,
          His guidance for their choices,
          His solving of their problems.

And they have found all these wonderful gifts because they
were willing to pay a price.
They have honestly called the roll of their sins . . .
                their laziness,
              their cheating,
            their bad temper,
           their tawdry use of sex,
            their selfishness,
          their vanity and greed,
and found—not only that they are forgiven—
but that they could conquer their previous habits,
lose former desires, and become, as it were, new creatures
altogether.

But there are others of you who shy away from religion and
make a detour around spiritual realities because you are
afraid it might "get" you . . .
      afraid you might feel urges which
would transform your lives.
Afraid you might have to give up some things you enjoy too
much, afraid of the adjustments which might have to be made.

Well, you are right.

True, joining the church is nailing one's colors to the mast.
But suppose you have nailed *your* colors to the wrong mast?
Or what is infinitely worse—suppose you have no colors to nail
to any mast at all?
Then for you the world is a flat featureless plane, a dull gray.
Is that your idea of a joyous life?

There is a price to be paid for spiritual reality.
It does not float down upon you, like tickertape from the
window of a skyscraper when you march in a parade.

Too long has the price of spiritual achievement been cheap-
ened.
I would not deceive you . . .
If you want God to be real to you, you have to meet His terms.
And those terms are not for cowards who want cushioned
lives.

Jesus Christ walks in no moral or spiritual twilight.
In the high noon of His love there are no neutral tints.

I need to be reminded, and you need to be reminded, that
with Christ looking over our shoulders, what we do,
> how we act in the classroom,
> what we do on dates,
> how we treat our parents and friends,
> what we say and think,
are either right—or wrong.

Before you complain again that God is not real to you, I suggest that you test your life honestly and courageously by
Christ's standards,
> and then *act* on what you find.

The result will surprise you as much as it did that nameless
woman at the well of Sychar long ago.
Try it—and come out from behind your wall of straw.

•VII•

*Late one autumn afternoon two young theological students,
David Simpson and Peter Marshall, were driving back to
Columbia Seminary in David's old Model A Ford. They had
spent the day with friends in Marietta, Georgia. There had
been a long afternoon of tennis and a rollicking evening playing games.*

*"My Ford had terrible springs, and stretches of the road
were bumpy," David was to reminisce years later. "Peter was
in a talkative mood. He got started on his idea of what real
preaching should be. Vigorously he discarded merely being
a conscientious student of other men's work; writing sermons
by putting their thoughts and quotations together like a patch-
work quilt.*

*" 'That's not good enough,' I remember he said, 'no matter
how fine the stitches or how careful the workmanship.'*

*"He talked about what he called 'pictorial preaching.' As
Peter warmed to his subject, his Scottish brogue got thicker
and thicker. . . .*

*" 'Look, David—isn't the problem of the poet, the play-
wright, the artist, the prophet, and the preacher really the
same—to make people see? What we have to do is to take
a passage of Scripture and so carefully and accurately recon-
struct the context of it that the scene comes to life. We see
it first ourselves. Then we take our listeners to the spot in
imagination. We make them see and hear what happened so
vividly that the passage will live forever in their minds and
hearts. It's like a newsreel from the Scriptures . . . a film from
the world's big drama.' "* [3]

99

For Peter Marshall that concept of preaching hammered out so early never changed; time merely perfected it. "Dawn Came Too late" is a classic example of one of his "newsreels from the Scriptures."

DAWN CAME TOO LATE

Hᴀᴠᴇ you ever come right up to the point of making a decision and then backed away—to your regret later on?
Perhaps it was the chance to land a new job,
>   to go on a trip,
>   to propose marriage,
>   to take a strong stand.

The moment confronted you, made your heart beat faster.
You paused . . . but did not act . . . and then it was too late.
>   Circumstances changed.
The opportunity never came again in quite the same way.

I have seen this happen when a man comes under Jesus' spell.
Suddenly he sees his life through Christ's eyes.
He know that his life is off-center, purposeless.
>   He feels trapped in wrongdoing.
>   He lacks zest.
>   He has clutched at happiness but it has eluded him.
Then he is offered the adventure of commitment to Christ.
Something stirs in him, like a bugle call to action.
He clears his throat, almost speaks, starts to move.
Then a counterforce steps in . . . "Don't be hasty," it says.
>   "Let's not do anything foolish . . ."
>   "Watch out for embarrassment . . ."
>   "There's plenty of time to think it over."

But that particular moment slips by and is gone forever.
He was on the brink of a move that would have changed every-

thing.
He was nearly Christ's—so close to greatness.

But nearly is not enough.

It has happened so from the dawn of time.
The story of Nicodemus is the story of such a man . . .

He might have been a disciple—but was not.
Nicodemus was a member of the Sanhedrin—the highest Jewish court.
The label John gave Nicodemus has stuck . . .
   "Nicodemus, which at the first came to Jesus by night."
Why did Nicodemus wait until it was dark?
Was he, perchance, afraid?

Suppose Nicodemus came while it was night simply because
he could wait no longer . . .
Suppose he had come—without wasting a minute—
   immediately after he had seen Christ for the first time?

Nicodemus knew the spot well.
He had sometimes sought refreshment of the spirit there himself when he could no longer stand either the heat of Jerusalem
               or its seething intrigue.

The tall man drew his beautiful outer cloak of striped linen
more closely about his shoulders.
It was frosty at night on the Judean hills.
He paused on the brow of Olivet to look out across the moonlit valley.
The Temple, which Herod was still rebuilding for the Jews,
towered over the valley of Jehoshophet and Hinnom,
   gleaming like snow in the moonlight.
Nicodemus sighed involuntarily as he looked down at the city.
Asleep, Jerusalem looked peaceful enough.
   But awake? It was a dirty city . . .
               a desperate city . . .

The dignified aristocrat knew only too well the machinations
at its heart.
The Nazarene—whether He knew it or not—was in real danger
of His life.

Stepping out of the shadaws, Nicodemus found Christ exactly
where Joseph had said he would.
Strangely, the Master seemed not at all surprised to see him.
In fact, it was almost as if He were expecting Nicodemus.

They talked for hours—those two—totally unaware of the passing of time.
There was a meeting of minds such as Nicodemus had never
known even in his youth, with his greatest teachers from Jerusalem, Corinth, or Alexandria.
In the Lord of Life, this master of Israel discovered fathomless
depths of mind and heart.

Nicodemus knew men.
"Here is no cheap fanatic," he thought.
"Here are clear eyes and a quiet voice."
      "Here is Manhood at its highest."
The talk was of spiritual regeneration—being born again, but
this time, not a natural but a supernatural birth.
A change in the inner man, without which no man can get
into the Kingdom of God.

At this point, Nicodemus asked what any one of us might have
asked,
      "How can a man be born when he is old?"   *John 3:4*

You and I have voiced the same doubts in different ways.
Suppose Jesus asks us to give up something we want to keep—
We want to have our fun first.
"Besides, there's plenty of time."
But is there?
How do we know that there is plenty of time?

Or we have answered in another way . . .
"I am what I am—nobody special.
Even though I'm still young, I have deeply ingrained habits,
                                not all of them good.
It just doesn't seem reasonable that I should begin all over
again and be somebody else . . .
Besides, who wants to be good?
I'm just not built that way."

And Jesus has answered, "Of course you're not built that way.
I'm not talking about a little repair work here and there,
                                a little increase in kindness . . .
                        a bit more generosity.
Something much more drastic is required."

"Ye must be born again"—not by education,
                                or culture,
                        or legislation,
                                but by regeneration.

But Nicodemus was the voice of man's skeptical question-
ing . . . "How can a man be born again?"

And Jesus answered quietly. Yes, there is a mystery here, Nicodemus, that you are not quite ready to understand.
    "The wind bloweth where it listeth, and thou hearest the
    sound thereof, but canst not tell whence it cometh and
    whither it goeth: so is everyone that is born of the Spirit."
                                        John 3:8

There are many things going on around us which we do not
understand and cannot explain . . .
                        but they are nonetheless true and valid.

There are some things in the Christian life about which it is
useless to argue, for they can never be proved by logic.
I do not fully understand regeneration.

But I have seen it take place.

I have seen men and women changed from above . . . completely . . .
Men reclaimed from habitual drunkenness to sobriety . . .
Criminals changed into respectable citizens . . .
I have seen men changed from egocentrics to outgoing men,
from grasping, greedy materialists into spiritually minded
men, suddenly aware of the winds of the Spirit.
And then Nicodemus asked, "How can these things be?"
Perhaps he meant, "Oh yes, I see.
                              All right, I believe you.
I believe that it is possible for a man to start all over.
But how? Tell me how?
How does a man begin? What does one do first?"

And then Jesus answered and said unto him—probably with
a twinkle in His eyes—
"Art thou a master of Israel, and knowest not these things?"
You, a leader of the people and don't know?
You, a teacher and interpreter of the Sacred Law and you
don't know how?

"It isn't something we can do for ourselves, Nicodemus.
Only God can work this miracle.
      He has to do it for us.
All that is required of us is our willingness to have Him make
us over.
He requires only our permission.
Our Father never violates a man's freedom of choice.
He wants for His sons only those who long to be.

"You see, Nicodemus, it is the old self-centered ego in us,
                              vain,
                        critical of other people,
                              wanting its own way . . .
                        that is what has to go.
Its painful character-surgery, painful—but necessary.

We can give God permission to slay that self-centered person in us, and He will.
Then the Spirit of God will come to live in us,

> giving us a new nature,
> a new set of desires,
> a new way of looking at things,
> even a new will.
> That is being born again."

Perhaps there was sadness in Christ's eyes as He made the strange statement that somehow, in order to achieve this re-birth, He—this Jesus—must be lifted up from the earth.

It was beyond Nicodemus, too mysterious, this talk of the blowing wind,
> blowing from the Unknown into the Undiscoverable . . .
These beautiful words, like the music of the spheres,
falling upon his ears:

"For God so loved the world, that He gave His only-be-gotten Son, that whosoever believeth in Him should not perish, but have everlasting life."   *John 3:16*

Christ must have felt an affinity
> a great affection for this man Nicodemus.
For it was your visit, Nicodemus, which gave us that precious revelation; your talk drew it forth.

You came out of your night—and a shaft of light pierced it.
You came out of your night, and now the dawn is breaking.

The two men fell silent, bound together by thoughts lying beyond the ability of words to express.
They stood . . . looking down across twenty miles of hilltops, watching the sun come up behind the blue hills of Moab, the misty hills.
And in the distance, cocks begin to crow.

"I must be going," said Nicodemus suddenly.

He looked into Christ's eyes and gripped His hand.

With long strides, the tall man retraced his steps down the rocky, winding path with the parting words of Jesus still ringing in his ears—words like an echo out of eternity:

> "Light has entered the world, Nicodemus, but anyone whose life is evil will avoid it; but one whose life is true will come to it, fearing it not . . . Men have preferred darkness to light. It is their choice. You and I know, Nicodemus, that their decision is already made . . ."

So the Master knew . . .

He knew . . .

Time passed.

It was now late in September—the time of the Feast of Tabernacles.

Many things had happened since that night when Nicodemus had first come to the Galilean.

Many people had been healed . . .

many miracles wrought . . .

many words spoken . . .

many prayers uttered . . .

many plots hatched, many schemes perfected.

The Pharisees were increasingly troubled by the following Jesus had attracted because of His miracles.

Many of the common folk were actually beginning to believe that He was, indeed, the Messiah—even as He had said.

That would not do!

On the last day of the Feast, the seventy-one members of the Sanhedrin solemnly assembled in the great Hall of Hewn Stone in the Temple.

Caiaphas had called them into session.

The question was: "What shall we do with Jesus?"

The discussion arose and fell like waves around the semicircle of distinguished men.

Caiaphas seemed impatient of discussion.

It was apparent that he wanted Christ put to death.

But some said, "Not yet. On what basis could you condemn Him now?"

Others sided with Caiaphas.

Anger—a quiet cold anger—welled up in Nicodemus.

He was hearing once again the faint sigh of wind through cypress trees,

    feeling a hand on his shoulder . . .

        seeing the pink dawn beyond a distant hillside . . .

hearing a quiet voice saying, "But he that doeth truth cometh to the light."   *John 3:21*

Suddenly Nicodemus felt that his own future was not important.

Did it matter what his compatriots thought of him?

Nothing mattered except honesty,

               fairness,

             justice,

          truth.

And Nicodemus rose from his stone chair and pulled himself to his full height.

A voice, calm, clear, used to controlling other men, rang out through the marble hall:

"Surely our Law does not condemn the accused before listening to his defense, calling reputable witnesses, and ascertaining the full truth . . ."

Caiaphas rose in his place—mockery in his eyes,

              a sneer on his lips:

"Are you a Galilean too? Nothing good comes out of Galilee. I'm surprised at you, sir. Is this some kind of September madness of yours?"

Nicodemus did not reveal to the Sanhedrin that he was willing
to stand with Christ whatever happened.
He did not announce that he was willing to follow Him and
trust Him all the rest of the way.
No—he did not do that. But he had spoken!
He had sought to defend Him on a point of Jewish law!
He had taken one step toward the light!

There was a strange peace in the heart of Nicodemus.
Already he felt those eyes, warm and appreciative, smiling
upon him.

Only once more do we see Nicodemus.
It is near the end of the narrative, some five months later.
The scheming Caiaphas has had his way: Judas had played
into his hands.

The Master had mounted His last pulpit . . .
    preached His last sermon.
The beggars waiting by the gates of Jerusalem would still need
their crutches and sticks, for He who might have freed them
from dependence on those extra legs was Himself dead.

After hatred had finished its work, "Joseph of Arimathaea,
being a disciple of Jesus, but secretly for fear of the Jews,
besought Pilate that he might take away the body of Jesus:
and Pilate gave him leave . . ."   *John 19:38*

He had prepared a rock-hewn tomb that the Master might be
interred with love and tenderness and that deep inarticulate
sorrow which had stunned the little band of believers.

Joseph came therefore, "and took the body of Jesus. And there
came also Nicodemus, which at the first came to Jesus by
night, and brought a mixture of myrrh and aloes, about an
hundred pound weight. Then took they the body of Jesus, and
wound it in linen clothes with the spices . . ." *John 19:38–40*

"And there came also Nicodemus . . ."
There is a sob in John's words.

Nicodemus, who first came by night, now comes in daylight.
But it is too late.
He can do nothing for the Master now except lavish the spices
on His body, and wish that he might have saved Him.

The Master had said that it was hard for a rich man to get
into the Kingdom.
   So Nicodemus found it . . .
      He had much to lose by taking a definite stand.
But he should have had the courage; now he knew it.

There in the Sanhedrin he should have said, "Yes, I am one of
His disciples. I believe that what He says is true.
I had a long talk with Him. I have never met a saner Man,
                    a kinder Man,
                 a wiser Man,
          Go ahead, excommunicate me too.
      I intend to stand with the Galilean to the end."

Instead he had taken but one timid step toward the light, and
that had not been enough to stem the dark tide.

Nicodemus might have stood with John, there at the foot of
the Cross, when the others crouched at the fringe of the
crowd, ready to run at the first sign of danger.

When the others forsook Him and fled, Nicodemus might
have been there . . . stood by Him, for the sake of that night
when they had together watched the dawn come up over the
hills of Moab.

Now it was too late.
   The Master was dead . . .
      "And there came also Nicodemus . . ."
         His tears lay on the white linen like diamonds.

Many of you—like Nicodemus—have come close to Jesus.
Perhaps you too have felt the nudge . . .
    the uneasy feeling in your own conscience . . .
        the tugging at the heart . . .
            the resolves that spring up every now and then . . .
                the longing to do something special . . .
                            to *be* someone . . .
Could not that be Christ calling you?

And you have waited . . .
    You wanted to respond . . .
        but you waited.

Remember that He will not force Himself upon you.
He will not assault you, or intrude where He is not wanted.
Christ will let you go through the years, using no restraint or
compulsion beyond the appeal that He is constantly making—
    to your better nature,
        to your loyalty,
            your gratitude,
                your recognition of the imperishables,
the hunger of your own young heart.

There are some terrible scenes in the Gospel narrations:
Jesus standing and letting the rich young ruler walk away from
Him.
And if the Gadarenes prefer their swine to His company,
He does not argue the point . . .
He enters the boat again . . .
    The wind fills the sails,
        slowly the vessel draws out.
            He goes as silently as He came.

If the inhospitable Samaritans do not want Him, He punishes
them in a far more terrible way than the disciples suggested:
They were for calling down fire from heaven on them.
Jesus does something more awful . . .
    He simply passes on and leaves them.

An hour may come when you will never again hear Christ's knock on your heart's door . . .

Eveything that happens to you from now on—in this life and throughout eternity—hinges on whether or not you stretch out your hand to open the door to Him.

The latch is on the inside.

Just one more step, Nicodemus.
Just one more step to take.
The dawn is coming.

It must not come . . . too late!

•VIII•

There was a boy who grew up in a town called "the Iron Burgh" because it is the center of the Scottish iron trade—Coatbridge, eight miles east of Glasgow. The child's environment was that of fire, smoke and soot . . . the roar and rattle of massive machinery . . . the flames of the furnaces on the night skies. A network of railways fanned out from the town to transport the finished boilers, firebricks, railroad wagons, the malleable iron.

As the boy grew, he wandered farther afield. He saw Clydeside where so many ocean giants ae built, with the tall cranes and the davits poking into the sky. He stood on the bank of the narrow, man-made canal listening to the sound of hammers and riveters, the yelping of the tugs. And his imagination soared. From there he could go to any spot in the world . . . the South Seas . . . China . . . Africa . . . India . . . Why not?

Often he bicycled to Blantyre where the missionary-explorer David Livingstone had been born. He would wander into the tiny stone cottage where David had lived. The beds were bunks in the walls with curtains pulled across them to shut out some of the bitter cold. David had gone to work in a cotton mill at ten, but he had taken his Latin book with him —and his dreams. The dreams must have reached far beyond Blantyre, the wee cottages and the mill. For he took one of the boats from Clydeside one day. He explored the heart of the Dark Continent, found the Zambesi River and Victoria Falls. He dealt a staggering blow to the African slave trade. His tired heart was buried in an African jungle, the rest of his body in Westminster Abbey.

112

*As the boy pondered all this, he knew that what had hap-
pened to David Livingstone and to many of his fellow countrymen—adventurers, conquerors of new frontiers, colonizers—
had not been happenstance. Something (was it God?) planted
the dream of destiny in a man's heart, and he went out in faith
to meet that dream. Then it was important that the vision
be worthy. There was a risk in reach. . . . Certainly there had
been plenty of risk for Livingstone, but ah, the adventure . . .
the deep inner satisfactions of contributing something to the
world! Then anything was possible with a dream big enough
and God's will behind the dream.*

*The boy who roamed and pondered was Peter Marshall.
He was to reach and to risk far beyond the horizons of his
native land. Yet always he would carry in his heart an undying
love for Scotland: for the Doric and the "braid Scots" tongue;
for Celtic love songs and poetry; for the sturdy independence
of the sons of the heath; for the mists, the windswept moors
with heather slanting, the low stone cottages; for "his ain
folk."*

THE RISK OF REACH

IT was an afternoon in the early summer; there was a strange
quiet on the battlefield.
In the bright sunshine, the air was balmy and had a breath of
garden in it.

By some grotesque miracle, a bird was singing somewhere
near at hand.
On the firing step, with his rifle lying in a groove in the para-
pet, stood a private soldier in field-gray, his uniform stained
with mud and blood.

On his face, so young yet strangely marked with the lines of war that made him look old, was a wistful faraway expression.

He was enjoying the sunshine and the quiet of this strange lull in the firing.
The heavy guns had been silent—there was no sound to break the eerie stillness.

Sudenly a butterfly fluttered into view and alighted on the ground almost at the end of his rifle.
It was a strange visitor to a battleground—so out of place—so out of keeping with the grim setting
    rifles and bayonets
   barbed wire and parapets
  shell holes and twisted bodies.

But there it was—a gorgeous creature, the wings like gold leaf splashed with carmine,
swaying in the warm breath of spring.

As the war-weary youngster watched the butterfly, he was no longer a private in field-gray.
He was a boy once more, fresh and clean, swinging through a field in sunny Saxony, knee-deep in clover
        buttercups
       and daisies.
That strange visitor to the front-line trench recalled to him the joys of his boyhood, when he had collected butterflies.
It spoke to him of days of peace.
It was a symbol of the lovelier things of life.
It was the emblem of the eternal, a reminder that there was still beauty and peace in the world—that somewhere there was color and fragility
    and perfume
   and flowers
  and gardens.

He forgot the enemy a few hundred yards across no man's land.
He forgot the danger and privation and suffering.
He forgot everything as he watched that butterfly.

With all the hunger in his heart,
with the resurrection of dreams and visions that he thought were gone, he reached out his hand toward that butterfly.

His fingers moved slowly, cautiously, lest he frighten away this visitor to the battlefield.
In showing one kind of caution, he forgot another.
The butterfly was just beyond his reach—so he stretched, forgetting that watchful eyes were waiting for a target.

He brought himself out slowly—with infinite care and patience —until now he had just a little distance to go.
He could almost touch the wings that were so lovely.

And then ... ping ... *ing* ... *ing* ... *ing* ...
A sniper's bullet found its mark.
The stretching fingers relaxed ...
   the hand dropped flat on the ground ...
For the private soldier in field-gray, the war was over.

An official bulletin issued that afternoon said that
   "All was quiet on the Western Front ..."
And for a boy in field-gray it was a quiet that no guns would ever break.[4]
There is always a risk—when you reach for the beautiful.
When you reach for the lovelier
                  finer
                     more fragrant things of life—
there is always a risk—and you can't escape it.

The risk is what makes the Christian life exciting.
   It is thrilling—make no mistake about it.
      It is an adventure.

As long as we live in this world, there will always be a risk in reach.

But there are many in our time who are abnormally afraid of that risk of reach.
They are afflicted with a modern disease.
The psychiatrists have ponderous names for the sundry phobias that afflict us poor humans . . .
and the names are as terrible as the disease.

Agoraphobia is the fear of open spaces . . .
while claustrophobia is the fear of being shut in . . .
and acrophobia is the fear of heights.
There are many people who are afraid to climb . . . and they will not leave the ground . . .
    to get out on the roof of a building
        or up in a tower
            or on a mountain.
To be up on any elevation and look down makes them dizzy,
    affects their sense of balance,
        strikes terror into their hearts.
They are afraid of that which is high.
They have acrophobia.

But acrophobia is not only the fear of high monuments
                                mountains
                            and flights in airplanes.
                    It may also be the fear of high ideals
                                high thoughts
                                    high ambitions.

There are timid souls who avoid high places because they are afraid . . .
But then there are others who avoid high ideals because they are content with low ones.
There are persons who do not have high ambitions because they are lazy.

Altogether there are a great many people afflicted with acrophobia.
Are you?

Not enough of you today are hitching your wagons to stars.
You think it enough to couple a trailer to your car.

Jesus remarked upon those who sought the small and shallow things of life,

"Verily, I say unto you, They have their reward."
Matthew 6:2

That is, they got what they went after, and that is all they will ever get.
That is what they deserve.
They take a tin thimble to the ocean and scoop up a few drops, for that is all they can get into a thimble.
It isn't the fault of the ocean they did not get more . . . that they did not plunge in and swim in the ocean's immensity.

The tragedy of this age is that people with minds to think and souls that are hungry are so afraid to reach up and seek the things that are high.
What a tragedy that personalities in this glorious twentieth century are afflicted with acrophobia.

The night sky does something to the star-gazer.
One does not remain the same after seeing a sunset,
    or gazing into the heart of a flower,
        or watching the tiny fledglings in a nest.

There is a silent uplifting importation from the Absolute.
It does us good to look up and see Orion driving his hunting dogs across the Zenith . . .
Or Andromeda shaking out her tresses over limitless space.

It enlarges the self to have studied great architecture . . .
   to know great art—the reds of Titian
        the sunsets of Turner
        the seas of Winslow Homer . . .
to have felt the spell of epic deeds . . .
to have swung to the rhythmic pulse of Homer . . .
to have trembled with the passion of Romeo
   or the tenderness of Francis of Assisi.

To have wrestled with Kant's categorical imperatives,
   the whirring of angels' wings in Milton's *Paradise Lost,*
to have been swept away on the surge of music in Beethoven.
To have engraved upon the heart the prologue to John's Gospel,
to march with the majestic affirmations of the Nicean Creed.

It does something inside a man.
It stretches him mentally,
   stirs him morally,
      inspires him spiritually.
He is a bigger man—sweeter, nobler, higher,
                 richer than he was before.

The uplift of adoration brings the humble but blessed beholder to the threshold of a worship which miraculously transforms him just by beholding.

Out of the horrors of the second world war came an expression of such worship—a poem written by a nineteen-year-old flyer who met his death serving with the Royal Canadian Air Force. His father was an Episcopal rector whom I knew in Washington.

Pilot-Officer John Gillespie Magee, Jr., called his poem "High Flight . . ." [5]

"Oh, I have slipped the surly bonds of earth,
And danced the skies on laughter-silvered wings.

Sunward I've climbed, and joined the tumbling mirth
Of sun-split clouds—and done a hundred things
You have not dreamed of—wheeled and soared and swung
High on the sunlit silence. Hov'ring there,
I've chased the shouting wind along, and flung
My eager craft through footless halls of air.

"Up, up the long, delirious, burning blue,
I've topped the windswept heights with easy grace
Where never lark, or even eagle flew—
And, while with silent, lifting mind I've trod
The high untrespassed sanctity of space,
Put out my hand and touched the face of God."

The Christian is to seek the things above—to seek them
   as the needle seeks the pole . . .
   as the sunflower seeks the sun . . .
   as the river seeks the sea . . .
   as the eagle seeks the ceiling of the world.

Thas was why Paul pleaded with the first-century Christians
to set their affections on thing above . . .
                  high things,
                lofty concepts
and "not on the things of the earth."

But it is so difficult for us to transfer our affections, for we
have fallen in love with toyland
                  and our playthings have become so dear.

It is so difficult for us to believe the truth: that this life is but
a preparation for a greater and more glorious one to
come . . . and that if we would only believe,
   if we only had enough faith and the right kind and were
   seeking the "things above . . ."
all our real needs—earth's trinkets for which we strive so
desperately—would be provided for us.

Once and for all, we must put out of our minds that the purpose of life here is to enjoy ourselves
> to have a good time
> to be happy
> to make money

and to live in ease and comfort.
That is not what life is all about.
You were put here for a purpose, and that purpose is not related to superficial pleasures.
No one owes you a living—not your parents, not your government, not life itself.
You do not have a right to happiness.

You have a right to nothing.
I believe that God wants us to be happy—but it is not a
> matter of *our right,* but of His *love and mercy.*

The time for drifting
> or sleeping
> or wishful thinking

or day-dreaming is over.
The state of our world today makes that a very dangerous pastime.

This generation of young people and all of you who are sensitive to what is going on around you, are called to a supreme adventure.
There is a great stirring in society.
The upheavals of life and the revolutions of multitudes across the world in desperate motion are indications that our world can never be the same again.

So do not ever underestimate what you can do. You have the courage to cast off your acrophobia
> and to dream big
> and to aim high—

if you do it with God's help.

Two years before I left Scotland, I had a small part in a re-
markable demonstration of what youthful vision combined
with Christian faith can accomplish.
Bert Patterson was a medical student in Glasgow University,
very much in love with Nessie Knight.
They had been friends through high school.
They were wholesome young people, interested in life
and eager to invest their personalities to some noble end.
Both belonged to a group of about twenty of us who went
around together.
We played football and cricket.
The girls had a hockey team.
We went to picnics together . . . took hikes . . .
Normal young people—fond of life
                     full of fun
with some of the virtues and most of the faults of young peo-
ple anywhere.

At last Bert graduated . . .
    secured his medical degree and volunteered to go to Africa
    as a medical missionary.
Before he left, he and Nessie were married.
Leaving his wife at home, he then went out to establish the
Scotch Presbyterian Medical Mission at Sulenkama, Africa.

Bert knew there was nothing in Africa for him but a grass hut
and a tremendous need.
He determined to build a hospital
                  a dispensary
              and a compound
before he could ask Nessie to come out to help him in his
work.

To those of us who were left behind there came the challenge
to do what we could to build that hospital and dispensary for
them in Africa.
Bert had gone out like a happy warrior to tramp the high road

of service and sacrifice . . .
Surely there was something we at home could do.

Money was scarce . . .
  Mission committees were hard up . . .
    The churches were giving all they could, but there were
    so many needs.

Now Nessie was quite small, but her heart was big, and she
had the spirit of a giant.
She organized us into a dramatic club to raise the money
needed to build the hospital.
She was director and coach,
    organizer and leader
of one of the craziest, maddest, and most thrilling ventures
with which I have ever been connected.

We decided to present two plays by Sir James Barrie—*Quality
Street* and *Dear Brutus.*
We determined to present the plays in one of Glasgow's
downtown theaters—the Coliseum—and to hire it for a week.

It was a fantastic sort of thing, I must admit, to think that a
gang of twenty young people could hire a theater for a week,
and do a good job of presenting such challenging plays . . .
    to do it in such a way as to raise enough money to build
    a hospital in Africa.
Nevertheless, I can only tell you what happened.

Sir James Barrie presented to us an autographed copy of the
plays that they might be auctioned and the money applied to
the fund.
Sir Horace Fellows, a noted conductor, not only agreed to let
his orchestra play, but he himself came on the opening night
to conduct.

Each one of us frantically sold tickets for weeks before the
production.

We enlisted all our friends in schools and in offices,
                    in restaurants and in picture houses,
                in university and church,
            in the stores and in the tramcars.
We secured the help of the newspapers.
There was something about the whole mad enterprise that
captivated our fathers and mothers.

Suffice it to say that the plays were successful beyond our
dreams.
The young people acted as if they were inspired, and who can
say they weren't?
And every night for a week hordes of people came to the
Coliseum theater and caught the spirit of it all, so that in the
end enough money was sent out to Bert to build his dispensary
and a compound—a place for him to work and live.
And Nessie went out to Africa at the close of the year to join
him in God's work.

Nor does the story end there.
The next year Nessie's sister, Jean, directed another of Barrie's
plays, *Mary Rose,* and played the lead herself to raise enough
money this time to build a hospital.

One of the Glasgow newspapers in telling the story called
Bert and Nessie "Pilgrims of the Lonely Way ..."
But I wonder if their way is so lonely after all!
Pilgrims of the Lonely Way ... Pilgrims unafraid to reach ...
They are in good company.
There are great people who walk beside them—a rich fellow-
ship dedicated to hard labor and austere lives in far-off places.
But the excitement
    the joy
        the adventure
            the deep inner satisfactions
of those who dare to reach sky-high more than make up for
any loneliness.

For no way can be lonely if it is the way Christ walks . . .
No way can be lonely if it is the way to which He calls you.

•IX•

"*The devil is real all right*," *Peter Marshall always insisted.* "*I know him well. He uses insidious, diabolically clever techniques. He is dedicated to corrupting lives and keeping men and women from achieving their God-appointed goals.*

"*Why is Satan always depicted as being of the masculine gender?*" *he liked to say.* "*The devil is no fool; he changes his sex. We associate with womanhood all that is pure, lovely, sweet, and wholesome. But Satan is not above taking on the guise of what we respect in order to accomplish our downfall. Consider Delilah and Samson . . . Jezebel and Ahab . . . yes, and many a modern woman.*"

He was speaking from experience. For six years after Peter's ordination to the ministry, he was a bachelor. As such, he was the target of many an aspiring maid and even some married women.

Often he received calls like this one: "*Dr. Marshall, I have an urgent problem for which I need spiritual help. Could you possibly drop by this afternoon? I would come to you at the church office, only I turned my ankle yesterday.*" *Quickly he learned to take his secretary, who would sit in an adjoining room during the conference.*

Once in a series of lectures at Gettysburg Theological Seminary, Peter warned the men about the temptations that assail a minister from these designing women: "*You are caught in a dilemma. If you are abrupt with them, they can accuse you of not wanting to help them. If you are courteous, they will be encouraged and make life miserable for you in many feminine ways.*"

When Peter was still a bachelor, one such woman had set a series of subtle traps in his way for two solid years. He had avoided them all. Finally the woman abruptly changed her tactics and confronted him in the privacy of his office with her plan to divorce her husband. She asked Dr. Marshall to join her in Mexico.

In telling me about it later, Peter said, "She couldn't understand when I spoke about my love for Christ and my responsibility to other people, so I finally told her bluntly that at that moment I found her the most unattractive woman I'd ever met. That did it!"

Of course, there were other areas where Peter wrestled with beasts in his own Ephesus. . . . There was the matter of using time correctly. He had no regular hours or office routine to give order to his day. He liked to stay up late; that usually meant a late start the next morning. He struggled mightily with procrastination on sermon preparation and on the serious reading that he knew he must do. Offers from other churches were attractive; did he sometimes dally with them too long?

Perhaps for him the most subtle and devastating trap of all was discouragement. When all other temptations failed, this one could always engage him in deadly battle. "Why isn't my leadership accepted?" he would moan. "Maybe I should quit, throw in the sponge."

Then was the time for us to remind one another that all discouragement is of the devil—to be recognized, fiercely resisted and overcome.

OUR FRIEND, THE ENEMY

To most moderns, the devil is either a swear-word
　　　　　　　　　　　or an allusion to archaic folklore.
Nowadays the devil has become a clown in pantomime . . .
　　　　　　　　　　　and hell a sardonic jest.

Quite in the mood of this gay, spoofing approach to the subject is the now-famous book *The Screwtape Letters,* written by the Oxford don C. S. Lewis.
The book is a series of letters from a senior devil, Screwtape, to his underling and apprentice, Wormwood.

Wormwood has been given the assignment of seeing to it that one average, middle-class Englishman never makes it to the Father's house.

But underneath the blithe, sparkling façade of the book, there are deep philosophical and spiritual insights.
Mr. Lewis wrote *The Screwtape Letters* not just as a humorous exercise, but for a reason.

He had important things to say:
That there is a Dark Power in our world ...
That this Evil Power has intelligence and wit ...

> was created by God ...
> was once good ...
> and went wrong.

That on this earth there is a war to the finish between God and this Evil Power ...
That we human beings are never so much in danger,

> or please the Evil Power so much,

as when we do not believe that he exists, or refuse to take him seriously.

"I know someone will ask me," Mr. Lewis writes in another place, "'Do you really mean, at this time of day, to reintroduce our old friend the devil—hoofs and horns and all?'

"Well what the time of day has to do with it I don't know. And I'm not particular about the hoofs and horns.
But in other respects my answer is, 'Yes, I do. ...'" [6]

In so doing, Mr. Lewis places himself squarely back into the stream of Jesus' teaching about the evil in our world.
In at least forty-three separate references recorded in the

Gospels, Jesus spoke of this Evil Personality, giving him a variety of names:

Satan . . .
the Devil . . .
the Enemy . . .
the Adversary,
Tempter.

A loving Heavenly Father is never the author of evil, Christ insisted.
He attributed to this Dark Power all disease

pain
depravity
sin
and death.

Hence the devil is one to be taken seriously indeed.
One does not take lightly the one responsible for a face eaten by leprosy with a gaping hole where the nose has been . . .
Or screaming children laid on the fiery arms of idols . . .
Or the lust for world domination that reduced hundreds of thousands of men to the level of animals through slavery . . .
Or the big business of prostitution.

If what Jesus had to say about the devil is true, then he is something more than an idea for a Halloween costume.
But if what Jesus taught about the Evil One is merely superstitious nonsense, then how could we take authoritatively anything else Christ said?

In Christ's eyes the stakes here are deperately high:
your immortal soul and mine,
where we shall spend eternity—either in the Father's house or lost from ourselves, our Maker, and our fellows.

Jesus warns us that the devil's techniques are insidious.
In our time we have heard a great deal about infiltration.
But the Communists did not invent it.

It started back in the Garden of Eden when a snake slithered his way into Paradise . . .
    and this technique has been used ever since.

There is no more perfect illustration of the way infiltration works than the Old Testament story of "Little Sunshine" or Samson.

Any young person would have admired Samson.
He was a powerful physical specimen . . .
    Head and shoulders above his companions . . .
        He had the easy grace of a born athlete . . .
and the wit of a toastmaster.

He loved life
    and practical jokes
        and laughter.
He was a born leader.

He had an open face, laughing and honest, a charm of personality which purchased for him indulgence rather than discipline from his parents—the discipline that might have saved him.

His mother and his father had been told before his birth that theirs was to be an extraordinary child, blessed with great gifts of body, mind, and spirit.
And so, in full anticipation of the radiant energy which would brighten their home, they named their son "Little Sunshine" or "sun-man," for that is the meaning of *Samson*.

And then, as the child Samson grew, another even more wonderful gift was added to the talents with which he had been born:
    the spirit of the Lord came upon him.

    "And the Spirit of the Lord began to move him at times in the camp of Dan between Zorah and Eshtaol."
        Judges 13:25

Even from the point of view of Samson's companions, rare
and awesome powers began to stir in him . . .
   not only unparalleled physical strength,
      but also the ability to sway men,
         to lead them.
And along with all this, there was his joy at being alive and
young, with the world at his feet.

He became the romantic outlaw
   the benefactor of the downtrodden
      the people's hero fighting the common enemy—the Philis-
      tines.
God was in the glory of this young man exulting unashamedly
in splendid strength and developing muscle.

   "Then went Samson down, and his father and his mother,
   to Timnath, and came to the vineyards of Timnath: and,
   behold, a young lion roared against him.

   "And the Spirit of the Lord came mightily upon him, and
   he rent him as he would have rent a kid, and he had
   nothing in his hand . . ."   *Judges 14:5–6*

Can you imagine what strength it would take for a man to
subdue a lion with his bare hands.

And then we have a touch that makes Samson seem lovably
modest:

   ". . . but he told not his father or his mother what he had
   done."   *Judges 14:6*

His father had always disliked braggarts.
Besides, most mothers are not fond of their darlings fooling
around with lions.
Better to keep that quiet!

Then Samson deliberately chose an insulting weapon with
which to swat Philistines:
   the jawbone of an ass.
Quite indifferent to the odds against him,
he dove into a free-for-all fracas, with the final tally at one
thousand Philistines.

So he goes cavorting through the pages of the book of
Judges...

                         full of riddles...
                         playing tricks...
                         and practical jokes,
with the firebrand stunt the craziest of all.

"Little Sunshine" caught three hundred foxes,
   tied them together in pairs by the tails, with a lighted
   firebrand knotted in the tails.
Then he turned the crazed animals loose into the enemy's
ripening cornfields ... vineyards ... olive orchards.

The tale must have traveled from mouth to mouth as rapidly
as the fire had spread.

Samson was now a giant in the community,
   the hero who won every contest,
      adored by the children,
         admired by the aged,
            envied by the other young men,
worshiped by the girls.

He could do no wrong—or could he?
We are not told when his downfall began, but it is not difficult
to piece the story together.
Was there ever a male hero who was not tempted by the
seductive young thing?
One common desire of youth then, as now, was to be popular,
                         to be sought after,

admired,

complimented,

invited here and there.

No one knows this better than the devil, for it was he who planted these seeds in the hearts of youth.

For any of us—as for Samson—the temptation is to put ourselves first, at the center of life,

  to play at being god.

"I want what I want . . ."

My will—or God's will.

In this case, God had a great plan for Samson:

> ". . . he shall begin to deliver Israel out of the hand of the Philistines."   *Judges 13:5*

"Little Sunshine" was meant to swat Philistines all right, but for a better purpose than personal glory.

More than that, he was meant to be a Nazarite . . .

 His body was to be kept clean of strong drink and sensual indulgence . . .

 No razor was ever to touch his head.

But the human will is always free.

God will force no man to obey Him nor will he shield any man from temptation.

The sin is not in being tempted but in yielding.

This is our battleground, where every human being faces a decision about God and the devil.

So Samson was tempted.

He saw a woman in Timnath, a daughter of the Philistines, and he took it into his head that he wanted her for his wife.

His parents protested and pleaded, but the pattern had been set years before . . .

They had never been able to resist their child's willfulness;

they could not now.

The devil came to Samson in a woman's guise; he often has . . .
he often does.

Samson married the girl, and it was a pathetic travesty of a marriage, because God was not in it.
Read the story for yourself in Judges.

So Samson lost his first battle with temptation—and we can be sure that it *was* a battle.
For God, having blessed Samson with unusual gifts, needed him.
There had to be a tremendous battle within, particularly that first time.

But after the first giving-in to temptation, our defenses are weaker the next time.
We have handed over our wills to this Evil Power,
    fraternized with him like the friend he pretends to be.
He has won control.
His sly suggestions infiltrate . . .
then contaminate . . .

    then dominate.

"Then went Samson to Gaza, and saw there a harlot, and went in unto her."   *Judges 16:1*

And so the man who with his bare hands had torn a lion limb from limb was victim of a snakebite in the tall grass of sensual indulgence.

The argument that desire alone is sufficient excuse for conduct is a philosophy as old as sex.
The unbridling of passion . . .
the exaltation of sexual pleasures torn from the context of life
and worshiped as the god of happiness—

this rationale has been given a fresh Freudian face in our century, otherwise there is nothing "modern" about it.

The temptation is always to purchase popularity by joining the crowd around the bargain counters of hell—when in exchange for an irrecoverable,

fragile,

precious thing—purity

the devil will offer the cheap, glittering baubles with which his hooks are baited.

But the truth is that the devil has no bargains.
"Take what you want, Samson.
We can settle up later . . ."

One of the devil's tricks is this:
When we choose evil, usually we get what we want at once and pay for it afterward.
When we choose good we have to pay for it first before we get it.

Most of us have found this out with as simple a matter as examinations in school.
If you chose good grades and a degree with honor, you had to pay months ago with hard study,
    the giving up of some pleasure and recreation.

But if you chose to have a good time, you began that long ago, and you have had your fun.
You did not pay then, but you are paying now in your frantic, last-minute boning for your exams, and your paying is not over yet.
There will be further deferred payments later in your life.

Make no mistake about it.
This Evil Personality is very real and very subtle.
He is real to me; I know him well.

He wants to persuade us to choose the things that we do not have to pay for right away.
Usually they are cheap and sordid things.

"You want it," the devil says. "Charge it.
I understand. I'm your friend. Take what you want."

But the bills always come due.
And what is more, they are not all presented to you.
Payments must also be made by those close to you, bound to
you through all eternity by ties of blood and bonds of love.
In Zorah, Samson's parents would worry . . . and hope . . .
                    and pray . . . and finally grieve.

There were other women after the harlot, and finally Delilah.
Samson was still trifling with the devil's baubles.
He thought he could handle them, only to find, when it was
too late, that he had flirted with temptation too often.

The story moves on.
   The scene changes.
      The music moves into a minor key.

Samson, his massive head in Delilah's lap, says, "I will go out
as at other times before, and shake myself . . ."
And then as you read, you catch your breath,
for the next words are so simple,
                    so terrible . . .

   "But he wist not that the Lord was departed from him."
                    Judges 16:20

The Spirit of the Lord had been pushed out of a man's heart.
No man can serve God *and* the devil.
Samson had long since made his choice, had clasped the
serpent to his heart.
He had had his fun; now was the day of reckoning.

The Philistines had him at last, and there was no shaking them
off this time.
The repeated yieldings to temptation had sapped Samson's
vital strength.

"I will go out as at other times . . ."
How often we have heard it: "I will pull myself together."
Ah, but this was not as other times:

> ". . . the Philistines took him, and put out his eyes, and
> brought him down to Gaza, and bound him with fetters
> of brass; and he did grind in the prison house."
>
> *Judges 16:21*

Bound and blind in the prison of the Philistines was Samson—
  the hero meant to deliver his nation from their hands.
The true nature of the Dark Power was out in the open now.
A wrecked manhood
  an empty shell of a person
    God's great plans all awry
      a broken heart
        gaping sockets where shining eyes had been.

But in his darkness "Little Sunshine" remembered the man
he might have been . . .
  He thought of the God he had abandoned . . .
    And once more he prayed to that God:

> "O Lord God, remember me, I pray thee, and strengthen
> me, I pray thee, only this once, O God, that I may be at
> once avenged of the Philistines for my two eyes."
>
> *Judges 16:28*

It was the last cry of a desperate man.
"Remember me . . . only this once . . ."

Some part of his old strength returned to him.
Three thousand of the enemy were gathered in a great pillared
hall.
They had sent for Samson to make sport of him.
So, groping his way, he found the two key pillars of the house,
              bowed himself with all his might,

and in a thunder of crashing beams, collapsing masonry, and screaming men and women, the house fell.

The tragedy had come full circle.
The story ends with a sob . . .

> "So the dead which he slew at his death were more than they which he slew in his life."   *Judges 16:30*

Now we begin to see why Jesus, who loves us
                                    and wills the good things of life for us,
wants us to know the true nature of the Evil Power with whom we temporize.
Then is one like Samson lost forever to his Father's house,
                                    his Father's love?

We cannot know.
The one thing we do know is that—according to Jesus—we can count on no blessed oblivion in death.
For Samson, as for all of us, the curtain comes down,
                              only to rise again.

Jesus warned us over and over that a lifetime of setting self-will up as king . . .
    of making the wrong choices . . .
                    inevitably leads down the broad road to hell.

He spoke of "the outer darkness" . . .
                "the lake of fire" . . .
                    "the everlasting fire" . . .
Not, as we might expect, so much to the murderers, the prostitutes, or the outcasts . . . but to the Scribes and Pharisees,
                        to His own disciples,
                    to the church people,
                        to the scholars and intelligentsia . . .
to them He had a great deal to say about hell.

You may not like it.

You may not believe in hell, but there it was, in repeated references—on the lips of this "gentle Jesus, meek and mild."

The twentieth-century sophisticate is inclined to say condescendingly, "Isn't all this merely a relic of a dark superstitious past when bogeymen were conjured up to frighten children into being good?

"If there is a God, He couldn't possibly permit such a place. I cannot imagine it . . .

I cannot entertain the thought . . .

Therefore I won't."

I remember in a humble restaurant in a poorer quarter of Atlanta, Georgia, seeing a card underneath the glass on the counter. The card said:

"Because you don't believe in hell is no sign you ain't going there."

Despite its crudity and bad grammar, there is an underlying truth in that homely observation.

Far too often we moderns are tempted to think that just because we reject an idea, it therefore ceases to be.

Certainly we need not discuss a literal hell.

I am not concerned that you believe in a burning pit,

a boiling cauldron,

the devil with a forked tail,

the smoke and the flames.

Personally, I think hell will be more terrible than that!

Suppose a soul passes through the curtain of death without the purging work of Christ—still soiled—with a record of crime

iniquity

sin and degradation.

Suppose that through all eternity he has to witness the playing
and the replaying of his record upon earth . . .
Or to use another figure of speech, as though he were in a
motion picture house, seeing the same pictures over and over
again.
Would not that be hell?

We are told in the Bible that the inhabitants of Hell . . .
those members of the lost legion . . . will be murderers,
                                    idolators
                                whoremongers
                                sorcerers
                        liars.
    Now the lust to kill or to inflict pain,
                        to abuse sex . . .
                            to crave drink
                                or narcotics . . .
these things are of the spirit, make no mistake.
They are spiritual urges.
We sin in the flesh . . . yes, but of the spirit!

These are sins of desire . . . and we desire, not with our body,
but with our spirits.
We desire with our souls, do we not?
The body supplies the vehicle of consummation . . .
                    the means of gratification of a base urge.

When the clock chimes for us, we leave the body behind, and
it returns to the dust whence it came.

But the soul . . . what of it?
It goes on, we are told—the unsaved soul to join the lost
legion . . . to swell the ranks of the hopeless outcasts.
It goes on—with its longings
                    its cravings
                        its lusts and passions—
                                on behind the curtain.

Suppose then, these damned souls still have their desires and
lusts . . . their passions and their cravings . . . gnawing—eating
—burning constantly at their personalities,
and they have no bodies with which to gratify them?
Would not that be hell?
What could be more terrible than the thought of those lost
souls completely turned over to the base passions which they
had deliberately chosen in life?

I think that in this connection the Old Testament injunction:
    "Choose ye this day whom ye will serve."   *Joshua 24:15*
or in the New Testament:
    "No man can serve two masters . . . God and mammon,"
has a deep significance.   *Matthew 6:24*

Let me remind you that God does not send anyone to Hell.
He permits the soul a choice . . . and if a human being has
chosen to gratify the lusts of the flesh rather than the longings
of the spirit . . .
        that soul may have to be left that choice!

What have you chosen?
What are you choosing—day by day?

The proof of how real Jesus knew Hell to be is that He came
to earth to save us from it . . .

    "For this purpose the Son of God was manifested, that
    He might destroy the works of the devil."   *I John 3:8*

In other words, the reason that the God-Man came among us
to live a while on the planet earth was to fight to the finish the
Evil Power.
Christ gave His life to make sure of victory.

He was willing to be scourged . . .
        lashed with leather thongs studded with steel . . .

willing to be spat upon,
>   smitten,
>   humiliated . . .
He was willing to be nailed to the cross with huge nails driven
through His hands and feet.

He was willing to endure such pain as we cannot imagine . . .
>   willing to burn up with thirst . . .
Willing to die suspended between earth and heaven . . .
Willing to be separated temporarily from His Father . . .
Willing to go even into hell itself.

"He was dead and buried and descended into hell . . ."
Millions in churches throughout the world repeat this every
Sunday in the Apostles' Creed.

How? Why? In what way did Jesus go into hell?
It is Peter who gives us some clues in his First Epistle.
Jesus' work of redemption on the cross would not be complete
if it included only those who were living,
>   or even those who would live in future centuries.

What of those—like Samson—who had lived before?
They must hear the good news too.
They must have their chance to embrace belief.
So, says Peter, during those three days, Christ's living Spirit
went and preached "to them that are dead. . . ."   *I Peter 4:6*

They too, must know that Jesus has offered us a way out . . .
the opening of our wills and hearts and minds to His cleansing,
>   the giving of our lives to His safekeeping,
>   the acceptance for ourselves of what He did for us on
>   the cross.

Even in this, our wills are free to accept or reject.
But let us soberly consider the price we shall pay if we reject
Christ's love.

He is the only One who can deal with our sins,
the only One who can open our inner eyes to perceive the
tricks of the devil within us,
> the only One who can supply us with the strength to
> resist temptation,
>> the only Friend who will never deceive us.

Others promise us sins excused
> discounted
> denied
> explained away.
But only at the foot of the cross do we ever experience the
beautiful divine contradiction of *sins forgiven.*

Here is the greatest miracle of all!
> that God loves men even in their hate . . .
>> that His heart yearns for us even in our indifference . . .
>>> that His pardon and His grace are waiting for us
>>> even though we may feel no need of either . . .
>>> that God, for Christ's sake, is willing to forgive
>>> sinners such as you and me.

• X •

I held the man's stickpin in my hand. It was not long after Dr. Marshall's death and I was going through his possessions. The tiny chip of a diamond in the pin winked at me. The story of how the pin came to be given to Peter Marshall had been told to me by our friend Marguerite. . . .

Peter had been invited to Marguerite and Bud's for dinner. There was nothing unusual about that. Those were his bachelor days, and he dined with this particular couple so often that he even kept a pair of house slippers in their coat closet. He and Bud were making sets of Chinese Checkers to give to several mutual friends for Christmas.

On that particular night, Atlanta was in the grip of a severe ice storm with many streets impassable. Peter made it anyway.

He had no sooner gotten inside the door than he took off his shoes, put his slippers on, and asked to use the telephone. His first words over the phone were, "Are you still out of pain?"

Apparently the answer was in the affirmative because he fairly shouted for joy. It seems that the woman to whom he was speaking had been suffering acutely for months. A battery of specialists were baffled, seemingly could do nothing for her. That noon Peter had gone to her home and had prayed for her healing.

Only a few Sundays before he had been preaching on prayer—about mountain-removing. He felt that he would be a hypocritical theorist not to rise to a challenge like this

143

woman's need. The extremity of her pain had given him bold-ness in prayer. He had suggested that together they claim Jesus' promise, "If ye abide in Me, and My words abide in you, ye shall ask what ye will and it shall be done unto you." What they had asked was that she be healed.

"I've never seen anyone more radiant or more exuberant than Peter was that evening," Marguerite told me. "So far as I know the woman was completely cured."

There was still a card in the bottom of the little box with the stickpin. The fine feminine handwriting was a bit faded. . . .

"I want you to have this gift as a tangible token of my gratitude for the mountain of illness that a loving God has removed from me."

THE ART OF MOVING MOUNTAINS

I AM sure that each of you has read this statement many times:

Prayer Changes Things.

You have seen it painted on posters which adorn the walls of our Sunday-school rooms.

You have seen it stamped on little metal plates,

read it in the Bible

heard it from the pulpit, oh, so many times.

But do you believe it?

Do you actually, honestly, believe that prayer changes things?

Have you ever had prayer change anything for you?

Your attitudes

your circumstances

your obstacles

your fears?

This is the way the Master said it:

> ". . . for verily I say unto you, If ye have faith as a grain of mustard seed, you shall say unto this mountain, Remove hence to yonder place; and nothing shall be impossible unto you."
>
> *Matthew 17:20*

Now that is certainly one of the most audacious claims about faith ever spoken.
Does it strike you as overstated?

Have you ever wondered why Christ chose this particular image—moving mountains—
                to illustrate the power of faith and prayer?
He might have said something about mountain-climbing, but no, it is mountain-*moving* which is mentioned as the expression of a robust
    virile
        and exuberant faith.

How it must grieve Him to see us go through life with such timid attitudes toward prayer.
Constantly He was appalled at men's lack of faith . . .
    "O men, how little ye trust Him!" He cried at one point.
                                    Matthew 12:28
And in another . . .
    "Why are you afraid? How little you trust God!"
                                    Matthew 8:26

And then He promised boldly:
    "If ye abide in Me, and My words abide in you, ye shall ask what ye will, and it shall be done unto you."
                                    John 15:7

For nearly two thousand years, Christ's words have challenged men to think big . . .
    to be bold for Him,
        to do great and audacious works in His name.

Yet too often we do not believe His promises.
And sometimes when our prayers are answered, we do not believe even then.
We charge if off to coincidence.
We search for what we call a "logical" explanation, for we do not want to be thought peculiar.
How he grieves over our lack of faith!

But prayer is the key to Christian growth.
Through prayer, God still works His miracles today just as He did when the first Christians had the audacity to think that they could convert the world.

Do you remember when the Roman ruler of Judea—Herod Agrippa—decided to stamp out the fanatical band of men who were followers of the crucified Galilean by throwing their leader, Peter, into prison?

Herod mounted a strong guard of soldiers to keep Peter in prison until after the Feast of the Passover.
Sixteen soldiers had charge of the prisoner.
Two of them were chained to him, one on either side, and they occupied the cell with him.

The others guarded the inner and outer doors of the prison, and Peter was secured.
He could not escape.

Meanwhile, in a house in the city, in the home of Mary, the mother of John Mark, Peter's brethren were gathered.
They were engaged in prayer.
They had been praying all week.

They were praying in earnest, praying with passionate conviction for something specific.
They were praying that Peter might be released from prison—

that the Lord would somehow intervene on Peter's behalf.
Peter was sorely missed.

He was the leader.

Nearby in the prison—strange things were happening.
Gates, chains, and guards could keep out friends and keep in
prisoners, but they could not prevent the coming and going
of the Lord's angels.

An angel of the Lord appeared at Peter's side as he lay asleep,
and a light that was not of men filled the prison.
Peter was commanded to rise up—the shackles fell from him,
and he stood free of the chains that had bound him, while his
two guards continued to sleep.
How was it done?
We are not told.
But the angels of God are not deterred by men.
Led by the angel, Peter followed as one in a dream, until the
cool night air outside the prison brought him to the realization
that he was a free man.

The church had been praying for a week that Peter might be
liberated and restored to them.
Here he was, liberated; the prayer was answered.

Still musing over the strange and wonderful thing that had
happened, Peter walked through the streets, deserted and still,
until he came to the house which served as a meeting place of
the brethren.
He knew he would find them there—praying!

Peter knocked for some time until a damsel came to the door,
and hearing the voice of Peter, she became so overjoyed that
she let him stand outside while she ran to the others with the
good news that their leader was delivered unto them.

Upon being told that their prayer was answered, they refused
to believe it and told the girl that she was mad.

But her story could not be changed.
She insisted that Peter was outside.

They next thought that it must be his ghost, because Peter
was in prison—they knew—and although they had prayed ear-
nestly that the Lord should set him free—they had not expected anything like this.
Maybe Herod had already killed him!
They thought of every possibility—save that they had gotten
what they had been praying for.

The question naturally arises: Why were they praying at all?
Their skepticism clearly demonstrated that they did not expect an answer.

We are not much better today after nineteen centuries of
practice in the art of prayer . . .
Not much more expectant after two millenniums of answered
petitions.
We have not much more faith . . . perhaps not as much.

We are like the old lady whose view from her front porch was
spoiled by an unsightly hill that not only had not beauty itself but also shut out much of the beauty that lay beyond.

The old lady wished again and again that the hill might be
removed, and then she came upon the promise in Scripture,
Mark 11:23.

> "For verily I say unto you, That whosoever shall say unto
> this mountain, Be thou removed, and be thou cast into
> the sea; and shall not doubt in his heart, but shall believe
> that those things which he saith shall come to pass; he
> shall have whatsoever he saith."

She decided to try, and one night she prayed that the hill
might be removed.

Next morning when she arose, her first thought was to go to the window and look out to see whether or not the Lord in the night had moved the hill.

Her comment was most revealing, and revealed why her prayer—like most of ours—was unanswered. She said, "Umph, well, it is still there, just as I expected."

We really do not believe in prayer.
Even as we pray, we do not expect results . . . and we hardly know why we bother to pray at all.

I have seen what prayer can do on many levels.
Take the matter of jobs—economic needs . . . down-to-earth things.

When I first landed in this country, at the Battery off Ellis Island, I had just enough money to last me two weeks.
So I immediately went after a job in New York City.
I was told that there were some openings in a steel construction job.
Still another skyscraper was going up . . .
When I applied, I was told that I could have a job on two conditions.
The first was that I had to join a union.
That was all right; I did not mind that.
But then the hiring man added, "See that guy over there? The one with the plaid flannel shirt? You have to pay him fifty dollars."

At that point, I did some quick thinking and praying.
And I decided that bribing someone to give me a job,
                                    indeed buying a job,
                                        was not right.
That was not what I understood by Americanism.
If I really believed Jesus when He promised,
"But seek ye first the Kingdom of God, and His righteousness;

and all these *things* shall be added unto you . . ."   *Matt.* 6:33
then I had to fulfill my part of the bargain.
And I did not believe that bribery had any place in the Kingdom or was a part of His righteousness.

So I did not take the steel construction job.
Instead I left New York City for New Jersey.
There I got a job with a gas and electric company.
We were putting down four-inch conduits across the Hudson
Tubes into Kearny and West New York.
My next job was assisting a molder in a Paterson foundry.
But during these months I was praying, asking God to show
me what He wanted me to do in this country.
I could not really believe that He had brought me from Scot-
land to the United States to dig my way across New Jersey
     or to fire a blast furnace.

Then came a letter from David R. Wood in Birmingham,
Alabama.
Dave had been a boyhood friend of mine in Scotland and had
emigrated the year before to the United States.
Dave wanted me to come to Birmingham.
He himself had found warm friends in the South, and he was
sure that he could get me a job on the *Birmingham News.*

One Sunday afternoon I went out on the back stoop with
Dave's letter in my hand.
It was a hot August afternoon in Elizabeth, New Jersey.
How can I ever forget?
And I prayed, I asked the Chief for directions.
     What did He want me to do?
     Was I supposed to go south?

I received the answer clearly, as clearly as my directions had
come to leave Scotland . . . "Yes, this is it. This is your next
step.
Go south and go immediately."

I went immediately—on a bus—with borrowed money.
And indeed that was the right step.
For, like Dave, I too found friends in the South—and a job
                                and opening doors
                                        and a way to go to seminary,
                                a wonderful new life,
the life God had planned for me.

You cannot have experiences like that and doubt any longer
that God can move mountains—even in our day.
Maybe you do not believe that prayer changes things, but I
can assure you that I, and many others like me, know better.
Prayer changes us . . .
        and changes other people . . .
        and changes circumstances.
Too many people today have an attitude of skepticism . . .
                                or disillusionment
                                or disappointment
                                or frank incredulity.

The people who say "I prayed . . . and it didn't work" too
often conclude therefore that prayer is unavailing,
        or that the prayer was not heard at all . . .
        or that if He heard, God did not care.

Now there is a great mystery here, and I would not for one
moment make light of it.
There is such a thing as unanswered prayer.
The Bible tells us of some of them, and there are those among
you who have addressed sincere petitions that are as yet unanswered.

Let us face this mystery honestly.
I cannot explain it— and it would be glib and dishonest of
me to try.

I can only say that there are times when God must say "No"

to our petitions, just as fathers and mothers at times refuse the petitions of their own children.

Let me make the point by modern analogy.
When you flick the electric-light switch in your room and the light does not come on, do you immediately conclude that it is not the nature of electricity to light up rooms?
Or that electricity plays favorites and just
does not like you enough to give you light . . .
therefore you will have no further use for electricity—
you are through?
No, of course not.
You know immediately that there must be some rational explanation for the failure of the light . . .
a faulty connection,
a broken switch,
a blown fuse,
or a burned-out bulb.

If you have prayed—and nothing happened—did you immediately conclude that prayer does not work?
Or that God does not care about you anyway?
Or that He can't be expected to know anything about your insignificant problems and affairs?
Or bother about them if He did?

Did it ever occur to you that there might be another explanation?
Have you ever thought that maybe you had a faulty connection—were not plugged in properly to that source of divine power and love?
I can hear you say: "What do you mean by 'not plugged in properly'?
What more can one do than just pray?"

Well, think again of plugging into a socket.
You have to be sure that there is nothing wrong with the plug itself.

It could have exposed wires—it could have a short-circuit—
   and the result would be either a blown fuse . . .
      sparks and a shock . . .
or nothing at all.

We can and often do short-circuit our prayers by faults within
ourselves—wrong attitudes like resentment . . .
               feelings of self-pity . . .
           envy or pride . . .
         or wrong actions.

We had better get this straight—we can't go on living a life
of self-will and self-indulgence, in and out of jams, and send up
a quick prayer for help and expect God to fix it all up, so that
we can go on as before.

I like this definition from the Presbyterian *Shorter Catechism:*
   "Prayer is an offering up of our desires unto God, for
   things agreeable to His will, in the name of Christ, with
   confession of our sins, and thankful acknowledgement
   of His mercies."

Most of us have not realized that anything which will glorify
God is His will.
And what Christ was telling us in the mountain-moving pas-
sage is that the circumference of things which will glorify
God is wider than we think.
And mountains are of wide circumference!

Hence if moving a mountain will glorify God,
then mountain-moving is within the province of God's will.
And we can be sure that petitions concerning the physical
              and spiritual health
            and daily happiness
          of human beings
        are squarely at the center of that will.

How boldly we may pray and how absolutely certain we may be of the glory of God is well illustrated in an event in the life of Martin Luther.

In 1540, Luther's good friend Frederick Myconius lay dying. Luther received a farewell letter from his friend, written with a weak and trembling hand.

Immediately Luther sent back this reply:

> "I command thee in the name of God to live, because I still have need of thee in the work of reforming the church . . .
> The Lord will not let me hear while I live that thou art dead, but will permit thee to survive me.
> For this I am praying.
> This is my will, and may my will be done, because I seek only to glorify the name of God."

The dying man had already lost the power of speech when this letter arrived, but within a short time he was well again. He survived Luther by two months!

Maybe you haven't known that there is a God who is ready and willing to do great things in you,
> and through you,
> and for you,
in answer to your prayers.

You will never know it until you really ask God for something—something specific—and find out for yourself.

Is there a mountain in your life you would like removed? Nothing is impossible with God.

> "If you, being evil know how to give good gifts unto your children . . .
> how much more shall your heavenly Father give the Holy Spirit to them that ask Him!"   *Luke 11:13*

"How much more God!"
Over and over Christ repeated these words—
    "How much more God!"

"Ask, and ye shall receive, that your joy may be full."
Ask—with faith that God keeps His promises.

Ask with faith just the size of a grain of mustard seed.
    Try it out!
        Take the Lord up on His promises!

Try a little mountain-moving . . .
and you will find it the greatest adventure of your life.

•XI•

For those who asked Peter Marshall to perform their wedding ceremony, he required—wherever possible—several conferences. As a result, there were a few occasions when he refused to marry a given couple.

Early in his ministry, he had written his own marriage ceremony. This had been typed and pasted in on top of the printed Order for the Solemnization of Marriage in his blue leather Book of Common Worship.

This was never a routine service, quickly dispensed with. Judging by dozens of letters, many a couple regard Dr. Marshall's wedding ceremony as one of the high points of their lives.

One of these brides was the sister of an FBI agent who knew Peter well. Martha's wedding was to be a small one in the Lincoln Chapel, nothing unusual about it. Yet years later, the FBI agent—not usually given to sentimentality—was describing the scene for me:

"Dr. Marshall stood before the flower-banked altar waiting for the wedding party. It was the gladness on his face that I can never forget. There was a twinkle in his eyes, a lilt to his voice . . .

" 'Dearly beloved . . . the marriage relation when rightly understood and properly appreciated, is the most delightful, as well as the most sacred and solemn of human relations. It is the clasping of hands, the blending of lives, and the union of hearts, that two may walk together up the

156

hill of life to meet the dawn—together bearing life's burdens . . . discharging its duties . . . sharing its joys and sorrows.'

"Some of the service he must have written just for Martha and Dick. I was so fascinated by the vibrancy of his voice, the buoyant joy that lifted every sentence to give it a memorable quality I had never before heard in a wedding ceremony.

" 'Marriage is much more than moonlight and roses, much more than the singing of love songs and the whispering of vows of undying affection. In our day, it is by many lightly regarded, and by many is lightly discarded. But marriage will ever remain, in the sight of God an eternal union, made possible only by the gift of love which God alone can bestow.

" 'Therefore we are still entitled to say that true marriages are made in Heaven, because that which, above *all* things, makes a marriage true and happy comes only from God. . . .'

"I hold dear to my heart the things Dr. Marshall told my sister and my brother-in-law:

" 'Remember Martha, that it was Love that gave you this man—and you, Dick, this woman—not this ceremony. . . Your marriage must stand and endure, not by the authority of the marriage license, nor by the strength of the wedding certificate—for these are only pieces of paper —but by the strength of your love and the endurance of your faith in each other and in Jesus Christ, without which no marriage can be truly happy. . . .'

"Then Dr. Marshall asked that Martha and Dick look at each other, rather than at him, as they spoke their vows. And as I stood there hearing those ancient, lovely words, In plenty

and in want, in joy and in sorrow, as long as we both shall live, *I knew why that moment would be unforgettable—not because of any particular words that Dr. Marshall had strung together, however fine—but because he had brought with him into the chapel the joyful presence of Him who attended the wedding feast and who blesses all true romance."*

THE ELECT LADY

Do you believe that true marriages are still made in heaven? That God cares about whom you marry? . . .
    That somewhere there is a particular person meant for you? Or do you think that such idealism is pious nonsense?

These are pertinent questions.
For you cannot believe in God the Father as Jesus revealed Him, and not believe that He cares about you as an individual. And if God is interested in you and in what you do, then would He not be interested in whom you marry?

Perhaps you think that falling in love is enough.
But we are so often wrong about love . . .
    Many of us do not recognize it when it comes.
        Many of us mistake sexual attraction alone for love. Surely here—with regard to marriage—we need God's help more than in anything else.
Is not the proof of that the dark shadow of divorce that lies across every hearthstone?
One marriage in every four now ends in divorce.
There is evidence that soon it will be one marriage in every three.

You need God's help in the realm of courtship and marriage because you are disillusioned and lost without Him.

Many already have tasted of a society which is debauched.
You see divorce organized as big business.
    You see society's daughters and sons taught to drink at an
    earlier and earlier age.
        You see mothers who covet popularity for their daugh-
        ters at whatever price, push them out into society like
        tempting bargains placed in a store window.

Some of you have tasted of the fleshpots.
You are prematurely old,
        not so much in experience
        as in disappointment.
Already you have haunted hearts.

Your defense against these wrongs is often an assumption of
indifference.
You cultivate a veneer of apathy and nonchalance as a shield
against being hurt.

But underneath the veneer there lurks a wistful, poignant
quest for some kind of enduring values, an idealism tested by
experience.
You must have solid ground beneath you, and this is precisely
what Jesus Christ offers.

When you refuse to let Him direct your dating,
                        your courtship,
                        your marriage;
you are cheating yourself of one of the greatest gifts of all.
How can I dramatize for you what you are missing?

The world loves romance and seeks it everywhere.
Nine out of every ten songs are about love.
Sex is exploited to sell everything from spark plugs to hair
tonic.
Hollywood has worn the subject thin . . .
                and thinner . . .
            until there is no substance left, only tawdriness.

The romance offered by the world is as a ring set with dime-store glass.
The romance God offers you is a pure and flashing diamond.
                         Synthetic . . . The real thing.
                         Ephemeral . . . Eternal.
                         Mockery . . . Fulfillment.
          That is the difference; think well before you choose.

But understand that you may have God's help with your romance only on His terms.
First of all, He insists that His children dream big.
Because He wants our happiness, He will settle for no cheap compromises,
     no tawdry substitutes,
          only the best for any of His.

God demands idealism with regard to sex.
Let us frankly face the fact that the keenest of all problems,
     the sharpest of all temptations
is to compromise personal purity and chastity.
That is where the battleground is.
And so—with no apologies and no equivocation—I challenge you to Christ's ideal for sex.

Dr. Harry Emerson Fosdick once confided in a sermon to his congregation at the Riverside Church, New York, how he battled this as a young man.
He decided to force himself to face the question of what use he wanted to make of sex in his life . . .
Did he want a Christian home with its deep fidelities and satisfactions,
     or a loose life of sensuality?
He was reasonably sure that he could not have both.

He chose!
In order to make that choice clear-cut and definite, he sat down and wrote a letter to the girl he was going to marry—

even though he had never met her.

The letter expressed his confidence that his wife-to-be was waiting for him somewhere,

> that at the right moment they would meet,
>> that in the meantime, he was going to keep his fidelity to her as true as if she were already his bride.

At the time Dr. Fosdick spoke about this to his congregation, his wedding day was some forty years in the past.

In retrospect, looking back over long years, he could say,

"That decision cost . . ."
Of course it cost!

"But how grateful I am for it, that I did not make the other choice and surrender all the deep and sacred satisfaction of these lovely years for a mess of pottage." [7]

Of course, those "lovely years" . . .

> "the deep and sacred satisfaction" . . .

would not have been possible had not the girl waiting for Harry Emerson Fosdick shared his idealism.

Perhaps we need to look again at what Christ's concept of womanhood is.

The emancipation of women did not begin in the twentieth century.

It began with Christianity, for Jesus Christ was the first to usher women into a new place in human relations.

Jesus accorded woman a dignity she had never known before and crowned her with a glory, so that she might be revered, protected, and loved.

The symbol of purity and chastity has traditionally been a white rose.

I wonder if it would not be more accurate to choose a gardenia . . . because the gardenia with its fragrance and the velvet of its petals cannot endure to be handled . . .

treated roughly
or bruised at all,

for its pure white petals will reveal every telltale mark of handling.

Jesus Christ both challenges you and promises to help you, so that when you stand before the altar to whisper your wedding vows—both you and your bridegroom will be able to lay upon that altar a gardenia without spot or blemish, for what is desirable in a bride is just as desirable in a bridegroom.

Any temporary sacrifice or renunciation is a small price to pay for the achievement of ideals which will yield later in your marriage, dividends of peace, of joy, and of happiness.
There was a time when many a bride brought her white offering to the altar but knew that it lay there alone.
For there prevailed the iniquitous "double standard."
This was the philosophy that permitted,
    even encouraged
a young man to sow his wild oats . . .
with the excuse that he was only young once.

So he might step over moral bounds in sexual adventures, but when he settled down, he had a right to choose for a wife a girl who was sweet, pure and chaste.

You can be sure that Christ's standard is no double standard.
Today's girls are quite right to reject it.
But the standards which many of you have substituted are not Christ's either.

Today's women have interpreted emancipation as the freedom to smoke like a man,
  to drink like a man,
   to use rough language, to swear,
    to work like a man,
     to treat sex as loosely as a man.

Women have copied the vices of men—in the name of progress!

But it is never progress to go in a downward direction.
It is not progress to lose ideals, to lower morality.
No girl ever became more desirable by losing her femininity,
                                                    or her innocence.

I have never heard a man say that a girl's mouth was prettier
with a cigarette hanging out of it,
            or that her hair smelled divinely of tobacco smoke.
I have neard no poetry rhapsodizing over a girl's smutty joke.

Will a modern child—grown-up—remember some faint unforgettable fragrance which always seemed to be in his
mother's hair?
Or will he remember instead the odor of scotch on her breath?

Will he tenderly recall that day he rushed unbidden into her
bedroom to find her on her knees beside her favorite chair?
Or will he remember her, dressed in slacks, putting off his
eager questions while she poured cocktails for her noisy
guests?

Perhaps today's women will not feel so triumphant about their
"emancipation" when they realize that men no longer feel as
romantic about girls as did their grandfathers.
If something sweet and mysterious has been lost, this so-called
equality is a poor exchange for the privilege of being different,
        of being a woman.

Is it too late?
What of those who have already tasted of this debauched
society?
Is it too late for Christ's idealism?

No, it is not.
Christ gave us a deeper concept of purity than anyone else
has ever conceived.
He added a new dimension to it.

He taught us that purity is not just for the untouched,
                                   the untried
                                   the untempted.

The knight who rides past with shield bright and armor un-
stained and unspotted may never have been in the fight.
                         The clean shield proves nothing.

That person who has never felt the temptation to do
anything ignoble,
      to lower his ideals,
            to listen to the honeyed whispers of sensuality . . .
that person whose life has been so sheltered that he has never
felt blowing on his cheeks the scorching blasts of passion is as
a ship that has never been launched.

That ship may be seaworthy—or it may not.
The sheltered person may have strength—or he may not.

Jesus Christ was too realistic . . .
                         knew human nature too well,
not to realize that each of us is tempted.
Not one of us remains untainted by impurity of deed or
thought.

And so in God's eyes the pure vessel is not only that which
remains untouched.
Pure is the vessel also which the Master has cleansed . . .
      in whom His spirit abides to keep us cleansed.
Else He could never have forgiven and accepted
                         Mary of Magdala . . .
                         Zaccheus . . .
                  the woman taken in adultery . . .
                  the Gadarene demoniac . . .
            Joanna, the wife of Herod's steward, Chuza,
      the women with the alabaster box of ointment . . .

He is the only One who claims to be able to forgive and to cleanse.

Over and over, He provides that glorious new beginning for haunted hearts.

Always His word is what it was to that nameless woman long ago:

"Go and sin no more.

Make a clean break with whatever it is that has dragged you down."

In order to get God's help with your dreams of romance, you will have to live out your faith that He is able to guide you,

live it out day by day,

episode by episode.

It has to be a practical faith.

You should talk over with Christ the questions that trouble you—the perplexities of dating,

the constant head-on collision between your ideals and your wish to be popular and accepted.

These matters you discuss constantly with your friends, do you not?

Then why not with Christ?

He has more wisdom to give you about dating than any of your friends could ever have.

Is it possible that society is on the wrong track today with regard to courtship and marriage?

Many sociologists, psychologists, and marriage counselors are rapidly coming to that conclusion.

They point out that our western dating patterns go back no farther than World War I ...

that we romanticists, who scorn the "arranged" Oriental or European marriage, need to take a new, hard look at the tragedies and heartaches which our hit-and-miss courtship, our customs are bringing.

We see society's sons and daughters pairing off at an earlier
and earlier age . . .
We watch a shocking kind of mutal exploitation:
     The boy trying to exploit the girl sexually . . .
     the girl exploiting the boy financially . . .
          exploiting being simply another word for selfishness.

And so the socioligists are convinced that we need a profound
and creative revolution, if we are to save the home as an institution.
What they have not led us on to see is that the revolution
must be in our hearts:
               no longer what can I *get* from the marriage I seek,
               but rather what can I *give?*

For you girls this may come down to some difficult questions.
For example, many girls today are unwilling to make of their
marriage a full-time job.

There is a conflict between hard economic facts and the
dreams of a home in the hearts of many young women.
But when a girl is unwilling to give up her name,
her career,
          her own selfish ambitions for her husband's sake,
          she had better stay out of marriage.

Beginning with what is often simply greed for a larger income,
greed for *things,* material possessions, household gadgets, for
many young women the accepted practice of working after
marriage has distorted their concept of what marriage really
is. In Christ's eyes, true love must be ever a giving of oneself.
In the case of a wife, bearing her husband's name,
          seeking to please him,
               creating with her hands a home for him,
                    bearing his children.

The creation of a home where memories abide does not de-
pend on possessions.

Gracious living is created by loving hands,
by a tranquil mind,
a heart in which God dwells,
a soul which knows beauty.
Calmness,
  serenity
    faith
      contentment
        tenderness,
manifesting themselves in the way a woman goes quietly about
her household tasks.

Such qualities are not furthered by hard, competitive days in
the office . . .
by the hurried preparation of meals after working hours with
no time left for the children.

The women I know who are the happiest, whose homes are a
joy to enter, are the ones who have made a clear-cut decision.
Often at economic sacrifice, they have decided that they cannot create a real home on less than full time.

But this kind of giving is possible only if there is a reciprocal
giving on the part of the husband—"Husbands, love your
wives"—not in terms of a popular song moaned into a microphone,
    not with a box of candy,
      or a corsage twice a year,
not with any of the sentimental slush that is so often a counter-
feit for love.

But "love your wives even as Christ also loved the church, and
gave himself for it . . ."   *Ephesians 6:25*
There is a concept of a husband's love!
That means something.

Look at Christ on the cross—there for us husbands is the
ideal . . .

There is Love giving Himself for His bride . . .
    self-sacrificing love—knowing no bounds,
   having no restraint,
  love even unto death.
Such a love can come only from God.

I have found that no marriage ceremony, however beautiful
and meaningful, will make two selfish people, governed by
self-will, into an unselfish couple.
There is nothing magical about the marriage ceremony.

No problem which any married couple can have is beyond
solution if they are willing to get down on their knees together
and ask God what to do about it.
It is not a question of what the husband wants—or what the
wife wants—but always, what does God want?

So many children have an imaginary character with whom
they live and gravely discuss everything.
A certain mother heard her five-year-old son carrying on a
conversation under the kitchen table with his imaginary play-
mate:
    "Who's the boss in your home, Johnny?" asked the un-
   seen guest. "Your father or your mother?"
"Neither," said Johnny. "God's boss in our home."
Here was a fortunate little boy who had seen his parents reach
out in the most practical way beyond self-will to find God's
will.

And that must be the pattern from the beginning of your dating right on into the home you will create, if you are to find the
romance that God has planned for you.
For human beings vary little from century to century.
The manifestations of self-will change, but not the selfishness.
Dreams linger in every heart—along with the temptations to
compromise those dreams.

But God can change our self-will, so that we can find the love
He has planned for us.
That is what happened to a woman I shall call Mary.

Her home is in a Southern city.
I know it well, for I have been entertained there often.
She is a woman of some means—her heart and her home
always open—with a hospitality that ministers both to the tired
body and the discouraged soul of many a guest.

I always think of her as the modern counterpart of the "elect
lady" of Ephesus to whom John wrote his Second Epistle.
"Elect lady . . ." What a charming way to speak of a mother
for whom the years have woven the brocade of gentleness she
now wears, always with her slow smile of understanding love!

Yet in the modern elect lady's past lay a surprising story.
I heard it from her own lips . . .
Years before, when she was a young mother, a three-year-old
son had been drowned.
Her grief was compounded by bitterness toward her husband
because the boy had been in his care for the day.

With the bitterness, a process of disintegration set in.
Mary had been a meticulous housekeeper and a fine cook;
                                     now she no longer cared.
Dust and disarray took over her home . . .
           In the garden were weeds and rank growth, like the
           debris piling up and up in her heart . . .

Nor did she care any longer about how she looked until—
until one morning a woman whom she had never seen before
knocked on her front door,
       marched into the living room,
           announced that she was in love with Mary's husband,
       John.

"Somehow I got through that dreadful scene," Mary told me,
"and got the woman out of the house.
Then I went to the kitchen, poured a cup of strong coffee,
                    sat down for a good cry
                and a long hard look at myself.

"Suddenly a bit of Scripture came out of dim recesses of
memory:
        'See to it that no root of bitterness spring up and cause
        trouble, and by it the many become defiled—'
"I saw it all then . . .
I had let the roots of bitterness about Johnny's death grow up
and fill my heart until there was no room left for love.
My bitterness and defiled our marriage and our home.

"Then I thought of the other woman, and I got mad.
How could I forgive that?
I cried some more . . . threw a cup across the kitchen where it
went crashing against the wall . . .
        beat my fists on the table . . . screamed, 'I won't . . . I
        won't.'

"But all the time a quiet voice inside me was saying. 'You
must. You must forgive.
        There is no other way.'

"Then I walked over to that large mirror there in the dining
room to take a good look at myself.
I was horrified at what I saw . . .
Once I had been considered the belle of our town.
And now—here was a woman with disillusioned eyes . . .
                        hard lines around her mouth . . .
                        hair stringy and unkempt . . .
No wonder my husband had been attracted to another
woman."

My hostess sighed . . . and smiled her slow smile, remembering.

"Everything came out all right.
Christ came again into our home.
John and I had twelve years together before he died—
              near-perfect years, the happiest of all.
I had a second baby boy—always a joy to us.
He is now a physician in Kansas City."

I looked about me at the shining mahogany,
      the freshly starched curtains fluttering in the night
      breeze,
          the roses in the silver vase, grown in the garden outside,
              the portrait of John . . .
The artist had captured on canvas the face of a happy husband.

And in imagination I saw behind Mary's shoulder so many
elect ladies who are called by God to create homes in which
love dwells . . .
A cottage in Georgia with wisteria trailing over the porch . . .
      a trailer home with a very young mother . . .
          a tiny apartment . . .
              a split-level in suburbia . . .
                  a square white house under an arch of elms in a
                  New England village . . .
                      a ranch house overlooking the ocean on the
                      Monterey Peninsula.

I thought of the mothers who preside over these homes,
              modern women, not at all like Whistler's mother.
They know all about germs and sanitation,
                  vitamins and food values,
              formulas and schedules.

They are tireless in providing for the physical needs of their
children—these modern mothers—
      ambitious for their future intellectual life—
          eager for their proper social development.

They will chauffeur their children anywhere, to dancing
classes . . . Scout meetings . . . the dentist . . . the movies.
They will attend PTA meetings and forums endlessly.
But as for spiritual nourishment for their children, many of
them have never given it a thought.

How could they—when they themselves do not know God in
a real and personal way?
They read the best-sellers, child psychology books—but the
Bible scarcely ever.
Perhaps it never occurs to them that God has wisdom and
guidance to give them about their marriage and their children.
Yet how our tired old world needs parents who are willing to
add to their knowledge of economics and sociology and psychology a knowledge of God.

We need young women who would rather be called "elect
ladies" than "the smartest young matron in town."
The nation cries out for couples who will build true homes—
whether they live in two rooms or ten . . .
whether starched white organdy curtains
or silk damask draperies hang at the windows.
You can have a home like that, if you will recognize that God
is the greatest asset to romance there is.
He thought it up in the first place!
Reach for His idealism, so that your home may be built on
spiritual foundations,
with your family life oiled by the grace of God.

"Where there is faith, there is peace;
Where there is peace, there is love;
Where there is love, there is God,
Where there is God, there is no need."

Only in such homes can we build the better world
of which we dream.

•XII•

The two girls found seats near the front of the church. After the last rich notes of Bach's "Here Yet Awhile" from the Saint Matthew Passion died away, Dr. Marshall arose slowly, looked up at the choir for a moment, as if smiling his gratitude for the sixty-eight loyal young voices.

Betty was thinking how much she liked the way he conducted a service. He never rushed from one part to another, but often sat in his high-backed chair for a leisurely moment, thoroughly relaxed, as if he too were worshiping—drinking in the refreshing quietness. Under the spell of such periods of silence, Betty could feel the brood of ills of the week past—all the noise and confusion of her government office—slipping away. Peace would come stealing into her heart. She had come to look forward to these services.

But now the musical voice from the pulpit was beginning. With a sigh of contentment she settled back in the pew. The sermon was about death—and immortality.

After the service on the way back to their 16th Street apartment, Marion said suddenly, "You know, Dr. Marshall's sermon today did something for me. I've been afraid of death all my life, ever since my collie Mac died when I was six. You've heard me talk about old Mac. Well, after hearing that sermon, I know I'll never be afraid of death again. It's great to be free of that fear."

Betty smiled at her friend. "I know. Dr. Marshall's confidence is catching. He makes death sound like an exciting adventure, like going to a glad reunion."

173

On Friday of that week, Dr. Marshall received a letter which read:

Dear Dr. Marshall,

Last Sunday a friend and I heard you preach on death! Afterwards she told me and my roommates that you had made death such a beautiful natural experience that for the first time in her life, she was no longer afraid to die.

She—Marion—was killed Wednesday in an automobile trip to Florida. It happened on the highway between Macon and Dalton, Georgia. She died instantly. Because she was so young (twenty-four), so full of life, so happy, it has been a deep shock to all of us who knew her. One of our greatest comforts has been to recall her comments on "Rendezvous in Samarra" which released her from the fear of death.

May God keep you as His comforter to us, who need Him so much.

Sincerely,
Elizabeth Durand

One Sunday a few months later—December 7, 1941—Peter Marshall and I drove to Annapolis where Peter was to speak at the Naval Academy. At the last moment he had an overwhelming feeling that he should change his announced topic and instead preach the sermon on death and immortality:

For what is your life? It is even a vapor that appeareth for a little time and then vanisheth away.

On the way back to Washington that afternoon came the stunning announcement of the Japanese attack on Pearl Harbor. The nation was at war. Within a matter of days many of the young men to whom Dr. Marshall had just proclaimed his ringing assurance of life after death, would be on the high seas. Some would not return. "Rendezvous in Samarra" provided prophetic strengthening for some of the midshipmen in their

time of need. I know this because Peter received several letters
from distant places thanking him for his message that fateful
Sunday morning.

RENDEZVOUS IN SAMARRA

"For what is your life? It is even a vapor, that appeareth
for a little time, and then vanisheth away." *James 4:14*
Whenever my mother spoke of plans for the future, she always
added—even in her letters—the phrase "God willing."
This is not just a pious cliché.
It is the clear recognition that her future was in God's hands.

The apostle James would approve this viewpoint.
For in speaking of human life as being a vapor, James was
warning those who make great assumptions for the future with
never a thought of God . . .
        "I shall go to such and such a city . . ."
        "I shall be there for a year . . ."
        "There are our business plans."
Such as these do not recognize that the issue of life and death
is in the hands of God.
Indeed, for every one of us, life is a fragile thing.
The messenger that summons us into the larger room may be
        visible or invisible . . .
        expected or unexpected . . .
The summons is just as imperative!

A matter of seconds and yards, that is all that was between
you and a crash on the highway the other day.
A tiny microbe—so small that your naked eye could not see it
—has called many a man away from the broken toys of this life.

History is filled with dramatic illustrations of the fragility of
life and the unexpectedness with which the summons may
come.

Perhaps no illustration is more vivid than the *Hindenburg* disaster in 1937 as it was described by Dale Harrison of the Associated Press.

It was the afternoon of May the sixth.
   Lightning flashed the sullen clouds.
      Thunder rolled up and down the skies.
         Rain fell . . .
            It was a dismal evening.

Out of the east floated the silver *Hindenburg* . . .
         like a graceful cigar . . .
            Germany's pride—a haughty triumph over nature.

For though the thunder clapped and the lightning flashed viciously, the silver thing rode softly on . . .
   unperturbed and unharmed.

She was late . . . many hours late, for the weather was bad and she was cautious.
Better late than never!
Men and women waited at Lakehurst—impatient.
They were anxious for the *Hindenburg* to come down, for they were going to London for the coronation.

The *Hindenburg* lazed along . . . Let the storm diminish.
Let the wind die . . . then she would come down.
No need to hurry.
   There were ninety-nine human beings aboard.
The lightning grew weary of its futile strikes
at the silver monster.
   The thunder crawled off . . . grumbling.
      The rain became desultory . . .
         The clouds broke ranks.

The *Hindenburg* began talking: "All is well," she said over her radio, "I am coming down."
   She was mistress of the sky.
On the ground newsmen and photographers loitered with movie-camera men and field officials.

Covering a *Hindenburg* arrival had become a dull assignment.
Nothing ever happened.

The *Hindenburg* pointed her nose to the ground.
From her sleek sides threads of rope dangled, reaching for the
handclasp of the ground crew.
Rain still fell, but softly now.
Passengers poked laughing faces from cabin windows.
                    Some waved handkerchiefs.
                        There were children at those windows too.

She dipped majestically—the haughty airship of silk
                                    and steel
                                        and dangerous gas.
It was six twenty-three.
From somewhere jumped a spark—a spark so small you could
hardly see it.
And in less time than it takes to tell, the *Hindenburg* exploded.

Flames leaped from her middle—flames of red and yellow
                        wrapped in black and purple smoke.
She hung there for an instant—as though reluctant to die.

From the flaming ship bodies dropped.
It was forty, fifty,
     or one hundred feet to the ground.
No one knew exactly how far it was.
It is difficult to be mathematical when men and women are
falling screaming to their deaths.
On the ground there were shouts to the ground crew:
                                    "Run for your lives."

Men and women dropped like flaming torches
                        or like sparks in the indifferent rain.
Some lay where they fell, forever still.
Others, incredibly, rose up and staggered away.
Many came through it safely . . . sixty-three escaped . . .
                        however incredible it seems.

Sixty-three emerged alive—scorched
                              burned
                              shocked
                              speechless
                     horrified . . . but alive.
A fool would call it "luck."

What shall we call it?
Thirty-six people died—in an instant.
At the last there was a feeble flame.
It crawled skyward and lost itself in the blackness of the
night.[8]

Yes, James, life is a vapor which disappears
                              slips from our grasp
                     all in an instant.

But most of us never think of death or dying.
        We act as though we had a long lease on life . . .
           As though we had immunity somehow . . .
                As though that cold and clammy hand would never
                be laid on our hearts
or the shrouds of that dread messenger never brush against us.
It is a foolish attitude to take about an inevitability.
For death is life's greatest, perhaps its only, certainty.

They betray not only their fear but also their ignorance who
say, "Let's not talk about death or dying.
        Let's talk of something more pleasant."

Of course, that is true to our modern pattern.
We are not willing to face unpleasantness, and when we are
presented with facts we do not like to hear, we call them
"propaganda" and dismiss them.

But what is there to fear?
What contemplation could be more pleasant than what awaits
us after death?

Here we have pain—and partings
>> tears and tragedies
>> work and weariness
>>> heartaches—disillusionments.

We grow old ... our eyes dimming ... hair graying ...
Desperately we try to camouflage the betraying years.
I assure you that the life to come is infinitely more pleasant to contemplate than any of that.
It is more pleasant than reading our daily papers with their stories of crime and human wickedness
> cruelty and violence
>> sordid tales of passion and greed.
It is more pleasant than the thought of atomic warfare.

For if the Bible is true and Christ has not deceived us, there awaits just behind the curtain a life that will never end
>> a life of beauty and peace and love
> a life of reunion with loved ones
>> a life to be lived in the very Presence of God.

There will be no more pain,
> no more sorrow, nor tears,
>> nor crying,
>>> nor parting,
>>> nor death after death.

Age shall not weary them, nor the years erode.
We shall enter into that for which we were created.
It shall be the journey's end for the heart and all its hopes.

And yet there are those among us whose actions—let us eat, drink, and be merry, for tomorrow we die—suggest that they believe in no better hereafter.

There never was a time when the conviction of immortality was more needed than in this day when materialism has so exalted present life as to make it all-important.

People whose vision of death is earthbound remind me of the caterpillar crawling along the warm earth, imagining that heaven for him will be an endless row of cabbages.

Then one day a second caterpillar with a more philosophical turn of mind would say to his friend: "You know, I believe that some day you and I will no longer have to crawl along the ground, but might even fly over that fence. What is more, we will not be puncturing cabbage leaves with our neat little holes and stuffing ourselves full of green stuff, but we might be sipping dew and living on honey."

His friend, fastening on him incredulous beady eyes, might reply: "I knew this night life would get you."
Or, solicitously he might say: "Poor old chap, you have been working too hard lately. You've cracked under the strain."

And when the time comes for him to "die," his caterpillar friends gather round—and extol his virtues.

"He was a connoisseur of cabbage. He was a good old caterpillar—now this is the end."
And so he is buried in a shroud—a chrysalis shroud that spins upon the twig, a shriveled, dry grave.

And yet, by and by, on a summer morning
the grave bursts open,
        the chrysalis breaks, and out of it emerges a moist,
        trembling, lovely thing that hoists into the fragrant air
delicate sails of beauty.

As they dry and gather strength, the butterfly becomes aware of a new world.
And when the gossamer wings are dry and their colors are fast,
        the butterfly takes off and, fluttering, sails over the fence
        to sip the dew and taste the succulent honey.

In our superior wisdom, we know which caterpillar is right.
We know that he goes to sleep a caterpillar and wakes up a
butterfly.
But do we know as much about our own beautiful destinies
after the long sleep?

There are none on whom the Reaper will not call.
Death does come to the archbishop,
>   to the king in his palace,
>   the beggar by the roadside,
>   and the rat in his hole.

But persons are not blown out like candles in the wind.
Infinity surrounds us.
>   Is it dead?
>   Is it empty?
>   Is it a shivering void where nothing lives?
Is it a cold space into which we are launched to evaporate and
disappear?

So we ask our questions and receive our answers.
Do we think our transformation will be any less beautiful
and startling than caterpillar into butterfly?
We have the witness of Personality—the sense of Identity
greater than the universe.
We are aware of a star;
we cannot conceive of a star being aware of us.

We know that we are here for a reason, otherwise earth would
become a mere picture house, and life the stupid walking to
and fro of shadows on a screen . . .
Religion would then be a silly symphony of jazz played beside
deathbeds to keep idiots quiet, to dull their jangled nerves as
they are about to plunge off into nothingness.
You can stand before a glass case in the anthropology wing of
a good museum and see laid out in a row of saucers the con-
stituent elements of the human body.

There is so much phosphorus
                    so much silicon
                iron
              carbon
           lime
          water, and so forth . . .
Enough iron, I believe to make a half-dozen tenpenny nails . . .
Enough lime to whitewash an ordinary chicken coop . . .
Enough phosphorus to tip the heads of a thousand matches.

There, they will tell you, is the human body—
What? There you are?
There I am? . . . No!
That may be my body—it is not I.
That may be the house in which I lived, but it is not the
tenant.

Moreover, the physicists and anatomists tell us that the cell
tissue and structure of the body changes every seven or eight
years—is completely rebuilt, re-created.

So "you" are not your body—for you are the same individual
who has seen several such cycles—yet you remain the same
person conscious of continuous existence.

Nor are "you" your brain.
Your brain cells change in every cycle of reconstruction.
Then how does it happen that I remember what I thought and
did and said with the old vanished brain of twenty years ago?
My memory tells me that I am the same "I" in spite of all
those changes in my brain.

Parts of the body—a finger, an arm, a leg—may be amputated.
Yet the person, the "I," is still there.
The violin will be laid down some day . . .
The old refrains that skillful hands have plucked from its heart
will be heard no more—but the musician will still be alive.

No half-mad humorist tossed the world aloft and left its destiny to chance . . .
No infinite juggler threw into space the ball of his creation and walked away heedless of where it fell.
No blind groper in the mists of creation let a handful of dust trickle through his fingers to fall in a shower of sparks and turn into stars.

"The meek shall inherit the earth," Christ said, but He did not mean six feet of it, not a hole in the ground.
The grave is not their final heritage.
There are a thousand insane things easier to believe than this.

Human personality will survive, else God would be the capricious universal joker who created toys in His own image so that He might break them . . .
laugh at their disfigurements . . .
and sweep them into the garbage cans of His own caprice.

To believe this makes life a jumbled mystery,
aimless and futile
human effort a farce
human hope a mockery
human sorrow the cue for the crackling laughter of insane gods.
Yet where can we find the reassurance the heart seeks?

Let us honestly face the fact that all the
arguments—philosophical and otherwise,
analogies—however close and persuasive,
testimony—all of it that psychic research can so far produce, are still not conclusive evidence for immortality.
They leave us in the twilight of an excruciating uncertainty.

The only proof—the final convincing proof—is to be found in Jesus Christ.

In Him is all the authority needed to garrison your heart when the waters threaten to engulf and the darkness closes in.

How? Because He has proved, and stands ready to prove, that what we can experience with our five senses is not the only reality,

> indeed, is far less real than the actualities in the realm of the Spirit.

It was through His resurrection that Christ demonstrated this to His first disciples.

These men and women had not expected Christ to rise from the dead.

When His battered body was taken down from the Cross, their hopes and their dreams had already died with Him.

For He had said that He was God incarnate in human flesh.

Surely God cannot die . . . and the fact was that He was *dead*.

Therefore when the news came thirty-six hours later that His body was gone,

> that He had been seen alive,

they were shocked, bewildered.

At first, they flatly refused to credit such an idle tale.

But then, as one by one and finally in groups they saw and experienced His presence for themselves, they were forced to believe that Christ was indeed alive.

It was unaccountable, but stupendous!

What else in life mattered beside news like that!

So they shouted it across continents,

> blazoned it over land and sea,
>> cried it, sang it, preached it, exulted in it.

Read the flaming words of those first preachers in the Acts of the Apostles and you will see that the "good news" of apostolic preaching was not Jesus' life—but His death;

> not His ethic—but His resurrection.

These first disciples knew that human personality would survive . . . because One who went into the grave and beyond, had come back to say:

> "Because I live, ye shall live also.
> Whosoever believeth in Me shall not perish but have eternal life . . .
> Whosoever liveth and believeth in Me shall never die."

But then, when we go beyond Christ's ringing assurances, we are somewhat startled to find that He does not give us more details of what we can expect behind the curtain.
I am convinced that His reticence is based not on either lack of knowledge or on His disinclination to tell us
but on our lack of capacity to receive it.
How would you describe to a deaf mute the Fifth Symphony . . .

> or the sound of rain pattering down . . .
> or a birdsong?

Have you ever tried describing a sunset to someone born blind?
How would you begin?
Then how could Jesus have conveyed to us the reality that lies ahead of us when there is no analogy within the range of our knowledge?

He invited us rather to a different sort of proof, to the extraordinary adventure of entering into immortality for ourselves here and now, by experiencing—

> even as did those first disciples—
> the fact of His aliveness.

For don't you see that no fishermen and tax-collectors and housewives—no matter how persuasive—could ever have won converts to Christianity merely on their say-so?
What happened was that an increasing number of men and women themselves met Jesus Christ.

Yes, this can happen today too.

Yes, it has happened to me—and to many another.
And this—only this—is the final proof of immortality.

An old legend tells of a merchant in Bagdad who one day sent
his servant to the market.
Before very long the servant came back, white and trembling,
and in great agitation said to his master:
"Down in the market place I was jostled by a woman in the
crowd, and when I turned around I saw it was Death that
jostled me.
She looked at me and made a threatening gesture.
Master, please lend me your horse, for I must hasten away to
avoid her.
I will ride to Samarra and there I will hide, and Death will not
find me."

The merchant lent him his horse and the servant galloped
away in great haste.
Later the merchant went down to the market place and saw
Death standing in the crowd.
He went over to her and asked,
        "Why did you frighten my servant this morning?
        Why did you make a threatening gesture?"

"That was not a threatening gesture," Death said.
"It was only a start of surprise.
I was astonished to see him in Bagdad, for I have an appoint-
ment with him tonight in Samarra."

Each of us has an appointment in Samarra.
But that is cause for rejoicing—not for fear,
provided we have put our trust in Him who alone holds
                        the keys of life and death.

For at last, each of us comes back to the strongest argument of
all—the Love that in earth's greatest mystery clothed itself in
clay like our own,

and, dying, left the low door of the grave unlatched,
so that God could come into our sorrows ...
so that a loving Father could speak
to the earth's dumb anguish
of the Glorious Day beyond our dying sun.

NOTES

Dr. Marshall always went into the pulpit with a complete sermon manuscript. These were typed in the unusual format he had devised, the blank verse, stair-step style now familiar to the many readers of *Mr. Jones, Meet the Master* and *The First Easter*. Sometimes during his Washington ministry, he destroyed many earlier sermons. Nevertheless at the time of his death, about six hundred sermon manuscripts were left.

Since these were prepared for oral delivery only, considerable editing has been necessary. In some instances, where there were several sermons written during the years and the same topic, I have used material from two, sometimes three messages, in every instance being guided by what I felt Peter would have done himself had he published the sermons during his lifetime.

Biblical quotations are confined to the King James (which remained Dr. Marshall's favorite) and a few from Moffatt's translation, which he sometimes used. And, as in earlier books, the reader will find instances where he paraphrased and elaborated on Scripture—one of his oft-used devices for interpreting favorite passages to his listeners. All scriptural references are given in the text except where the quotation is a phrase or brief sentence.

For me the sermons presented here bring back many memories—of the man and of the occasions on which the sermons were delivered. I have included a few of these memories in the brief introduction to each sermon.

[1] Jean's mother thought I would like to see the theme, and sent it to me shortly after Dr. Marshall's death. She was right—I treasure it.

[2] Paraphrased from Montague, C. E., *Rough Justice*, Doubleday & Company, Inc., New York, 1926. Used with permission.

[3] This reminiscence was part of a memorable letter which I received late in July 1953 from the Reverend David Simpson, then pastor of the Second Presbyterian Church of Fort Smith, Arkansas. David had just finished reading *A Man Called Peter*. The book had sparked "a reliving of Peter's and my seminary days."

[4] Paraphrased from Remarque, Erich Maria, *All Quiet on the Western Front*, Little, Brown & Company, Boston, 1929. Used with permission.

[5] The poem "High Flight," by Pilot-Officer John Gillespie Magee, Jr., R.C.A.F., is reprinted with the permission of his mother, Mrs. John Gillespie Magee.

[6] Lewis, C. S., *The Case of Christianity*, The Macmillan Company, New York, 1943, p. 40; and Goeffrey Bles, Ltd., London. Used with permission.

[7] Fosdick, Harry Emerson, *On Being Fit to Live With*, Harper & Row, New York, 1947, pp. 54–55. Used with permission.

[8] The Dale Harrison Story of *Hindenburg* disaster is used by permission of the Associated Press.